AF837325

Acting on Faith

Acting on Faith

Religious Development Organizations in Northwestern Argentina

Laurie A. Occhipinti

LEXINGTON BOOKS

A Division of
ROWMAN & LITTLEFIELD PUBLISHERS, INC.
Lanham • Boulder • New York • Toronto • Oxford

LEXINGTON BOOKS

A division of Rowman & Littlefield Publishers, Inc.
A wholly owned subsidiary of The Rowman & Littlefield Publishing Group, Inc.
4501 Forbes Boulevard, Suite 200
Lanham, MD 20706

PO Box 317
Oxford
OX2 9RU, UK

Copyright © 2005 by Lexington Books

All rights reserved. No part of this publication may be reproduced, stored in a retrieval system, or transmitted in any form or by any means, electronic, mechanical, photocopying, recording, or otherwise, without the prior permission of the publisher.

British Library Cataloguing in Publication Information Available

Library of Congress Cataloging-in-Publication Data

Occhipinti, Laurie A., 1968–
Acting on faith : religious development organizations in Northwestern Argentina / Laurie A. Occhipinti.
p. cm.
Includes bibliographical references and index.
ISBN 978-0-7391-1110-9 (cloth : alk. paper)
1. Community development—Argentina, Northwest. 2. Community development—Religious aspects. 3. Non-governmental organizations—Argentina, Northwest. 4. Argentina, Northwest—Economic conditions. I. Title. HN270.Z9C658 2005
361.7'7'0982—dc22 2005016163

Printed in the United States of America

™ The paper used in this publication meets the minimum requirements of American National Standard for Information Sciences—Permanence of Paper for Printed Library Materials, ANSI/NISO Z39.48–1992.

For Joe

Contents

Tables

Acknowledgments

As I have proceeded with this work, I have incurred debts of gratitude that I can barely begin to express. My path has been eased by friends in the communities where I worked who spent countless hours with me, by total strangers, such as a woman in a small town in the province of Salta who offered to let me stay in her home when I appeared to be stranded, by thoughtful academic advisors and colleagues who pointed me in the right directions, and by family and friends who bore with me through the traumas and joys of research and writing. This work carries my name, but it bears the stamp of many wise minds and kind hearts.

It seems that convention is to thank anthropological spouses last, but I find that is where I would like to begin. My husband, Joseph Occhipinti, has been an intimate partner to me in this work, and has offered unstinting, unfailing support and encouragement. He shared the often difficult experience of fieldwork in rugged conditions with a smile and an ingenious turn of mind. His discerning comments and human insights have improved this work more than I can measure. I would like to thank him for all that he has done—he has saved me from the raging currents of rivers both literal and metaphoric.

The six months that I spent in Iruya and its surrounds were enriched by the hospitality and warmth of the people there. While I hesitate to list names for fear of neglecting anyone, there are a few I would like to offer special thanks to. Flavia Choque and her family in Iruya opened the happy chaos of their home to us, and we spent many enjoyable hours in their company. Her father, Don Isobel Choque, and his family generously allowed me to stay with them for days on end in San Isidro, fretting over my travels and work as if I were their own and patiently showing me how things were done in the "*campo*." Gloria and Nora Federico always welcomed us warmly, as did Minoru at Molinas. José Angel Ayala cheerfully shared his cultural insights, and I would also like to thank him for allowing Joe to accompany him on a long visit to the interior villages, which would not have been possible otherwise. Bette Molina helped us, as she helps everyone, in every way that she could, and in more ways than she knows. I would like to thank María and Nicolas Rodriguez in Río Grande, who offered both their hospitality and their assistance. Nicolas was a tremendous help with my household survey. I am grateful to the schools and teachers in San Isidro, Colanzulí, and especially in Campo Carreras, for allowing me to stay with them on various occasions. A collective thanks goes to the *mamas cuidadoras* of

Campo Carreras, who met my endless questions with patient good humor and unflagging interest.

In Los Blancos, I would like to extend my deepest gratitude to the Wichí community of Kayip. The families there welcomed us, sheltered us, and taught me much about their ways. To all of them, my warmest thanks. I would also like to thank the caciques of all of the Wichí communities near Los Blancos for their help and support. Our stays in Kayip were made even more pleasant by the company of Nimia Gomez, the director of the school in Capitán Page.

Both of the NGOs with which I worked generously opened their doors to this research. I would like to thank Alicia Torres of OCLADE for allowing me to work with that organization and for facilitating my work in Iruya. Lucia Nanni introduced me to the communities working with OCLADE near Iruya. Pablo Frere of Fundapaz enthusiastically welcomed me and Joe, and shared his own experience and wisdom on the work of that organization with the Wichí. The entire Fundapaz team in Los Blancos was exceptionally generous in their participation in this project, sharing their work and their daily routine. Their unstinting support lends this work much depth and insight which it may otherwise have lacked.

In the academic world, I have also accrued debts of gratitude. At McGill University, Don Atwood and Laurel Bossen provided much direction and support throughout my graduate work there, and I would like to thank both of them. I would also like to thank Kristin Norget and John Galaty for their many valuable suggestions. Colin Scott provided a bibliography which proved invaluable for sections on indigenous ecological knowledge, as well as helpful suggestions on chapter 5. Elmer Miller offered invaluable advice and suggestions on an earlier version of the text, especially the sections on the Wichí. Gastón Gordillo and Silvia Hirsch brought together a number of anthropologists working in Argentina at the AAA meetings in 2000, which was an enlightening experience. In Argentina, I would like to thank María Angela Aguilar for her warm welcome at the Universidad Nacional de Salta. Many thanks are also due to Cristobal Wallis, who opened his extensive library to me and allowed me to gain access to a number of sources which would otherwise have been unavailable. I would also like to thank Cristobal for his suggestions and guidance that led me to the Wichí communities near Los Blancos. In Buenos Aires, Morita Carrasco introduced me to the indigenous community at Derqui, another side of indigenous life in Argentina.

I received technical support from friends that made my work much easier. Richard Shaughnessy and Michael Chapman lent me computers to take to the field. John Lincicum found a creative way to back up my data remotely so that I felt secure using those computers.

My friends and family have been unfailingly supportive of my career trajectory which has taken me so far from them at times. Monique Skidmore shared the joys and travails of fieldwork. Megan Miller kept me sane, and also made invaluable suggestions on various drafts. My son, Paul Occhipinti, also should be thanked for putting things in new perspective!

McGill University was generous in its financial support for this research. I am very appreciative of the J. W. McConnell McGill Major Fellowship which supported me throughout the work for my Ph.D. Additional fieldwork funding was provided by the Graduate Faculty and by the Society for Technology and Development (STANDD), both of McGill University. I am grateful for this support.

Introduction

The impulse to make the world a better place is understandable to those of us who have traveled through the remote (and sometimes, not so remote) regions of the world that are often referred to as "underdeveloped." For people from the relatively prosperous parts of the globe, the extreme material poverty that is often encountered is difficult to behold. It is easy to understand how people of good faith and goodwill may dedicate themselves to changing such conditions.

Religious development organizations are often founded out of such efforts. Missionaries, priests, and other religious workers, on finding themselves in a remote region as part of their religious mission, decide that they simply cannot address spiritual questions without paying some attention to the very real conditions of material poverty of their would-be congregations. Their efforts take on many different forms, from simple charity to programs of full-fledged economic transformation.

The process of economic and human development is never a politically neutral, technological procedure, but a process of social and economic change. It is influenced by a global discourse that favors urban centers over rural peripheries, by the economic realities of an international capitalist market, and by trends and fashions among economists and international development agencies. The work of small development organizations is shaped and mediated by such forces. Religious development organizations operate within another context as well, that of their own spiritual and philosophical tradition, an element which may sharply distinguish them from their secular counterparts.

Local cultures, however, are not a blank slate upon which development projects may be writ. As these organizations proceed about the work of economic development, they are thrust into cultural encounters that condition and transform their efforts. Missionaries and development workers are plunged into a negotiation with local people and their way of life. Economic development, as it is actually enacted in local communities, is a complex process of resistance, attraction, and accommodation.

Particularly in indigenous cultures, development entails a process of cultural as well as material change. Local people are neither unanimous nor uncritical in their responses to programs and projects brought to them by outsiders, however well meaning. "Local development" is thus conditioned by negotiations over material and ideological resources: the quest for assistance, the acceptance of some outside interventions, and the rejection of others. It is intensely political, as visions of the present and of potential futures are examined and exchanged.

This research explores the visions and voices that suffuse the process of local development. It considers two case studies of religious organizations working in indigenous communities in northern Argentina. In these remote communities, increasingly involved with and affected by the global capitalist economy, NGOs act as mediators between local and dominant discourses of poverty, of equality, and of managing social and economic change. Religious NGOs, like their secular counterparts, must mobilize ideological resources to gain support from both local communities and their own sources of financial and technical support. I argue that specifically religious idioms of development emerge as religious organizations bring their ideological legitimacy to bear on questions of equity and development.

At the same time, this research is equally interested in the role of the local community in the process of development. Ideas about material and cultural change that an NGO brings to a community are met with varying degrees of skepticism and interest. In indigenous communities, engaged in a fervent dialogue with the dominant national society about identity and rights, "development" is an intensely contested and powerful discursive sphere. Taking into consideration the multivocal and often conflictual political context of any rural community, some individuals and groups mobilize to use both the ideological and material resources provided by NGOs, changing the local political and social, as well as economic, context.

The World of NGOs

Development theory has traditionally dealt with the economy at a macrolevel, rather than considering how economic changes affect people at the local level. Various schools of development theory have tended to paint the world with a very large brush. The unit of analysis is the nation, or even the global region, and the measurements of economic growth are at the level of entire industries or sectors of the economy. In this large-scale approach, institutions, rather than individuals, communities, or households, are the object of study. Macrolevel theories, whether based on liberal or marxist economics, share some of the same problems: a tendency to ignore local cultures, and a lack of historical specificity.

Throughout the world, there are numerous nongovernmental organizations working in the field of economic development. NGOs have become, in recent years, a major conduit for the funding and administration of development projects. According to the *Human Development Report* of the United Nations, the global total that was transferred to international NGOs by governments between 1970 and 1990 increased from under $200 million to $2.2 billion (UNDP 1993, 88). By 2002, more than $7 billion in aid to developing countries flowed through NGOs (UNDP 2002, 5). Globally, there are more than 37,000 NGOs, nearly one-fifth of which were created during the 1990s (UNDP 2002, 5).

Some organizations, such as the World Bank, USAID, or the IMF, are large and well known. Such international organizations promote particular sets of interests, derived from the interests of the large capitalist nations that provide both their funding and their mission. These large agencies tend to be part of the "development machine" (Crush 1995), promoting large-scale projects that may contribute little to improving the conditions for or addressing the interests of local rural people. They focus on *economic* development, measured by indices of GNP and economic growth, rather than *human* development, including issues such as illiteracy, infant mortality, and political empowerment. There is a substantial body of literature on the dynamics of these kinds of large-scale agencies and projects (see, for example, Payer 1991; Escobar 1995; Price 1989; Scott 1998).

There are also innumerable small agencies and organizations working to promote development. These take many different forms: they may be sponsored by international or national charities, religious organizations, or corporations; they may be locally or externally initiated; they may work in agriculture, health care, education, or other fields; and they may be linked to a greater or lesser degree with other organizations. In fact, "the heterogeneity of the universe of NGOs defies most analysts" (Carroll 1992, 23). In the last twenty years, many international organizations have become less involved in managing development programs directly, preferring to act as "partners" who transfer knowledge, technology, and money to smaller, locally managed organizations (UNDP 1993, 89). Most development programs are managed through a combination of central and local organizations with institutional linkages that include financial aid, technical assistance, regulation, representation, and informal influence (Leonard and Marshall 1982, x). The ability of NGOs to create and use such networks may be one asset that they bring to local economic and institutional development, as they are able to create institutional ties between the most marginal individuals and groups and the political system, the market, and funding from larger organizations (Carroll 1992, 181).

Little research has been done on the role of these microagencies in the process of economic development. The question of how NGO programs function in a local community—whether they are effective in promoting economic and human development, who benefits and who stands to lose, how local people gain access, and so on—have not been extensively explored, despite the large sums of money moving through such organizations and the increasing role of NGOs as institutional actors within the international development community. Small NGOs act as the principal agents of development in many regions. They are the interface between global development organizations and local communities, yet they are a "black box" in our understanding of the politics of development (Peters 1996). There is thus a need to understand how they define themselves, to examine the processes through which development is enacted on the local level and in daily praxis.

Religious organizations, the focus of my research, are an important segment of the NGO community. Throughout the world, there are countless NGOs sponsored by local, national, and international religious groups. Nearly every major Christian denomination in the West, from Catholic to Mennonite, funds and staffs some NGOs directly while supporting others indirectly. Some authors suggest that religion and religious organizations are "essential mediums" of development throughout the world (Quarles van Ufford and Schoffeleers 1988; Van Kessel and Droogers 1988). Yet only recently has there begun to be academic research on such organizations—how they operate in local communities and their impact on the world of development organizations (see, for example, Bornstein 2003; Marostica 1998; Mayotte 1998). This dearth of scholarship may be compared to a relatively abundant literature on other aspects of religious organizations, such as missionization, the growth of liberation theology, or the role of churches in national politics. Recent scholarly attention suggests that religious organizations may play a particularly potent role in the process of local development, as they are well placed to mobilize both material resources and a discourse of moral legitimacy.

An analysis of this religious idiom of development means moving beyond a perspective that privileges either the symbolic aspect of religion or the material forces of political economy. Anthropology has tended to treat religion and politics separately—religion as a symbolic system without an inquiry into the social conditions and forces that shape it, and politics as power structures isolated from cultural forces (Bax 1987). Instead, they need to be understood as mutually conditioning processes of meaning and power. Recent works on development have focused attention on the issues of power, language, and discourse in shaping social action (for example, Ferguson 1990; Scott 1998; Escobar 1995). This body of literature has opened up exciting and important questions and directions for anthropological research.

For NGOs that are part of larger religious organizations, the interplay between changing material conditions and ongoing ideological negotiations may be particularly highlighted. Religious development organizations operate within particular ideological frameworks when creating and developing development programs. These frameworks are different, in important and significant ways, from those of mainstream, nonreligious NGOs. Van Kessel and Droogers (1988) suggest that as long as development is seen as a technical, economic problem, the focus of development efforts will be on economic, technological fixes. In contrast, a specifically religious idiom of development will be focused on the ultimate goal of creating a morally desirable social order—however that may be defined.

Numerous authors contend that small NGOs have the potential to promote alternative development, development which promotes the relative empowerment of rural people, particularly those who are poorest, in ways that would increase the choices available to them as well as their ability to act upon those choices (see, for example, Elias 1989; Sen 1992, 1999; Hyden 1983). This may be especially true because of the tendency that has arisen for international organizations to work indirectly, by sponsoring and supporting locally based organizations and initiatives. Although there has been a great deal of praise and optimism about the prospects for alternative development, we need a better understanding of how the strategies and approaches of NGOs are themselves discursively constituted, and how this discourse shapes NGO "solutions" to discursively defined "problems." Religious organizations offer a particularly fertile ground for this kind of research, as they themselves construct a discourse that claims higher purposes than the merely material. In approaching these issues, great geographic and historical contrasts within Argentina provide a challenging but rewarding area of research. This book examines the view that NGOs are effective agents of economic and human development, and considers the effects of a religious discourse upon local development goals.

The Setting: Argentina

Geographically, Argentina encompasses several major ecological zones; beginning at its southernmost tip, one finds cold, barren hills with a small and scattered population. This landscape yields to the lush and fertile pampas of the central plains, which contain the great majority of the nation's population and is the seat of political and economic power. To the west, running the length of the country, rise the formidable Andes Mountains. In the northwest, the geography and climate more closely resemble the nation's Andean neighbors than the capital region. Finally, in the northeast lie lush tropical wetlands and rain forest extending to the border with Brazil, Paraguay, and Uruguay.

The population of the country is similarly diverse and heterogeneous. Unlike most other South America countries, Argentina has a relatively small indigenous population, concentrated in the north. European immigration to the region surrounding Buenos Aires has made this a cosmopolitan city often compared to great European capitals. Economically, the country's history has been tumultuous, with periods of great prosperity based on the export of abundant agricultural produce and a solid industrial base alternating with cycles of phenomenal inflation and crises spurred by debt and depression. Politically, Argentina has enjoyed periods of tranquil democratic rule and has also suffered through some of the most repressive military regimes in the hemisphere.

The province of Salta, the focus of this research, is clearly on the periphery of the Argentine nation politically, culturally, and economically. In many ways this northern province more closely resembles Bolivia and western Paraguay, which border the region to the north, than the center of the nation-state of which it is a part. In the mountainous west of the province, there is a relatively high concentration of indigenous peoples, who share many cultural features with the Quechua-speaking peoples of Bolivia. The mountains quickly drop off in the east of the province, where the Wichí and other former hunter-gatherers share their territory with poor white farmers. The economy of the rural areas is based on subsistence agriculture combined with wage labor on plantations, making it one of the poorest regions of the country.

Development and Underdevelopment in Argentina

Argentina is a vast, complex nation. Its image as a "developed" nation is belied by the conditions that are encountered in its remote rural areas. While Argentina is one of the more prosperous of the Latin American nations, the benefits of economic development have been unequally distributed. Frequent periods of military rule and political unrest, combined with economic policies favoring wealthy landowners and industrialists in the *pampas,* have left peripheral regions with a marginal economic base and little political clout (Corradi 1985). The province of Salta in the Andean northwest is one of its least developed regions. There is little industry, and its agricultural base is heavily dependent on tobacco and sugar, both of which have suffered recent decline (Aguilar and Sbrocco 1995). Small farmers, both mestizo and indigenous, produce subsistence crops and have little involvement in the market.

There are differences of opinion on why Argentina has been in a state of chronic instability since the 1920s, despite its high literacy rates, high living standards, relatively homogenous population, productive agricultural economy with a solid industrial base, and highly urbanized population. James Scobie blames Argentina's troubles on the failure of Argentine nationalism to act as constructive force, the overinvolvement of the military in politics, and the uneven development of the nation (1971, 219-231). Other theorists, notably Cardoso and Faletto (1979) and Frank (1967) in the dependency school, have attributed Argentina's unstable situation to the vagaries of the global capitalist economy and its position in the semiperiphery. They argue that the economic core nations, the United States and Western Europe, have exploited the resources of Latin American countries like Argentina through colonialism and commerce in such a way as to siphon off the surplus production and create underdevelopment in the periphery.

The political turmoil in Argentina during the entire twentieth century, and continuing into the twenty-first, has inhibited its economic growth, despite its rich natural resource base and well-educated population. Ongoing struggles between the central pampas region, which contains about two thirds of the population, and the interior provinces have contributed to uneven development. A political system constructed on patronage, the lack of controls on the power of the military, and an entrenched elite have contributed to the manipulation of the Argentine political economy to redirect economic surplus to a small proportion of the population. Periods of dictatorship and the strong centralized government of Perón with its intensive government investment in, and regulation of, industry, have been punctuated by brief democratic interludes.

Since the return to a civilian, democratically elected government in 1983, Argentina has undergone a series of social and economic reforms. Raul Alfonsín, a human rights leader of the Radical Party, won the October 1983 election but inherited an external debt of $39 billion (U.S.), four hundred fifty percent inflation, and high rates of unemployment at a time when austerity programs were being required by international finance (Andersen 1993, 306). The poor economic situation led to a 1989 election victory by Carlos Menem, the first time in over fifty years that one civilian president succeeded another (Snow and Manzetti 1993, 187). Menem's government instituted a program of economic reforms focused on stabilizing the currency, privatizing government-owned utilities and firms, decreasing government spending, and deregulating the economy. This was the situation that prevailed when the indigenous communities and organizations that I worked with were in the process of trying to complete land claims. Since that time, Argentina has endured a severe economic crisis in 2001-2002, and several changes of government—peaceful, if not all democratic. I address the impact of these recent developments on the indigenous communities of the northwest in my conclusion.

Methodology

Developmental processes, multidimensional in scope, manifest themselves most significantly in local contexts. Thus, an intensive study of a community offers the opportunity to understand the unfolding social changes that accompany development. With this in mind, my research provides a case study focusing on the political, economic, and social impact of development, through a detailed and grounded analysis of two case studies. A focus on the ways in which development discourse is created and enacted at the local level brings more attention to the cultural dimension of economic change, while not losing sight of the relations of power that shape the interactions between development agencies and the local people they purport to serve.

I spent twelve months in Salta, from November of 1996 to November of 1997. My first month in the field I spent developing contacts in the NGO community and choosing field sites for the study. I eventually chose two organizations that were willing to cooperate with me in this study, the *Obra Claretiano de Desarrollo* (Claretian Development Project or OCLADE) and the *Fundación para Desarrollo en Justicia y Paz* (Fundapaz). Both NGOs were informed of the nature of my research and agreed to my presence. In exchange for their cooperation, I promised to write each NGO a report that summarized my findings. Ultimately, just as anthropologists develop more or less friendly relationships with individual informants based on personality, hidden motives, and other intangible and often invisible reasons, so I developed a much closer working relationship with Fundapaz and its staff than with OCLADE.

From December 1996 until May 1997, I lived in the village of Iruya, in the Andean highlands, working with OCLADE. While I had little contact with most of OCLADE's administrative staff, I did have good relationships with many of its volunteers, who generously opened the way for my work in the communities near Iruya. My relationship with OCLADE, which had initially seemed quite promising, ended up being rather distant. Because most of OCLADE's administration was based in Humahuaca, a larger town some hours drive from Iruya, I was not able to observe administrative meetings. In fact, on one occasion when I made the trip to Humahuaca to attend a meeting, I was politely but firmly requested to leave. I believe that tensions among some of the individuals involved in the NGO's administration led to my being viewed rather suspiciously by other staff members. I had limited access to OCLADE's documents, except for those intended to reach a wide audience (i.e., formal publications and reports). However, my reception in the community of Iruya and my relationships with local residents, OCLADE volunteers and the parish priests, were unfailingly warm and welcoming. My focus was on the people and local culture, and my perspective on OCLADE's programs that of the "end user."

Iruya serves as the administrative and market center for a number of smaller villages, most of which are inaccessible by road. My time in the region, like that of the NGO that I was studying, was divided between Iruya and its satellite villages. I was based in Iruya. My husband Joe and I rented a room in the center of town, in a building owned by the municipal government. From there, I made frequent trips to the villages that were within several hours walking distance. I concentrated on the villages where the NGO was most involved—San Isidro and Rodeo Colanzuli. At times, I went to the villages accompanying a member of OCLADE's staff, and attended the meetings that they conducted as part of their business in the villages. More often, I went on my own, spending several days talking to local residents, observing community meetings, participating in fiestas and other community rituals, and visiting people as they went on with the business of their daily lives. Both in town and in the outlying villages, I engaged in intensive participant observation in the community and conducted numerous interviews. I also conducted a detailed survey of sixty-seven households, gathering information on income, agricultural practices, NGO involvement, and household size and composition. In order to conduct the survey, I had the help of three research assistants, who were able to reach households that I could not have, because of distance and time considerations.

From May until November of 1997, I worked in the town of Los Blancos, the base of Fundapaz in the province of Salta. During the time that I was in this region, known as the Chaco, I developed close personal and professional relationships with the staff of Fundapaz. My first month in Los Blancos, I lived with one of the couples who worked for the NGO, and shared meals and a busy schedule with them.[1] During this time, I accompanied Fundapaz staff as they traveled to the communities in which they had programs. I attended nearly all of their meetings during this time, both staff planning meetings and those that they held in the communities. This intensive introduction to both the Wichí and *criollo* communities in the area established a strong base on which to build during the rest of my time in the region.

Because of the difficulties involved in local travel, I concentrated on just one of the Wichí villages. There were three villages I could have worked in: Los Blancos, Misión San Patricio, and Kayip. After careful consideration, I chose Kayip because of its mixed economy and its accessibility. Kayip was also suggested to me by the director of Fundapaz as the community that "demanded the most" of the organization. The high expectations that this particular community has of the NGO, and subsequent negotiations in the relationship by both parties, proved to be a fertile ground for research.

For the remaining months that I spent in the Chaco, I spent half of each week in a small house that Joe and I rented in Los Blancos, and half in Kayip, where the community generously let us stay in the community center. The days in Los Blancos were variously spent at meetings with Fundapaz staff, reviewing documents, visiting the other Wichí communities with Fundapaz on their regular round of meetings, and typing up the notes from my days in Kayip. During those busy days, I engaged in participant observation, conducted numerous formal interviews, and spent countless hours conversing with members of the Wichí community. I also attended NGO meetings in the community when they coincided with my time there. Joe usually accompanied me on my visits to Kayip, and his presence proved invaluable. There were some taboos on my interactions with young men, particularly those who were unmarried. Joe, who has considerable training and experience in social science research, was able to act as my research assistant in these interactions, providing a social legitimacy that I could not have attained as an unattached female.

Collecting economic data in Kayip presented a particular challenge. The Wichí, unlike the people of Iruya, do not keep careful track of their incomes and expenditures. Their subsistence is based partly on day labor, partly on subsistence agriculture, and partly on hunting and gathering.[2] This mix is irregular and varies daily. It also varies much more radically with the seasons; I was there during the dry season, when natural resources are most scarce and wage labor most important. A detailed socioeconomic survey, as I had done in the highlands, made little sense in this small village. Instead, I took a complete census of each household: family members and available labor, animals, household gardens and enclosures. I then conducted a time-allotment study of adults, tracking what productive activities they performed each day. This provided a snapshot of how households met their subsistence needs. I periodically compared the information I collected with the impressions of Fundapaz staff and members of the community, in order to gauge both the accuracy of my results and their perception of seasonal variation.

Throughout this work, the names of most individuals have been changed in order to protect their privacy. The only exceptions to this are public figures, such as bishops and politicians. The names of the communities and NGOs have not been changed; to do so, without changing geographic and ethnographic details that are essential to the case studies, would have been disingenuous, as they would be easily identifiable to anyone familiar with the area. Throughout my fieldwork, I endeavored to get informed consent from all of my informants. Both NGOs were aware of the nature of my research and agreed to participate. In Kayip, formal permission was requested from and granted by the community. In Rodeo Colanzuli, I worked closely with the Centro Vecinal, whose leaders and members agreed to allow me to conduct research. In these communities and in the others where I found myself, I explained the nature of my work to people I interviewed and spoke with at any length, and obtained oral consent from them. At times, especially in communities where I visited infrequently, I was occasionally mistaken for either a member of the NGO staff or a foreign missionary. Although I cannot be certain that I was always successful in conveying my own anthropological mission, I did try to be clear about the nature of my work and my relationships with the organizations that were my frequent companions. Because of the nature of anthropological fieldwork, in which every conversational encounter is a potential bit of data, the extent to which I explained what I was doing varied from a simple statement that I was a North American anthropologist doing research to a full-blown description of my project.

Local Voices

In the chapters that follow, I offer a picture of communities and organizations and the relationships between them. I am often trying to understand and portray the feelings, opinions, and experiences of the people whom I met there. No anthropologist, and indeed no individual, can claim to speak for the people with whom they work. As has been intensively discussed in recent years, anthropological texts are a particular kind of representation, culturally and historically determined (see, for example, Clifford 1988; Geertz 1988). However, I am inclined to agree with the comments of Steve Gudeman and Alberto Rivera (1990, 3) that:

> The anthropological text is a controlled communication that the author uses to persuade or critique, invent, justify, or reaffirm a theoretical position. . . . To be certain, one must be wary of adopting the view that the "facts" are "there" to be collected. But according to the recent "textualists," the claim to have had the "experience" of "being there" is itself a rhetorical figure, a culturally and his-

> torically dated ideology used to justify the authority of the text in which it appears (Clifford 1983, 1988). . . . We take issue with this view that would pass over the special anthropological practice of listening to other voices and [would] evade consideration of the many skills anthropologists have developed and learned, used and refined, in their research.

In my research, I have engaged in "the special anthropological practice of listening to other voices." In my writing, I have tried to remain true to what those voices told me. To be sure, I am not trying to speak for them; I speak about them, based on my own admittedly imperfect understanding of what they were trying to say.

It is no longer revolutionary in anthropology to understand that a village is not an indivisible entity. "[A] view of an authentic culture as an autonomous internally homogenous coherent universe no longer seems tenable in a post colonial world. Neither 'we' nor 'they' are as self-contained and homogenous as we/they once appeared" (Rosaldo 1988, 87). People in small communities have a variety of interests and viewpoints. Even in a remote, unstratified society like that of the Wichí, groups and individuals within a single community may have wildly differing interests and values. During the course of my research, I tried to be sensitive to these varying interests and viewpoints. Insofar as it was possible to identify these schisms in the community, I endeavored to take them into account, interviewing people from the widest range of the divisions within the community. In my portrayal of these communities and organizations, I similarly have tried to convey the diverse and often dissonant voices and viewpoints that together spoke the whole.

Adelante

The chapters that follow explore the meaning of "development" in the two communities where I worked, and consider how development has been defined and enacted by various actors, from the NGO to local individuals. These visions of development have concrete effects, as demonstrated in an examination of the communities' efforts to gain legal title to land, and the role of each NGO in that process. In considering these two organizations, and two communities, I have struggled with the notion of making comparisons. Any kind of direct comparison between these two cases becomes problematic, if not impossible—I am looking at two very different cultures and at two very different organizations. The "variables" in a direct comparison would be unwieldy at best, and in reality are simply too divergent. Instead, I have tried to approach this work as offering two case studies, each of which sheds a different perspective on the role of religion in development and on the role of small NGOs in an indigenous community. From this perspective, the two case studies offer intriguing possibilities for looking at this question through different lenses. Both organizations are based in a progressive Catholicism. Each has developed a relationship in the community in which it works over many years, and each is deeply respectful of both the native culture and the agency of the people it works with. They work in the same province, and so share the same legal and political context, while their staff moves through the same networks. By placing these two studies side by side, I hope to open a broader perspective, one which has the potential of seeing beyond the personalities, quirks, or coincidences of a single case, and gain some understanding of a wider picture, a picture of a mode of development connected to religious ideals, played out in indigenous communities.

Chapter 1 begins with a detailed description of Iruya, its people, and the NGO that works there, OCLADE. It discusses the geography, economy, and culture of the region. Chapter 2 provides a similar context for Los Blancos and Fundapaz. Chapter 3 then moves on to examine development discourses. Beginning with a review of recent work on this issue, the chapter then proceeds to consider the role of small NGOs in creating and putting into practice such a discourse. The work of Fundapaz and OCLADE is determined to a large extent by the ways in which each organization envisions the needs and possibilities of the indigenous communities where they work. The ways in which this discourse is created and sustained in these organizations, and how this conflicts or coincides with local ideas about development, forms the second half of this chapter. Fundapaz and OCLADE are both influenced by the development discourse that prevails internationally, but their particular practices and goals are also informed by their religious backgrounds. Both were founded out of a progressive Catholicism inspired by liberation theology, and their work and discourse carry this religious underpinning forward. The emergence of a religious idiom of development is the subject of chapter 4.

Chapter 5 then turns to an examination of land tenure practices in the two communities. Much of the legitimacy of their claim to land is based on their status as indigenous communities. This specifically indigenous right to land is explicitly based on claims to historic reparation, but it is also seen to be constituted by a unique emotional and spiritual tie of an indigenous culture to its territory. This chapter considers the role of land and landscape in the cultures of Iruya and Los Blancos, the particular ethnoecologies that underlie ideas about development. Finally, chapter six reviews the land claims cases that have been pursued, and recently won, by local residents in both communities. It gives special attention to the role of each NGO in land claims issues, and how this role has been determined, at least in part, by their broader views of development and the role that each has defined for itself in the community.

Notes:

1. My husband was in the United States during that month.
2. One of the reasons I chose Kayip was that it was the most "intermediate" of the three communities in terms of this mix of subsistence strategies.

Table 1: Key Features of Each Case Study

	Iruya	Los Blancos*
Ethnic group	Kolla	Wichí
Satellite communities	San Isidro, Río Grande, Colanzulí, Campo Carreras	Misión San Patricio, Kayip, Cacique Abregu
Community size (including satellite communities)	5,000	1,000
Environment	Mountains, valleys	Chaco (dry monte or bush)
Economic base	Subsistence agriculture and herding, some migrant labor	Mix of hunting and gathering, subsistence agriculture, wage labor, herding
Religious affiliation	Catholic (80%), Evangelical (20%)	Anglican (nearly 100%)
NGO	OCLADE	Fundapaz
Type of NGO projects	Health and education, child nutrition, cooperatives, animal health, community organization	Infrastructure development for subsistence agriculture, craft production, community organization
Landownership before reclamation	Mostly private (fincas)	Government

* The information in this table refers only to the Wichí communities around Los Blancos. There is a significant *criollo*, or white, population in the region as well.

Chapter 1: Iruya and OCLADE

History, Geography, and Ethnography of Iruya

The village of Iruya is located in the mountainous northwest of the province of Salta. The image of this remote village, with its single church spire dwarfed by the surrounding canyon walls, is nearly ubiquitous in the tourist literature found in the provincial capital. But only a few hardy tourists make the daunting ten-hour bus trip over unpaved roads, through narrow passes, and fording several rivers. Those who do often are drawn not only by the stunning natural beauty, to which the glossy photos scarcely do justice, but also by the promise of an "untouched" local culture. While contemporary anthropologists scorn such a static view of any rural culture, the casual visitor is struck by the isolation of this community, by the distinct local culture, and by the daily routines of its inhabitants, regulated more by sun and season than by clock and stock market.

The village of Iruya, which numbers about 600 residents, serves as the administrative center for an eponymous *departamento* of about 6,000.[1] The "interior" villages are located from two to fourteen or more hours walking distance from the center, over terrain which is rugged and at times impassable, even on foot. Some of these interior communities are nearly as large as Iruya itself, while others are the home of only a few families living in scattered homesteads. Residents of the interior villages journey to Iruya to sell their produce and purchase manufactured goods, to complete government transactions, and to obtain health care. The communities are linked to the center and to each other through numerous kinship ties, commercial relationships, and social bonds. They share a common culture and worldview, but there are some differences between them, particularly in terms of local economy.

An outline of the culture, economy, and history of Iruya provides a background for the case study which follows. In many ways, the region is distinct, both culturally and economically, from the high *altiplano* or *puna* of nearby Bolivia, and even more so from the central areas of Peru or Ecuador. Information on the local economy and indices of human development in Iruya situate the following discussion on development projects. I conclude the chapter with a description of the history and organization of the *Obra Claretiano de Desarrollo* or OCLADE, a Catholic NGO active in the region.

Iruya: The Setting

The road to Iruya starts about 20 kilometers up the national route from Humahuaca, a larger town that is a center for both tourism and commerce. The turnoff is unpaved for the next 45 kilometers, which takes nearly three hours by the bus that runs between Iruya and Humahuaca four days every week. Although not considered "highlands" or "puna" locally, the community is located in a narrow canyon at about 9,000 feet above sea level. The interior villages range in altitude from just slightly higher than Iruya to about 11,000 feet above sea level. The landscape is very dry, with views of beautiful canyons and valleys that attract the occasional tourist. The road is just barely visible in places, a track that winds through the hills. The first sign of habitation again are the green fields of Rodeo Colanzulí across the canyon as the descent begins.

From there, the road, just barely wide enough for the bus, runs along the cliff wall halfway up one side of the canyon, passing an occasional homestead. The first sight of Iruya is the church steeple as you come around one of the turns. Then it vanishes again for a few minutes, reappearing as the road begins its final ascent into town. The plaza in front of the church is where the road ends. Across the canyon, you can see the little houses that make up the "*banda*," arranged along one narrow path that climbs up until it gets too steep.[2] The houses are made of adobe and almost vanish into the hillside. The church has a single bell tower, a wide front with a big plain cross and the words "Save Your Soul" emblazoned on one side.

The streets of Iruya are narrow, paved in rough cobblestones. They are barely wide enough for the few trucks that bring supplies to the many small shops, but there is no other traffic here. Most of the houses are made up of a series of small rooms arranged around a central courtyard, and in town, each presses up against its neighbor. The houses right in the center are plastered, painted white or pastels. Further up and down the hill, the houses are more likely to be unadorned adobe. The roofs are mostly corrugated metal, although a few are the more traditional plaster over cane. The streets all have steep inclines, as the town is perched on the side of a hill between two river valleys. At the very top of the hill sits a telephone antenna, in vivid contrast to the little cross and shrine that have been there much longer. The secondary school is the highest building up the hill, about a block up from the hospital.

The town has a system of potable water, if an unreliable one, supplied by a system of filtration tanks just below the top of the hill. There is a diesel generator located on the road below the church, which provides electricity eight hours each day during the week and six on weekends. There are a number of small stores which are stocked with minimal amounts of manufactured goods, including clothing and sneakers, canned foods, candy, wine and soda, and fresh produce, including things which are not generally grown locally such as onions and fruit. Such goods are usually purchased from trucks which arrive occasionally from the city, or purchased by members of the community on sporadic shopping trips, often to Bolivia. A few of the more prosperous shop owners have their own trucks.

The village of Iruya functions as the commercial and administrative center of the *departamento.* It is the center of the municipal government, which includes many satellite villages.[3] Residents of the smaller villages in the "interior" make periodic pilgrimages to buy manufactured goods and sell some produce, visit the hospital, complete their official business in the municipal offices, or, more rarely, to make a trip outside of the *departamento.* The population of Iruya itself is approximately 600, making it the largest center in the *departamento,* which has a total of 6,000 inhabitants. The municipal government owns a large television antenna that is aimed to receive the one or two channels that broadcast this deeply into the mountains.[4] A single telephone was installed in 1997, but two-way radios, located in the hospital and the municipal offices, provide a more reliable means of communication.

The Interior Villages

The villages of the interior are far smaller, some with only a few isolated households. Some are more than a day's walk from town, and only Rodeo Colanzulí has a road that is passable all year.[5] They are connected to Iruya and to each other by networks of well-worn and well-traveled footpaths. Most interior residents rely on burros, mules, and horses for transportation. The interior villages are much more isolated than Iruya and have far fewer of the basic services that exist in town. San Isidro is the only interior village with electricity, with a generator that provides two hours of power each evening to part of the community. There are no televisions, and radio broadcasts depend on the weather and the listener's exact position in the rugged terrain. There are no phones, and two-way radios are few and far between, usually located in health outposts. Most of the interior villages do not have a reliable source of potable water, using water directly from the rivers or from springs.[6] In each village, there are one or two tiny stores, similar to those in Iruya but smaller.

The Local Economy

The most important economic activity in the villages of the interior is subsistence agriculture. The majority of households have less than one hectare of land (see table 2), with very few households possessing more than two hectares. A household's land is nearly always divided between several small plots; some households may have as many as ten or twelve small fields under cultivation, some close to the house and others a kilometer or more away. Growing conditions vary tremendously, both regionally and in the microconditions of each plot. As elsewhere in the Andes, variations in altitude create microclimatic zones, which are used in vertical patterns of land distribution (Fonseca Martel and Mayer 1988). Households typically maintain some rights to land at a range of altitudes in order to maintain their ability to diversify their production. At relatively lower altitudes, an agricultural zone is intensely cultivated. The land is plowed using teams of animals, usually bulls, or with picks and shovels.[7] Chemical fertilizers and pesticides are not used; most households use some organic manure as fertilizer, and rotate fields between crops, fodder, and fallow, the cycle depending on the location of the fields and the household's particular needs.

Table 2: Landholdings in the *Departamento* of Iruya, 1996-1997

	Landholding	None	Up to 0.5 ha	Up to 1 ha	Up to 2 ha	More than 2 ha	Un-known	Total
Interior villages	Number of Households	1	19	8	3	5	2	38
	% of House-holds	3%	50%	21%	8%	13%	5%	100%
Iruya	Number of Households	3	22	2	2	0	0	29
	% of House-holds	10%	76%	7%	7%	0%	0%	100%
Total Number of Households		4	41	10	5	5	2	67
Total % of Households		6%	61%	15%	7%	7%	3%	100%

Landholdings measured in hectares (ha).
(Based on survey of households, May-June 1997.)

Irrigation systems are simple, using gravity-fed channels that divert water from rivers and streams at higher altitudes. Irrigation is communally managed, with households retaining rights to specific time segments and under obligation to assist with maintaining the communal channels.

The most important subsistence crops are potatoes and maize. Families usually raise these crops only to meet their own subsistence needs, not for the market, since transportation is difficult and the prices for both of these crops are quite low. Most families also raise some garden crops to meet their own needs to the extent that local conditions permit. Many vegetables which are part of the local diet, such as tomatoes, do not grow well locally and are nearly always purchased.

Higher grasslands are used as pasture for domestic animals and as a source of fuel for cooking and heating. Most households raise small herds of goats, sheep, and cattle for their own use. They may have a horse or two for transportation, and often burros for hauling produce. All of these animals are grazed on the nearby hills during the summer, then usually are moved to the lowlands for the cold winter, a journey of several days. A few households also raise chickens or pigs.[8] In San Isidro, which is located in a small valley and is somewhat more temperate than Rodeo Colanzulí, many families raise fruit trees and sell fresh or dried fruit. At higher altitudes, peas and fava beans are more common cash crops. The yearly income from the sale of such agricultural produce is generally quite small, with most families earning only a few hundred pesos after the harvest (see table 3).[9] Because transportation is so difficult, households in the interior villages closest to Iruya are somewhat more involved in market production than those in the more isolated settlements further from town.

In Rodeo Colanzulí, which has the advantage of a seasonal road, buyers come from the outside to contract directly with households for their produce. However, there is only one intermediary to whom nearly all households sell their produce. The terms of trade are generally unfavorable, as he exchanges manufactured goods and foods for produce, often leaving the family in debt until the next harvest, when the cycle is repeated. Farmers in other villages bring their produce directly to Iruya, usually using burros. From there, it is sold in small quantities to local merchants who resell it in town, or sent out by truck or bus to seek a better price in the market at Humahuaca. If a farmer chooses to send produce to outside markets, the price of transportation, paid in advance by the producer, often is equal to half or more of the final price that he or she will receive. This is generally only considered worthwhile for light, relatively expensive items with a limited local market, such as dried fruit.

Some households supplement agriculture with wage labor (see table 3). There is little steady employment available in the interior, this being limited to a few jobs working for the municipality, schools, or as part-time "*mamas cuidadoras*" for preschool programs run by OCLADE. The total number of such steady positions is about fifteen in Rodeo Colanzulí (of a total population of 534), and ten or eleven in San Isidro (where the total population is 318).[10] There is also sporadic day labor available to men within the community, mostly for construction projects sponsored by the government. Such work is highly sought but very irregular.

In the village of Iruya itself, sources of income are more diverse (see table 3). Many village families maintain small plots of land on which they grow subsistence crops and have a few large animals. This subsistence farming is usually secondary to wage earnings, supplementing them and providing a safety net in an uncertain labor market. In Iruya, most families have some income from wage labor. Sources of employment are limited, and jobs working for the government—directly, in the offices of the *departamento*, or indirectly, in the hospital and schools—are the most common. Other Iruya residents work as unskilled or semiskilled laborers, usually on a temporary or daily basis. Many families run small stores, selling groceries, beer and wine, inexpensive manufactured goods such as clothing and shoes, and other necessities to their neighbors and the residents of the interior. Most of the manufactured goods sold in these shops are purchased in nearby Bolivia, where prices are much lower.

While many Iruyan families continue to rely largely on a subsistence economy, the region has become much more highly integrated into a larger international economy where production is aimed at national or global markets, cash is essential to survival, and access to transportation has increased. However, the impact of capitalism is uneven within the community, depending on local cultural practices, social stratification, access to means of communication and transportation, and the ability of some individuals to take differential advantage of a changing situation (cf. Bourque and Warren 1981). Historically, highland areas were able to trade items like wool, meat, and potatoes for products from neighboring lowland regions, including fruits and vegetables and wooden items such as bowls, tools, and furniture. Because most lowland areas and urban communities are now fully involved in capitalist production, the traditional system of trade between regions has broken down, leaving many highland crops with much less value. Highland residents still have access to lowland products, as well as to the manufactured goods which have supplanted some items, but need cash in order to purchase them. Residents of Salta's highland areas have increasingly turned to migrant wage labor as an alternative source of income. Ricardo Abduca (1995) argues that a dependence on migrant labor in the region has led to a decrease in the productivity of land controlled by rural communities, as much of the labor force has been siphoned off. He points to increases in highland poverty and the decreased autonomy of rural producers as some of the consequences of this shift. Abduca notes that such a dependence on wage labor has arisen as a result of a long historical process, beginning with coerced labor during the colonial period. Until as late as the 1920s, rural producers were required to work in exchange for usufruct rights to land. Abduca finds that migrant wage labor has continued to increase since the 1970s, mostly on sugar plantations, as rural producers are increasingly involved in a cash economy.

For families in town as well as those of the interior, migrant work is common, as families send one or more members to work in plantations. As in Eastern Bolivia, there is a fluid relationship between subsistence cultivation and wage labor, with people moving in and out of both systems (Gill 1987, 4). Migrant labor represents a significant income for many rural families, particularly those located near commercial areas where wages may be somewhat higher. Formerly, sugar plantations within the province hired large numbers of workers, both men and women. In recent years, the mechanization of the sugar harvest has dramatically reduced the jobs available to Iruyan migrants. The jobs that remain are often filled by Bolivian workers, rather than rural migrants; the plantations prefer foreign workers who are not covered by Argentina's labor laws and may be paid much lower wages (Whiteford 1981). Iruyan migrant laborers generally must travel much further afield to find seasonal agricultural work, going as far as Rio Negro and the province of Buenos Aires in the south, where there are fewer foreign workers. This kind of work represents an important source of income, especially as money returns to the village in a large lump sum. Often, this money provides capital that is invested in increasing a family's landholdings, purchasing stock to start a small store, or buying a truck. In other households, it merely provides the cash that is needed to get the family through the year. Migrant labor is seen as a hardship, as the strongest workers of the household are gone for the entire growing season. Few families engage in migrant labor on a yearly basis. Instead, it is usually undertaken by young adults, who use the money earned to establish their own household or to supplement farm income for a large family where several workers remain at home.

Table 3: Description of Household Income in Iruya

	Iruya	Interior
Percent of households reporting income from employment	52%	43%
Average of reported employment income*	$291	$222
Percent of households reporting income from sale of agricultural produce	24%	49%
Average reported agricultural income †	**	$337
(Median reported agricultural income)	**	($240)
Percent of households reporting income from self-employment♦	24%	8%
Percent of households reporting income from migrant labor	21%	27%
Percent of households reporting income from other sources ‡	38%	35%
Percent of households reporting no cash income	3%	19%
Total number of households surveyed	29	37

All figures in Argentine pesos.
* This figure is based on households that reported some income from employment only.
** Information on income not reported.
† Of those households reporting some agricultural income.
♦ "Self employment" includes small shops, restaurants, and other home businesses.
‡ Includes pensions, sale of craft products, and irregular wage labor.
Source: Survey of households, May-June 1997

Migrant labor also takes the form of young people who leave the region to work in the city, usually Salta. This "life cycle" migration is common. In most such cases, young men and women leave the village, often for a period of several years, and accept low-paying jobs in the city. Young men usually work as unskilled laborers, often in construction, while young women find positions as housekeepers or watching children. Of course, some of these young people never return, choosing to remain in the city. Often, however, after a few years, they return and take over their parents' landholdings or purchase some land of their own. This kind of migrant labor does not usually provide a significant nest egg, since the cost of living in the city is considerably higher. In many households where the landholding is too small to support the typically large family, however, this pattern of migration may relieve some of the population pressure on the land. For some young people, who are exposed to urban lifestyles by television and radio and in their schools, where most of the teachers are from urban areas, the desire to experience a different way of living, which seems more glamorous than farming, is irresistible.

Being Kolla: Local Culture

The great majority of the people in the *departamento*, particularly in the interior, are part of the Kolla culture that spans northwest Argentina.[11] There are very few individuals within the *departamento* with European roots, as most of the large landowners never settled in the area but maintained their estates by proxy. Their agents also did not settle in the region but visited periodically to collect rents. The families who do claim European roots are few and are concentrated in the town of Iruya itself. Some other families trace their family tree to rural communities elsewhere in the provinces of Salta or Jujuy, but the vast majority trace their roots within the *departamento* itself.

The Kolla culture is part of the Andean cultural region and shares many traits with highland people in nearby Bolivia (about 80 kilometers away as the crow flies) as well as the southern Andes. Locally, as throughout this part of the province, the people refer to themselves as Kolla, a term that was previously considered pejorative but has recently been reclaimed by some indigenous leaders and is now generally accepted in the region.

Archaeologically, the local cultural antecedents are unclear. The area around Iruya shows clear archaeological evidence of habitation since the pre-Incan era. The region was incorporated into the Incan empire but remained peripheral to Incan expansion which generally followed a line further to the west. Pre-Conquest settlements near Iruya were located along important trade routes between the high puna to the west and the lowlands to the east. Some Incan ruins dot the area, marking defensive sites and trade routes. There is some debate among archaeologists of the region regarding which group or groups inhabited the area, but pre-Conquest information is scarce, as little excavation has been done in the region. "At the time of the Inca conquest [approximately 1100-1200 AD], the whole Andean region was divided into an almost unbelievable number of small political units, for many of which we do not even have the names" (Rowe 1963, 185). In the mountainous region where Iruya is situated, there were at least four distinct tribes: Ocloya, Churumata, Paypaya, and Osa (Reboratti 1996, 41). Of these, the most important was the Ocloya, who inhabited the region between Iruya and Nazarena, a town to the north. All of these indigenous groups were agriculturalists, growing maize, potatoes, and a root called *oka*, using terraced irrigation systems, and raising camelids. Land was owned communally, with plots assigned to households and transmitted through both male and female lines (Cushner 1982, 72).

During the colonial period, there were significant ecological changes in Iruya, as the Spanish replaced local systems of management and tenure, as well as crops and animals, with those that they brought from Europe (Reboratti 1996, 54-55). Llamas were pushed to higher altitudes as the European herd animals, which fared poorly at the higher elevations, took over the lower grazing lands. Transhumance was introduced during this period, also to accommodate the less well-adapted European animals. Cattle, sheep, and goats were more destructive of native plants than native camelids and caused more erosion. There was a degradation of pasture, combined with increased erosion, especially at higher altitudes. At the same time, there was a shift from irrigated agriculture to seasonal agriculture and overall productivity decreased, as the population decreased and land use became more extensive.

Because of constitutional changes that require indigenous peoples to have a history of continuous occupation in order to be entitled to certain legal protections, the issue of archaeological antecedents is hotly debated. Some authors, and at times the government, claim that the local population is not in fact "indigenous" according to this legal definition, arguing instead that they are the remnants of historical, post-Conquest migration from Bolivia (cf. Reboratti 1996).[12] Some claim that the cultural similarities between peoples of southern Bolivia and northwestern Argentina must be indicative of such migration. They further claim that the "Hispanicization" of local people—the loss of an indigenous language, of many religious rituals, and of other visible signs of cultural difference—is so thorough that the claim to an indigenous status has become invalid. This argument, generally mobilized in support of exclusionary political goals, such as denying local rights to landownership, ignores a long history of the active suppression of the indigenous language by the government and by white colonists, the eradication of public displays of local religious beliefs by the Church, and a pervasive racial discrimination that has led many local people themselves to assimilate as much as possible into the dominant population. It is also based on an approach to culture that focuses on the maintenance of "traditions" and a kind of catalog of traits, rather than a more nuanced view of contemporary indigenous peoples.

For these and other reasons, the issue of ethnic identity as Kolla and as "indigenous" is contentious and complicated throughout the region, and perhaps particularly in the valleys (Occhipinti 2002). Many individuals, especially in town, choose not to refer to themselves as Kolla, due in part to many years of prejudice and discrimination against native people in this part of the country. Because of the prejudice and ambivalence about the term, even asking people if they considered themselves to be "Kolla" was a topic that had to be approached carefully. I had a lengthy conversation one day with Juan Pablo, a soft-spoken middle-aged deacon in San Isidro, who tried to explain the local reluctance to identify oneself as Kolla:

> For my father, the word "Kolla" was a proud word. But people my age, they don't accept this. They don't consider themselves to be indigenous. Some accept it. But there are others who don't like to say "Kolla." When we go to the sugar plantations—I used to go—we would get there on the bus and they used to say, "Kollas from Iruya, shitty Kollas."

Instead, people often refer to "local culture" or "our culture," without invoking a specific identity as Kolla or as indigenous.

There are clear ethnic and cultural differences between the local people and what could be called the "dominant" Argentinean culture, differences recognized both locally and by outsiders (Merlino and Proaño 1994). Even when the people of Iruya migrate to nearby urban Salta, they feel a strong cultural distance from the *criollo* poor there. In some ways, the people of Iruya have lost many of the most visible markers of culture. There are no native speakers of Quechua within the *departamento*, for example; even the oldest residents say that their own grandparents spoke Spanish.[13] The *ayllu*, a kinship form that is still prevalent in other parts of the Andes, has disappeared; kinship is reckoned bilaterally, but with no reference to the extended family forms of the *ayllu*.[14] "Traditional" forms of dress, bright skirts and shawls for women and handwoven wool trousers for men, are gradually being replaced by more ubiquitous mass-produced clothing. Some skills, such as weaving on hand looms, are gradually being lost, although they are still practiced. Other visible markers of culture persist. Women carry their children on their backs, wrapped snugly in ponchos or shawls. Local fiestas are celebrated with *coplas*, a traditional musical form, and with *chicha*, a mildly alcoholic corn-based drink. These visible signs of culture are only the markers of cultural differences; the Iruyan culture itself cannot be quantified in a list of traits "lost" or ineluctably changed. A worldview persists in Iruya in conversation with changes that have occurred, and are occurring, in its relationship with the dominant culture of northern Argentina.

In the last several years, some of the reluctance to claim an indigenous identity has diminished, and Kolla identity is emerging as an important facet of political and cultural interactions, both within the *departamento* and in the relations of the local communities with the larger regional and national systems. Clearly, the awareness of the land issue and its inextricable tie to indigenous identity has played a significant role. Kolla identity has been politicized, invoked by urban dwellers and organizations that many local residents feel have lost their connections to the community. At this level, an internationalized discourse of indigenous rights has taken some precedence over local cultural differences and the needs of local people. However, this political struggle has had direct and concrete benefits for local people, as it has spurred the national government, in particular, to reconsider indigenous land claims throughout Argentina, including Iruya (see chapter 6). The emphasis on indigenous rights and an identity that incorporates an idea of being indigenous and being Kolla has also had emotional consequences for local identity. As a sense of indigenous identity has been revalorized, more people have been willing to lay claim openly to an identity as Kolla, using the word not as an expletive but again with a sense of pride.

OCLADE

In Iruya, as in perhaps most isolated rural communities throughout the world, nongovernmental organizations (NGOs) have taken on the role of promoting programs of human and economic development. The most important NGO in Iruya is the *Obra Claretiano de Desarrollo* (Claretian Development Project), better known as OCLADE. It is a development outreach program of the Claretian order, a Spanish missionary group that has charge of the Catholic Church throughout the prelature of Humahuaca, a district that spans the northern part of the province of Salta and most of the rural areas of the province of Jujuy.[15] OCLADE, as an NGO, is closely tied to the regional Church both financially and administratively. In addition to Iruya, OCLADE works in about six other *departamentos* throughout the highlands, all within the prelature.

Historically, OCLADE has been most active in areas of health and education in Iruya. This focus is in part due to the personal skills and interests of some of the people who were key to founding the organization, and also as a response to historic needs of the community. OCLADE has also acted as an important conduit of material resources into the community; projects have provided materials to construct systems for drinking water, for irrigation, and to build health posts. There have also been several attempts to create productive associations and cooperatives in both agriculture and the production of craft goods. While these had some success in the short term, they met with long term failure, and none of them are currently active in the community.

The History of the Obra Claretiana de Desarrollo (OCLADE)

OCLADE administers development programs throughout the prelature of Humahuaca, which covers a rather large area in the provinces of Salta and Jujuy, including most of the puna (*altiplano*) of northwest Argentina, as well as the sub-Andean valleys directly to the east (including the *departamentos* of Santa Victoria Oeste and Iruya). This area may well represent one of the poorest geographical regions in Argentina, with high indices of illiteracy, infant and child malnutrition, and unemployment. Because of the size of the area and the difficulties of transportation and communication, particularly in the rainy season (December-March), the resources of OCLADE are sometimes spread thin.

Before the mid-1970s, this region was served only by itinerant priests from Salta and a few German missionaries who traveled around occasionally to the villages.[16] In response to requests from these priests and some of their parishioners, the Vatican ordered the bishop of Salta to find a missionary order willing to take charge of the region (Olmedo Rivera 1990, 265). In 1968, the bishop reached an agreement with a Spanish order called the *Misioneros de la corazón de María*, or Claretians [*Claretianos*]. This link represented an infusion of personnel and resources into the region which had not previously had such an active Catholic presence. The Claretians began a program of active outreach and missionization designed to increase participation in the Church and improve the Church's visibility and presence in rural communities. According to Jesús Olmedo Rivera, a Claretian missionary working in the puna for a number of years, the order wanted to create an atmosphere that encouraged integrated religious evangelization with a respect for the distinct nature of the local culture and a program of "human development with a liberational dimension" (1990, 266).

In 1969, the prelature of Humahuaca was created. This administrative unit, which is smaller than a diocese, had a degree of autonomy greater than that which had existed previously in the region and its own bishop. The Claretians continued to increase the numbers of missionaries in the region. They expanded their physical base, constructing parish houses and meeting facilities in several locations. By the mid-1970s, they also began to augment their role in providing social services, such as homes for the elderly, youth centers, and an employment center. From this beginning, a number of development programs took root.

In 1982, the bishop held an assembly of the prelature, open to everyone living within the region, to discuss what the Church needed to do to contribute to the spiritual, economic, and social development of the communities. As a result of the assembly, which took the form of a series of meetings, development ("*la promoción humana*") emerged as an important issue. A new objective took its place in the mission statement of the prelature: "To achieve for the people, and with the people, complete human development [*la promoción humana*] as a sign of liberation, understood as the step from less humane living conditions to others more humane and liberating" (Olmedo Rivera 1990, 277). A priest was appointed to deal exclusively with development questions. It was decided that a separate, autonomous organization should be formed to deal with questions of development, and thus OCLADE was created, with the mission of supporting the communities of the prelature in their development efforts.

The Organization of OCLADE

In the thirteen years since OCLADE was founded, some of its projects have continued while others have ended or been abandoned. In 1996, another assembly of the prelature was held, with one of its goals to reevaluate the projects and programs of OCLADE as well as the development problems and needs of the communities within the region. In preparation for this meeting, Church representatives visited people living within the prelature over a period of three months, completing a large socioeconomic survey. There was then a period in which groups were formed at the level of the prelature to consider the major issues that emerged from the survey. As a result of the survey and the meetings which followed it, OCLADE has undergone a number of organizational and programmatic changes, many of which were still taking shape at the time of my research.

In 1997, OCLADE had about twenty-five people as full-time paid employees, including an administrative council of nine people (five laypeople and four clergy), three drivers, and a number of promoters who coordinate specific programs. The administrative council and the majority of the promoters are not from the communities of the prelature, but come from urban regions of Argentina, including Salta and Buenos Aires, and from Spain. Beyond this paid staff, there are also numerous people working at the local level, all of whom are unpaid or receive only a very small amount of money from the organization. There are forty-five "*mamas cuidadoras*" (child care workers, or "caring mothers") for example, who work in an infant health program and seven "popular educators" who work in a program for women, all of whom receive a small stipend for their work.[17] At the local level, the bulk of the work is done by these and other volunteers. The Church, more generally, trains over a thousand people, mostly to lead local Bible studies, but they also often deal with social problems. One of OCLADE's administrators characterized the work of such volunteers as "our most important support. If it weren't for them, we wouldn't be able to do anything."

OCLADE's funding comes from various religious intermediary organizations, both Catholic and Protestant, from nonreligious development organizations, and from several government programs. The Claretian order provides funding for much of the organization's infrastructure, such as vehicles, office equipment, and administrative salaries. International funding agencies support specific programs: Misereor, a German Catholic agency, finances social programs, for example, while the InterAmerican Foundation provides funding for salaries for promoters. The Argentine national Catholic Church pays for some mass communication programs, including publications and a local radio broadcast. Many of the women's programs operate with funding from Bilans, a Protestant Church organization based in Holland. There is also some other funding from municipal governments, UNICEF, and several other international funding agencies, while the universities of Salta and Jujuy collaborate in research projects. About twenty-five percent of total funding comes from some level of the government.

The administration of OCLADE is based in Humahuaca. Until 1997, all of the decisions about programming were made centrally by an administrative group. As one of the consequences of the 1996 assembly of the prelature, administration has been decentralized to some degree. OCLADE formed a number of smaller administrative teams that now make many programming decisions on a departmental level. The team for Iruya includes the promoter, one or two other people who work closely with OCLADE in Iruya, and several other people who work with the organization in other capacities (who are not based in Iruya). This group meets periodically to manage much of the administration for local projects. For example, it evaluates project proposals presented by communities and decide which should be funded, and it deals with problems that arise within ongoing projects. This decentralization is a positive step, as more decisions are made by those who are more closely involved in the community. However, further steps towards decentralization could improve the ability of local people to participate in the organization's decision-making process. At the present time, none of these team members comes from Iruya, and their regular meetings are not open to the participation of individuals from the community or other interested parties.[18] Increased participation at the administrative level of people from the community would enable OCLADE to be more sensitive to local concerns and cultural practices, as well as more accountable to the population it serves.

OCLADE's Work in Iruya

The *departamento* of Iruya was one of the first communities in which OCLADE began to work. One promoter works in the community, principally with the "Yachay" program. This project runs child and infant feeding programs and a preschool program in several communities in the interior. There are several other projects in the *departamento*, including an animal health program that delivers vaccines to most of the communities in the *departamento*, a women's program, which was more active in the past but still has groups in several communities and is beginning an adult literacy project in San Isidro, and an economic development program which works through funding "mini-projects" in the communities.

While OCLADE has worked in the village of Iruya in the past, and was a principal actor in community efforts to expand hospital services in the 1980s, its work in the *departamento* now is primarily in the interior communities rather than in town. The principle behind this, according to people who work closely with the organization, is to try to bring resources to those who need them most. In practice, however, OCLADE tends to concentrate its efforts in the communities that are most accessible to town, rather than those which are smaller and more remote. San Isidro, for example, is about a two-and-a-half-hour walk from town, while Rodeo Colanzulí is about three hours but may usually be reached by the road, a trip of just one hour in a truck. All of the preschool programs and child feeding centers are located in the villages that are within a half-day's walk to Iruya. Some of the more remote villages participate in other programs, such as the animal vaccination program. These efforts usually depend on local volunteers, often the laypeople most involved in the Church in those remote centers, who coordinate their efforts with the promoter and the local priests.

Conclusion

Iruya, like many other Andean communities described in the ethnographic literature, is located on the margins of the capitalist economy and on the periphery of the nation-state. Its isolation is not only geographic, but cultural, economic, and social.

Iruya has not been "left behind" as many of the glossy tourist brochures proclaim in their romantic zeal to portray the community as a "step backwards" in time, a relic of a former pristine and even precolonial culture. Instead, it is a community that, although on the margins of the capitalist system, is structurally integrated into that system. Throughout the Andes, including the northwest of Argentina, highland villages practicing subsistence agriculture survive on the margins of the capitalist economy. While many local practices are rooted in indigenous traditions, they have been specifically organized by colonial and post-colonial policy and legislation, and now exist within the political, legal, and economic frameworks of nation-states (Sallnow 1987, 106-107). Iruya's very poverty and isolation are the outcome of a long process of domination and exploitation, as the region's land and labor were subordinated to the interests of those in larger centers of power.

For local residents, capitalism has not "penetrated" unevenly, but it is experienced unevenly. Like peasant farmers throughout the world, households maximize their use of resources, carefully estimating the risks that they are able and willing to take, and balancing these against their ability to meet the needs of the members of the household (Netting 1993). Some households and individuals may be better placed than others to gain some advantage from a market economy, whether as a result of their household structure and position in the household cycle, their access to roads and to good land, a small store of capital that may have been gleaned over several generations, or, as is often the case in Iruya, kinship or other ties to local authorities and politicians.

Changes in the global economy and in Argentine society have their effects locally. Paradoxically, Iruya is being both pulled closer and further marginalized. Economically, the resources that Iruya has to offer are becoming less significant. Competing inexpensive labor from neighboring Bolivia and the ongoing mechanization of large-scale agriculture have replaced local workers on plantations. The land of the *departamento* is marginal at best for agriculture, and distance and the difficulties of transportation over the mountains further reduce the possibilities for commercial production. At the same time, technical advances in communication have increasingly exposed the residents of Iruya to the dominant society, as television and radio have become more pervasive, telephones and communications have improved, and even transportation has become more easily accessible.

The increased fluidity of contact with the dominant society is not without its own paradoxical consequences. The icons of national identity are celebrated and displayed perhaps even more vehemently than in larger cities. This enthusiasm is due in part to an insistence on inclusion in national society from a region and a local culture that has never taken such inclusion for granted. At the same time, the differences between the local culture and the national become more apparent. A local ethnic identity as Kolla has found its resurgence as a response. This tension between indigenous identity and national identity is played out not just between groups or factions, although this is certainly one arena, but within individuals.

In the *departamento* of Iruya, the majority of the problems of economic and human development are long term and structural: a low level of agricultural productivity, poor access to markets caused in large part by geographic isolation, discrimination, a lack of employment, little infrastructure. These problems can be ameliorated, but only with careful, long-term planning, the active involvement of the community, and the meaningful investment of resources. Short-term solutions create a dependency on outside interventions and do not resolve the underlying issues: child malnutrition is the result of poverty, and a focus on improving the productivity and income of households will address such a problem in a meaningful way. OCLADE has taken on a major role as an actor in the process of development—from charity to bureaucratic programming to locally initiated projects. However, development has social, cultural, and political, as well as economic, ramifications. The impact of development goes beyond increasing household incomes—where it has that effect at all—to changing daily praxis.

In subsequent chapters, I will examine how certain relationships—between local and dominant cultures, between households and their land, between the members of households—are the objects of development as much as are incomes and crop yields. I will also consider how OCLADE creates and employs a particular moral discourse, one which emerges out of its Catholic environment, to justify and explain its development work, and the impact that this discourse has on the actual accomplishments of the organization. First, however, I will move on to examine a second case study, one which offers interesting contrasts to Iruya and OCLADE.

Notes:

1. A *departamento* is an administrative district, best comparable to a county. I distinguish between the village and the larger *departamento* of Iruya where I feel this clarification is significant.
2. "*La banda*" translates loosely as "the other side," usually meaning the opposite bank of a river, but I also heard it used to refer to the opposite side of railroad tracks, canyons, and even roads. In Iruya, "*la banda*" is the neighborhood across the river from town.
3. Iruya is one of two incorporated municipalities within the *departamento*. The other, Isla de Cañas, is located on the other side of a ridge to the east. Travel between the two

municipalities is difficult, and uncommon, as they are about a week's walk apart over terrain impassable by any vehicle. Isla de Cañas is accessible by road from the east, through Oran.

4. One is the national Argentine channel, the other is broadcast from nearby Bolivia.

5. There are seasonal roads to San Isidro and to Higueras. However, these roads, which follow the river beds, must be reconstructed each year at the beginning of the dry season. Even during the winter, only sturdy trucks or four-wheel-drive vehicles can pass.

6. While this water is generally safe, it is untreated and vulnerable to outbreaks of bacteria.

7. The only tractors in the local area are owned by the government: one by the *departamento* and one by a provincial road crew that has its headquarters midway between Humahuaca and Iruya. Both of these tractors are used for road maintenance, for heavy hauling, and to remove other obstacles. The town government's tractor is used occasionally at the beginning and end of the wet season to bring heavy supplies to some of the interior villages. There are no tractors used in agriculture: the fields are generally too small, too irregular in shape, overly rocky, and very often too sloped for tractors to be practicable.

8. There are no llamas in Iruya or the interior villages, although I was told there "used to be." There are wild vicuñas, a smaller camelid, in the higher hills near Colanzulí, which are sometimes illegally hunted for their very valuable wool.

9. At the time of my research, the Argentine peso was equivalent to the U.S. dollar, and was linked to the dollar. The peso was devalued in 2002, and has fluctuated tremendously since then. At current writing, $1 U.S. is equivalent to about three pesos.

10. This population data comes from data collected by health care workers (*agentes sanitarios*), who take a household census every three months, going door to door to all of the dwellings in the *departamento*. The data used here come from the census dated March 14, 1997. I am grateful to Armando Tacacho and the hospital in Iruya for sharing the data from this census with me.

11. Kolla is variously spelt Colla, Koya, or Coya.

12. In fact, there is little concrete evidence of such a migration, much less than there is for a history of continuous habitation.

13. There are a few words of Quechua that have been absorbed into the local Spanish dialect, and many place names are based on Quechua words.

14. In fact, the only time I heard reference to an "ayllu" during my stay in the community was in a document in Rodeo Colanzulí, where it was used synonymously with "community."

15. A prelature is an administrative region of the Catholic Church, similar to a diocese.

16. For a detailed history of the Catholic Church in the Humahuaca region during the colonial period, see Olmedo Rivera 1990, 256-266.

17. The amount of these stipends range, up to about seventy-five pesos per month.

18. Including the anthropologist.

Chapter 2: Los Blancos and Fundapaz

> If we study history, it says that the whites are more nomadic than the indigenous peoples, because white people came from other countries to exploit the riches of [the people here] and to conquer the land that they occupied. . . . We are a little nomadic, but only to search for food, but not in order to damage or persecute anyone.
>
> Mbyá man, Misiones Province[1]

While Los Blancos is only about 200 kilometers from Iruya as the crow flies, it could hardly be more different in terms of its landscape, ecology, and inhabitants. To the east of Iruya, the mountains drop off through a series of nearly impassable river valleys, giving way to verdant semitropical forest and plantations near the city of Oran. This lush landscape quickly changes as one travels further eastward, becoming increasingly dry and monotonously flat. Along the single unpaved highway, cultivated fields of sugarcane and stands of citrus fruit are replaced by cacti, thorny brush, and an occasional tree too gnarled to be felled.

Los Blancos is located 15 kilometers from Salta's provincial border with neighboring Formosa. The town itself is a minor outpost along a poorly traveled route, isolated during the rainy season when the road becomes impassable for weeks at a time. The population of the town is neatly divided by recently abandoned railroad tracks that run a few hundred meters from the road: *criollos*, or whites, on one side, and the indigenous population, the Wichí, on the other.[2] The physical boundary between the two is a spatial reminder of the nearly palpable social and cultural gulf that separates them.

The Wichí are one of numerous indigenous groups of the Chaco, a large, flat expanse in the center of South America. The Argentine Chaco is the home of a number of indigenous groups belonging to two major linguistic families: Mataco-Mataguayo, which includes Mataco (Wichí), Mataguayo, Chorote, and Chulupí; and Guaikurú (also commonly spelt Guayacuru), which includes Toba, Pilagá, Mocoví, and Abipón. The region came under Spanish and then Argentine control at a much later date than the Andean highlands.

The indigenous people of the Argentine Chaco, while culturally distinct in many ways, also share numerous cultural features and similar historical experiences; I draw on studies of some of these other ethnic groups, particularly the Toba, where they seem comparable or relevant to the Wichí. I begin this chapter with a consideration of the ethnography of the Wichí, looking particularly at the "timeless past," a description of the culture "before" its integration with the dominant culture and economy. I then look at the history of the region in order to understand local dynamics of cultural change which have occurred, here, over a relatively short period of time. I move on to consider the present situation of the Wichí in Los Blancos and the surrounding communities, focusing particularly on their economic situation. The second part of the chapter presents the NGO that is most actively involved in Los Blancos and the surrounding communities, *La Fundación para Desarrollo en Justicia y Paz*, or Fundapaz.

Ethnography of the Western Chaco

The Wichí live in the western part of the Gran Chaco, between the Pilcomayo and Bermejo rivers in northern Argentina and along the frontier with Bolivia.[3] Early Anglican missionaries estimated the Wichí population at over one hundred thousand at the turn of the century, a number which fell to just thirty thousand by 1927 (Makower 1989, 62). Today, the official census puts the Wichí population in Argentina at just over six thousand. This tiny figure is considered low by many of those working in the region, who offer estimates as high as twelve to twenty thousand (for example, Alvarsson 1988, 32-35). However the population is counted, it is far from homogenous. Many Wichí live in urban areas in the northern part of Salta, working as unskilled labor in the cities, while at the other extreme, small groups in rural areas continue to practice hunting and gathering as their primary or, rarely, only form of subsistence.

Even before white settlers arrived in the region, the Wichí were not a unified, homogenous group. In the ethnographic literature on the Wichí, they are generally divided into three linguistically and culturally distinct subgroups: Güisnay, Véjoz, and Noctenes. The Los Blancos region is home of the Véjoz; locally, they call themselves in Wichí, *lewet taiñi*, or people of the monte. The major differences between the populations include some differences in dialect as well as differences related to use of river resources. All of the populations utilized the resources of the rivers and the monte, although relying more heavily on one or the other. There were significant trade, kinship, and social networks between them.

Before white settlement, the Wichí, like most of the other indigenous peoples of the Gran Chaco, based their subsistence on hunting and gathering. Small groups moved seasonally in patterns that allowed them to make the most of the resources that the region provided. Settlements were temporary, and their location depended on the availability of water, certain plants, and the migration of animals that were hunted for food. Women were the primary gatherers, and also harvested from small horticultural plots, while men practiced hunting, fishing, and the collection of honey (Alvarsson 1988, 161-193). Generally, work by both sexes was done in groups. In the decades and centuries since the Chaco was incorporated into the colonial system, occasional wage labor and a trade in handicrafts were also important.

The Wichí, like most of the groups of the Chaco, reckon kinship bilaterally. Residence was uxorilocal, but this was flexible, depending on the preferences of the individuals involved and the resources of each extended family. Traditionally, marriage customs included a strong preference for band exogamy (Braunstein 1983; Alvarsson 1988, 90-95). Researchers differ on the importance of clans (*wikyi*) in Wichí kinship and social organization. Alvarsson (1988, 118-122) finds that the *wikyi*, or clan, has diminished in social and political importance in recent decades, and has been transformed into a social category which still influences marriage choices. In the Pilcomayo communities, clans continue to play some social role (Wallis, personal communication) while in the communities near Los Blancos, clan organization is no longer politically significant. José Braunstein (1983, 1974) notes that Wichí society possessed a high degree of flexibility of organizational structure, linked to kinship ties across territories occupied by progressively larger social units. The flexibility of rules governing marriage preference and residence allowed the Wichí to continually reorganize groups according to the availability of resources in progressively larger territories.[4]

Communities consisted of flexible family-based groups, which grew and divided depending on the availability of resources and individual preferences and personalities. Within a group, food and other products were distributed to all of its members. Leadership was situational and flexible; the person who was considered most skilled—usually an elder—was respected and his or her opinion sought and highly regarded, but he or she was not in a permanent position of authority. Conflict of any sort was scrupulously avoided within a group. If there were serious disagreements, one of the individuals or factions would often leave the group rather than provoke a confrontation. Self-control (Dasso 1999, 141) and good-will (Palmer 1997) are central themes in Wichí norms of social behavior.

The reciprocal obligations entailed by kin relations prevented individual accumulation. In the traditional Wichí economy, prestige was accorded not by what one had, but what one gave. Redistribution was seen as an *obligation*, rather than as a "generous" *choice* of the individual (Von Bremen 1987, 20). Redistribution did not imply that everyone in the community shared every resource equally. Instead, people in certain positions were understood to have an obligation to give, while people in other positions had the privilege to receive. When a hunter returned from a successful expedition, members of his group were entitled to share in the bounty of his success. The hunter himself was secure in the knowledge that on another day, when his luck was poor, one of the others would share with him.

I have so far outlined the "traditional" culture of the Wichí, the salient features of social organization that anthropologists in the past often relied on to classify a culture. More recent critics have justly drawn attention to this classic ethnographic portrait as ahistorical, noting that it ignores the dynamic of internal change as well as the tremendous changes wrought in New World cultures by a long history of colonialism and the development of the modern state.[5] "Contact," except in very rare instances, is not a sudden event, but a process structured by economic, military, and political relations (cf. Gupta and Ferguson 1992). Like indigenous peoples elsewhere, the Wichí and their culture have been tremendously affected by the consequences of colonialism and white settlement, as well as by the incursion of outside technology and goods, among other things. Europeans moved in to the Chaco as early as 1585, setting off a long process of pressure on indigenous groups and their territories, resistance by the peoples of the Chaco to European incursions, and the restructuring of previous political and economic systems (Braunstein and Miller 1999). In the case of the Wichí, a cultural history should not emphasize their isolation, but recognize a long history of relationships among the indigenous peoples of the region and with the dominant society, mediated through economic and military dominance.

The recent history of the Wichí is one of territorial marginalization that dramatically accelerated with the construction of the railroad and the accompanying colonial expansion. Although the Wichí, like other groups in the Chaco, were working as migrant laborers on sugar plantations beginning in the nineteenth century, oral histories recounted by people in Los Blancos mark their settlement in mission villages in the 1930s and 1940s as a historical moment dividing the "traditional" past from the present moment. Their traditional culture is not relegated to the "timeless past" but is in fact a part of living memory. What is now the eldest generation are those who first settled in the mission villages. Their memory of a nomadic lifestyle based on hunting and gathering makes the contrasts that they see between "before" and "now" dramatic and poignant, as they emanate from personal experience and memory. As we will see, the ongoing negotiation of the transformation from hunting and gathering to some other form of subsistence is the crux of issues of development for the Wichí.

History of the Wichí

A More Recent Conquest

The western Chaco was incorporated into the colonial system relatively late, although Spanish interest in the region began as early as the 1540s, when several expeditions passed through the region. Many of the Chaco tribes, but not the Wichí, adopted horses during the seventeenth century, permitting the expansion of territories. There was a decline in hunting, fishing, and gathering, and an increase in fortified settlements, social stratification, and political centralization, as well as increased commerce and warfare between aboriginal groups and with the Spanish.

There were some attempts to incorporate the indigenous tribes of the western Chaco into the Spanish colonial system. Beginning in the late 1600s, there were several attempts at Catholic missionization, largely unsuccessful and with seemingly little impact. In the early seventeenth century, the area which roughly corresponds to the Chaco Salteño[6] was missionized by Jesuits rather unsuccessfully. After the expulsion of the Jesuits in 1767, Franciscans took over mission efforts, but they "found the Toba very fickle" (Makower 1989, 12) and chose instead to establish a mission with the Wichí in 1779, near the current site of Misión Chaqueña near Embarcación. This mission had two priests and twelve soldiers and was abandoned in 1794. The missions of this early period were unsuccessful, Katharine Makower states, because of "intertribal fighting" and a low level of trust of the missionaries by the Indians (1989, 13). The Franciscans abandoned another mission near Oran in 1882, after numerous battles and attacks.

The area remained a frontier with little peaceful contact between the indigenous people and Spanish settlers until significant *criollo* settlement of the western Chaco began in the 1840s. At this time, a Bolivian expedition reported meeting 12 indigenous groups with a population of at least 40,000 (Carrasco and Briones 1996, 198). Until the mid-1880s, the control of the Chaco was mainly indigenous. At that time, however, there was an expansion of the agricultural frontier, spurred by the goals of the Buenos Aires elite to advance "civilization" and "progress." A series of forts was established and military expeditions began in 1884. Despite the existence of several treaties that had previously been signed recognizing indigenous rights to the land, the government began the military campaign referred to as the Conquest of the Chaco. The military forces met with considerable, if unorganized, resistance by the native groups. The war dragged on from 1884 until 1916.

The violence of colonization was followed by the violence of economic exploitation. The subjugation of the indigenous tribes of the Gran Chaco had explicitly economic ends, expressed by leading military and political figures of the day:

> I do not doubt that these tribes will provide cheap laborers to the sugar industry and to the lumber works [in the Chaco] as some of them are doing in the haciendas of Salta and Jujuy, and indeed I consider it indispensable to also adopt an adequate system to permanently situate them in convenient locations, limiting the territory that they are allowed to occupy with their families to the effect of modifying their customs little by little and civilizing them. (General Benjamín Victorica, head of the military campaign in the Chaco Salteño, 1884, quoted in Carrasco and Briones 1996, 200)

From 1880 to 1920, most of the labor for a new industry of sugar plantations was recruited from the Gran Chaco, especially among the Wichí (Reboratti 1996, 71-72). Many Wichí, along with members of other indigenous groups in the region, worked as migrant laborers for the plantations in deplorable conditions at near-slave wages. Most of their work was paid not in cash, but in clothes, food, and manufactured goods (Makower 1989, 66-67), barter goods which the Wichí probably preferred to cash. Until the end of the nineteenth century, the Wichí continued to work on the plantations sporadically, combining this labor with traditional activities.

The development of Oran and Embarcación as centers for sugar plantations in the early 1900s intensified contact between indigenous tribes and white settlers in the western Chaco. The construction of a railroad linked Oran and Salta with cities further to the east began in 1909. In the meantime, increasing numbers of white (*criollo*) settlers began to arrive in the region. Following the course of the railway, they founded towns and established ranches, precipitating continued conflicts with the indigenous groups over land, water, and natural resources. The natural forests were cut first to use on the railroad and then to use as fencing in the pampas of Buenos Aires (Carrasco and Briones 1996, 202). The introduction of cattle to the newly denuded Chaco began a process of environmental degradation that continues to the present time.

Anglican Missionization (1910-1982)

As General Victorica noted, in order to exploit the labor of the Chaco tribes in nascent agricultural industries, it was necessary not only to conquer them militarily but to "civilize" them. In particular, it appeared necessary to constrain the nomadic practices of the indigenous peoples in favor of permanent settlements, thus both opening land for secure white settlements and at the same time concentrating a labor force that would be dependent on paid labor. The force finally accomplished these ends was neither military nor economic, however, but religious. After the failure of early Catholic missionaries, the Catholic Church had not made any concerted efforts at converting the Chaco tribes. Anglican missionaries who entered the region beginning in 1910 were able to successfully establish a series of mission villages. Katharine Makower, in a history of the missions, comments that despite the "good intentions" of these early missionaries, the missions were in fact used by business interests, especially oil companies, as a means of opening up the Chaco (1989, 45). The Anglican missionaries may have been well intentioned and even unwitting allies in the exploitation of the indigenous peoples and their lands, but the missions that were founded in this period concentrated the population, allowing *criollo* occupation and settlement and contributing to a loss of control by the indigenous people over resources.

Guadalupe Barúa argues that missionization was a far more significant medium of cultural change for the Wichí than previous involvement in migrant labor (1985, 31). On the plantations, migrant groups tended to remain isolated, apart from *criollos* and other indigenous groups. Family groups tended to migrate as a unit, meaning that there was less social contact with others. The groups returned to their native territory with consumable goods and food which were then shared with those who had not gone.

The Anglican attempt at missionization was far more successful than earlier Catholic efforts, in part because during this period Wichí leaders were looking for white allies to aid them in their defense as *criollo* settlers and the military encroached on their lands. Additionally, they were struggling against efforts by plantation owners to increase their control of the migrant labor force (Von Bremen 1987, 28). In just a few years, most of the Wichí had settled in the permanent mission villages, unable to continue their former nomadism and independence because of a reduced land base and military expeditions. The sedentarization encouraged by the missions "is synonymous with the disorganization of Indian societies" (Braunstein and Miller 1999, 19). By this point in time, the Wichí had lost most of the land to which they had previously had access to white settlement and plantations, and had become a crucial labor force that allowed the plantations to operate profitably.

Makower describes the general conditions of the time of the founding of the missions in the early 1920s (1989, 38-39). The railroad had just recently been completed, bringing an influx of settlers. This caused an increase in diseases and deaths in the indigenous population. As stated earlier, the missionaries estimated the population of the Wichí to have decreased from one hundred thousand around 1900 to just thirty thousand in 1927 (Makower 1989, 62). There were occasional punitive military expeditions against the indigenous people. Often, the military was called in by *criollo* settlers in an effort to consolidate their control over land. There was a high participation of the Wichí, as well as the Toba and others, in seasonal work on the sugar plantations. The migration of entire families to the sugar fields for eight or nine months each year continued through the 1930s and 1940s. This labor migration brought an increase in illness and drinking. The money that was earned was usually spent quickly, often gone before the end of the agricultural season.

The Wichí made a rapid transition from nomadism to settlement in the Anglican missions, a shift which was costly in terms of health and independence. Makower provides the following quotation by Richard Hunt, one of the early missionaries, to explain the wholesale conversion of the Wichí to Anglicanism:

> They had been harassed by white settlers, often ill-treated and despised, cheated and browbeaten. The idea of a friendly foreigner and a safe refuge appealed to them, and in the course of a few months some six families came and settled there [in Misión Chaqueña], each with a house and garden, and with freedom to come and go as they liked. (1989, 40)

The Wichí perspective is presented in a statement by Guilfredo Ibarra, an elder and pastor in Misión Chaqueña during Makower's visit in the late 1980s:

> Evil spirits had instilled into people's minds the idea that people would come who would eat them. It was my father, the Capitán, who placated them and settled their minds about accepting the missionaries. He said, "I'll go and see them. If they eat me, I don't care. If they don't, then you can follow me." (1989, 40-41)

The missionaries, like the white settlers, followed the course of the railway into the interior of the Chaco. The railroad was extended from Embarcación to Formosa in the early 1930s. This allowed the missionaries to spread further into the interior from their base at Algarrobal (now known as Misión Chaqueña) just outside Embarcación. In 1933, at the request of a cacique who was familiar with the missionaries from his people's yearly migration to the sugar plantations near Algarrobal, Misión San Patricio was established on the edge a lagoon (Makower 1989, 96). In 1934, the first eight converts of Misión San Patricio, including the cacique (chief, or leader), were baptized. The missionaries began the gradual evangelization of the "surrounding villages" (Makower 1989, 96), which gradually came to include settlements at Los Blancos and Capitán Page.

According to Makower's detailed history of the founding of the missions, even the presence of the Anglicans failed to end the conflicts between the Wichí and *criollo* settlers. As Misión San Patricio was being constructed,

> the peace was shattered not only by the sounds of building work and the arrival of [the cacique] Feliz Paz and large numbers of Indians moving on to the mission, but also by protests from settlers who had been there first and resented the arrival of a crowd of "goat-stealers." (Makower 1989, 97)

The missionaries themselves were generally regarded with suspicion, and often dislike, by the *criollos*, both because they were English and because they lived with the indigenous people (Barúa 1985, 25).

The pressure for the Wichí to move into mission villages was accentuated by the Chaco War, from 1932 to 1936. Conflict over supposed oil deposits in the Chaco resulted in war between Bolivia and Paraguay across the Gran Chaco, with devastating results for the indigenous populations, who lost their land and became tied into a cash economy (Alvarsson 1988, 28-29). This war only indirectly affected the Wichí population in Argentina through the movements of troops and neighboring populations.

Makower describes the 1940s as a difficult period for the missions. The state and other outside interests were gradually able to follow the missionaries into the interior, establishing schools, government outposts, and projects to build infrastructure, sponsored by the government of Juan Peron (Makower 1989,

128). Religiously, she notes, "backsliding was widespread" (1989, 125), which the missionaries saw demonstrated in a resurgence of traditional dancing "with its attendant immorality," as well as in the reemergence of other practices condemned by the Anglicans, such as the use of coca and alcohol. The missionaries bemoaned continued "witch-doctoring," their term for any traditional healing practices, which usually involved a spiritual component.

There were other transformative changes going on as well—many of which must be considered as at least as important, if indeed not more significant, than missionization. The Wichí were less able to practice hunting and gathering because of a steady loss of territory after the railroad entered. As migrant labor to the sugar plantations became more difficult and less desirable, more of the Wichí began to work as hired labor for local *criollos*. According to Makower, the Wichí:

> found it hard to make the cultural change to wage-earning. They did work at their gardens, but not only was the climate often against them but the settlers' cattle would often break in and wreak havoc among the crops. (1989, 125)

The 1940s was also the Perón era, and Makower says that the Wichí gained more political consciousness and awareness of the nation as projects sponsored by the government entered the region.

In the early 1960s, the Anglican missions were revitalized with an influx of over forty new missionary workers to the Argentine Chaco (Makower 1989, 141). There was an effort by the church to shift away from old policies and structures of authoritarianism and protectionism in favor of a more autonomous control of the local church by the indigenous communities themselves. The communities favored this change, which came with assurances that they would have increased support if any real difficulties, especially problems with the *criollos*, arose (Barúa 1985, 26). The church gradually began to shift the leadership of local churches to indigenous leaders. A Bible Study Institute was founded at Misión Chaqueña with the goal of ordaining indigenous ministers. Older men were often ordained based on their willingness to act as pastors and on their moral character, without formal study (Makower 1989, 141).

The 1960s also saw a continuing decrease in the material living standards of the Wichí (Makower 1989, 155-156). There was less work available in the sugar plantations, as mechanization and the import of labor from other regions, including the highlands, replaced the Wichí, who were seen by plantation owners as an unreliable labor force (Reboratti 1996, 71-72). Wichí settlements were beginning to feel the effects of overgrazing of the monte and of deforestation.[7] By the late 1960s, there was an increase in attention to the material problems of the indigenous people by the Argentine press (Makower 1989, 157). As a result, the government began some welfare programs, most importantly a program of food distribution which was badly implemented. The Anglican missionaries began to become involved in these government projects (Makower 1989, 157).

By the 1970s, the Anglican church was administering its own development projects. One of the largest projects was located near Misión Chaqueña, and drew Wichí families from throughout the region, including the communities near Los Blancos. The project established a large agricultural station, much like a finca. The project ultimately failed, in part because nearly all of the British missionaries were expelled during the Falklands/Malvinas War in 1982. As one of the missionaries at Misión Chaqueña today recounted,

> It was a big plantation—they cleared all of the monte around and put in commercial crops. It was a big project, with big farm machinery, and lots of money. . . . The timing was bad. It was the period just before the Falklands, and the primary problem was that the currency was very unstable. It all just collapsed. And once the missionaries left [because of the Falklands], the Wichí couldn't run it.

The failure of this project caused both the Wichí and the British Anglicans to reevaluate the prospects of such large-scale development projects. According to the same missionary,

> The project brought money into the community, lots of money. When the project collapsed, there was some bitterness on the part of the Wichí—they felt, justly, that their expectations had been raised and then dashed.

While the Anglican church remains important today in the Wichí communities, its role has diminished considerably. After the expulsion of the missionaries in 1982, Guadelupe Barúa finds that there was an increase in shamanistic practices, with "ceremonies of exorcism and healing in the Anglican church building itself" (1985, 27). In Barúa's study (1985, 28), she also finds an increase in conflicts between the indigenous Anglican pastors and traditional shamans, the separation of some groups from the mission communities, a search for outside groups to replace the protective role of the Anglicans, and an increased outmigration of young people. Since the democratization of the Argentine government, relations with England have thawed, and British missionaries have returned to the region, but in much reduced numbers. In the communities near Los Blancos, there have not been any resident missionaries for many years, and there are only occasional visits from missionaries based at Misión Chaqueña and Juarez.

Cultural Changes

Since the early 1940s, the Wichí have changed from a nomadic to a primarily sedentary lifestyle, and their subsistence strategy has shifted to a reliance on wage labor, supplemented by raising sheep and goats, planting small gardens, and some hunting and gathering. Changes in residence patterns and in the subsistence base, as well as the widespread adoption of the Anglican faith by the Wichí, have been accompanied by tremendous cultural changes.

The degree to which individuals in any community depend on wage labor as opposed to subsistence farming, hunting, and gathering depends primarily on the proximity of white communities. Even in the most isolated communities, there is some involvement in wage labor, especially by men. Although hunting and gathering still remain an important element of subsistence, they are limited due to environmental degradation caused by the presence of herd animals throughout the region and the overexploitation of certain plants and animal species. Wage labor allows increased access to highly desired manufactured goods and commercially available foods such as flour, sugar, and rice.

Patterns of labor have changed even within "traditional" activities of hunting and gathering. Gathering has become less important to subsistence strategies, but remains a significant activity. Many staple food items are purchased. Techniques of food preservation used by older generations fallen into disuse; Alvarsson suggests that food preservation in the past was only practiced when necessary, and has been supplanted by wage labor that carries families through the "lean" season (1988, 214). Men's fishing and hunting remains a collective activity, but the fish and animals are sold as often as they are consumed.

These changes are remarked upon by people in the communities. The elders, in particular, have a vivid memory of life "before." A wife of a cacique, an older woman who frequently came to visit me, explained:

> Before, there was no bread, like this. We didn't have bread from flour. Just *chaguar* [an edible native plant with many uses]. We took off all the leaves and cooked it with honey. . . . I didn't know bread like this. Then when the gringos came, they taught the people to make bread. To take the flour and mix it with fat and put in some water. That was when everyone went to live in the mission. Then the people started to have flour and sugar. Before, there wasn't any. We didn't have sugar—they went out looking for honey, that was all. And we had all of the fruits, then, that grow in the monte. It was nice, very nice. I knew how to find all of the fruits of the monte. . . . The men hunted—they caught iguana, rabbits, all of the animals. Then, it was nice. There were lots of animals then. I go out, I see something. Now there are hardly any. . . . There in San Patricio before, they hunted iguanas. . . . They would hunt, then bring it back. And they would have it, and someone else would share it. Everyone would come and have some. They shared it all. Now people are stingy! Some, yes, some share a little, but a tiny piece and that is all. There isn't a big meal for everyone, like before. And others come with money—they want to sell it for money. They won't share if you don't have money. Before, we didn't have money. We didn't use money.

Such a narrative illustrates the thoroughgoing nature of the changes brought by missionization. This was not merely a shift from a nomadic lifestyle to one which was sedentary. Instead, settlement in mission villages represented a radical change in cultural praxis. In this recollection, an elderly woman was describing how her daily diet had changed. New foods were not just introduced—the staples of daily consumption were replaced. The entire process of food acquisition and consumption shifted from one which was collective in nature and reliant on the utilization of wild resources to one which was individualistic and dependent on participation in a cash economy. As in nearly any oral account of Wichí history, missionization is invoked here as the marker of this shift.

The dependence of the Wichí communities on the Anglican church meant that they had to adapt, at least to some degree, to its structures, and to adopt some of the practices and beliefs espoused by the missionaries. As in nearly any case of missionization, these changes went well beyond the religious to encompass nearly every sphere of life. The Anglican missionaries have been described by many researchers as relatively sympathetic to the indigenous culture. However, as Barúa notes (1985, 22), this sympathy only extended to the point of not interfering with the missionaries' own agenda, which included particular religious beliefs accompanied by what they believed to be appropriate social practices, all garbed in a well-meaning paternalism. The British missionaries rejected shamanism and traditional fiestas, banning such events in the mission villages. They also introduced new forms of authority and hierarchy. The missions reinforced, but changed the meaning of, traditional cultural practices such as ideas of solidarity, the role of the family, and the role of elders.

The spiritual life of the Wichí was dramatically changed by missionization. Traditional Wichí spiritual beliefs were animistic, with spirits as powerful forces that were a fundamental component of the natural world. Those who were powerful within the band—the shaman and some elders—were seen to have knowledge of spirits which allowed humans to interpret the spiritual world and to communicate with it (Métraux 1939, 92-97). Persons who possessed knowledge of spirits were able to use this knowledge to manipulate the spiritual, and thus the material, world. Anthropologist Alfred Métraux, who worked with the Wichí in the 1930s, described their eagerness to understand Protestantism:

> It is the general opinion of all of the missionaries with whom I discussed the question that the Matako are most eager to accept protestantism and that those who take the new faith do so seriously. They are not only interested in the exterior manifestations of religion, but they understand perfectly the moral problems and the subtilities of faith. The Matako who ask for baptism do so because they feel a genuine need for religion and the converted Indians do their best to adapt their living to new rules. (1939, 4)

The very separation of spiritual knowledge from other spheres of life, such as economic success, was alien to the Wichí. The indigenous people saw potential white allies—missionaries, anthropologists, and development workers, among others—as people who knew how to manage new knowledge, and could share it with the Wichí (Von Bremen 1987, 19). Anglican missionaries, in particular, were eager to teach the Wichí and to share their explicitly spiritual knowledge. They promoted studying rather than insight as key to knowledge (Miller 1970, 18). An elderly Wichí pastor described the importance of this process of teaching and learning:

> The missionaries came and they taught people the word of God. Before, the people didn't know about God. They believed in other gods. They didn't know about the Bible. No one had come to teach them before the missionaries came. Then the missionaries came, and made the missions. They came from very far away, to teach the people.

In the communities around Los Blancos, Christian religious knowledge did not supplement indigenous knowledge, but in fact replaced it. Traditional beliefs were rejected, in large part because the missionaries condemned traditional religious practices. Because spiritual practices were an integral part of other aspects of traditional life, many rituals and cultural practices were rejected as "evil" or tainted by their connection with evil spirits. A church leader, an elderly man among the first generation on the mission, remarked on traditional culture:

> I don't understand the traditional culture. Some people understand it, but I don't know. It didn't have love, almost. Because they didn't know that God is above us all. No one taught that there is God in heaven. When the missionaries came, they said that there *is* a God above.

Other features of social life were changed by the process of missionization, although less deliberately. The former fluid structure of bands as the main social unit has been replaced by settled mission villages. The mission villages are not isolated, self-contained settlements, however, but exist as units within a strong network of interrelated villages. Ties between villages remain strong, and there is a great deal of mobility of individuals between different communities. In practice, a "community" cannot be understood simply in terms of a residential grouping, but as a wider network between settlements, organized according to overlapping ties of kinship and filiation. Within villages, the extended family remains important to the distribution of food and other goods, but now the family exists not as a mobile autonomous group but as a unit living in close proximity to others. Food and goods are not distributed or shared freely between families except where there are strong kinship ties.

It is still the extended family, rather than the smaller household, which is the primary unit of production and consumption. Physically, the living arrangements of most extended families comprise a group of small buildings, each occupied by a nuclear household, arranged around a central open space or courtyard. The composition of extended families varies, but they generally comprise several households. They may include an elder couple and their grown children, spouses, and grandchildren, or a set of siblings and their households. Individuals, especially young adults, may move freely between different households to which they have some kinship claim, even if these are located in different villages. A young person, for example, might live with his or her parents, grandparents, or spouse's family, or occasionally with other kin. Living arrangements can be dictated by personal preference, by the ability of a household to support another member, by proximity to employment opportunities, or by a change of residence at marriage or separation. The flexibility of residence patterns is an echo of past practices of mobility in order to maximize resources and minimize conflict. Moving in order to avoid a conflict is in fact fairly common.[8]

Changes in economic activity have brought radical changes to the practice of sharing and redistribution, and, to a lesser extent, to the principle of egalitarianism. While they remain the ideal cultural practices, under present circumstances resources are now generally shared only within the household and with the extended family group. While daily incomes, whether in cash or in kind, are not typically shared within the community, the redistribution of resources that does occur continues to prevent the accumulation of wealth. When any individual or household begins to accumulate more than is necessary for its basic subsistence, others in the extended family make claims upon those resources. Numerous ties of kinship and filiation ensure that most families have some claims on most of the other families within a village. Because there is such a high cultural value placed on sharing, and so little emphasis on personal wealth as a source of prestige, a person's refusal to share would be seen as "stingy," and would create a source of tension within the community. Moreover, there is little sense of the "Protestant work ethic"—the idea that one has worked hard to earn whatever wealth one possesses. Rather, Wichí values include generosity, a balance of work and leisure, and an emphasis on community (Alvarsson 1988, 56). The Wichí culture echoes a vision of the world as an abundant place (see Von Bremen 1987).

Although there have been visible, quantifiable changes in their means of production, the Wichí generally have *not* adopted what we might call a capitalist system of production. Despite their participation in a larger regional capitalist economy, the Wichí, as a group, have not adopted most of the ideas, behaviors, and cultural practices that underlie capitalist production, and lack the capital to participate in any way other than as laborers. There are some individual exceptions to this. Some Wichí have become smallholders, purchased cattle, and set up small farms much like those of their *criollo* neighbors. For the most part, however, the Wichí in the province of Salta live according to the distinct cultural practices and community norms which I discuss.

Patterns of leadership within Wichí communities have also changed. Contact with white society, from the earliest colonial period, demanded that there be a permanent leader, a *cacique* or chief, who could speak for the group. Traditionally, leadership was flexible and situational, frequently invested in elders as role models and as possessors of knowledge. In traditional culture, there was a role of *niyat*, or spokesman (not exclusively, but most often, male), which was generally filled by a household leader who was seen to have skills in mediation and influence over others (Alvarsson 1988, 130). In the communities around Los Blancos, the positions of *niyat* and cacique have merged, but the individual in this position indeed acts primarily as a spokesman, convening meetings, helping the community reach consensus, and acting as the official spokesman vis-à-vis the government and other external agents. This position is passed from one generation to the next not according to a strict rule of inheritance, but through the assessment of the community on who is most fit to provide leadership. While each community has an acknowledged *cacique*, he has little power within the community, acting only as a leader among equals.[9]

In fact, leadership remains diffuse and situational. Pastors (also referred to as *encargados*), who may or may not also be caciques, have a great deal of authority and influence. Younger men, more fluent in Spanish and often more familiar with the dominant society, often take on the role of "community representative" in encounters with the larger political system. Within a village, community, or extended family, decisions are made through a process of negotiation and consensus, led by elders, with each person's opinion carefully voiced and considered. In relations with the outside world, representatives or caciques have little authority to make decisions or commitments on the part of the group. Instead, they act as a medium of information between the group and the outside world, conveying a collective opinion or position. Women almost never act in such "official" capacities but are actively involved within a group in egalitarian decision-making processes.

The Wichí Communities near Los Blancos

In the region of Los Blancos, there are four major Wichí villages: Los Blancos and Cacique Abregu, both located adjacent to the *criollo* town of Los Blancos; Kayip, located adjacent to the town of Capitán Page; and Misión San Patricio, located near the settlement of Resistencia. There is also a much smaller Wichí community located near Los Blancos called La Pantalla. Los Blancos is the largest of these communities, with approximately four hundred inhabitants. The highway that runs through the center of town is touted as an important route for trade between the provinces and with Paraguay, located to the northeast, but it is impassable for months during the rainy season, and during the dry winter months one can count the number of trucks that rumble through each day.

The natural environment limits agricultural productivity in the region. This part of the Chaco is semiarid, with mild and dry winters and humid and extremely hot summers. Los Blancos receives about 450 millimeters of rainfall annually, most of it concentrated during the summer, when temperatures of fifty degrees centigrade are not uncommon (Fundapaz Annual Report 1988/89, 11). Because of soil conditions, the rain that does fall during summer storms does not infiltrate the ground, but remains close to the surface, creating a dense mud that makes agriculture, as well as transportation, extremely difficult. Besides poor soil conditions and a lack of water for irrigation, numerous insects and pests make any kind of agriculture difficult.

Most *criollo* households rely on the production of cattle, goats, and sheep. However, for most households, this provides a marginal income at best. Unlike the fertile regions in the southern part of Argentina, the Chaco does not provide adequate natural fodder for large animals, and cattle, especially, require a large area of land on which to graze. Near Los Blancos, one cow requires from 15 to 40 hectares of grazing area.[10] The low productivity of the grazing land is compounded by extensive environmental degradation. Cattle, in particular, tend to cause considerable damage to the soil and natural ground cover, which causes erosion and localized desertification. As one travels through the area, such degradation is easy to see. Goats, while somewhat less destructive, have little market value and are raised primarily for household consumption, as are sheep. Most *criollo* households have a garden for household use, and some grow fodder to support their herds. Projects promoting similar small agricultural constructions in Wichí communities are being sponsored by Fundapaz and the provincial government, but these have had limited success to date. Because of a lack of water for irrigation, poor soil conditions, and seasonal extremes of temperature and rainfall, commercial agriculture has not been successful locally.

The physical relationship of the Wichí settlements with the larger *criollo* towns is a large factor in the economic strategy of people who live in each village. In the communities closest to towns, wage labor is the primary form of income for most households. Thus, in Los Blancos and Abregu, most of the Wichí work for their *criollo* neighbors. In both of these communities, women as well as men participate in wage labor. In Kayip, which is located next to the much smaller town of Page, the wage labor that is available is not sufficient to support all of the households, and there is more reliance on hunting, gathering, and raising sheep and goats. Women there participate in wage labor only occasionally. In Misión San Patricio, the most remote of these villages, there is little wage work available, and subsistence farming and animal husbandry, as well as using wild products, are much more important to household subsistence strategies.

In all of the communities, wage labor primarily takes the form of irregular day labor. There are few steady, reliable positions of any sort. Typically, men go around to their *criollo* neighbors daily, asking if there is any work available. Day labor may consist of building or repairing fences, caring for animals, construction of houses or farm buildings, cleaning trails, or other unskilled physical work. Women work much more rarely, occasionally finding employment washing clothes or caring for small children. Older men may have a sort of patron-client relationship with a particular *criollo* household, and this may provide a slightly more reliable source of work. This patron relationship does not usually take on the emotional ties that are often found in Latin America, with the creation of fictive kin relations through *compazdrago* (godparents), for example; rather, there is simply a longer term employment arrangement, with an unspoken agreement that the *criollo* household will offer work to a particular man before any others.

The typical daily wage in 1997 was from eight to ten pesos for a man, and about half that for a woman. However, the Wichí are often not paid in cash, but directly in the form of food—a sack of flour, sugar, or rice, or a couple of kilos of meat, items which are readily available in local shops. When payment is made in kind rather than in cash, the value of the products obtained is usually considerably lower, often half or less, of the standard daily cash wage. Most Wichí workers accept this arrangement as long as they feel that the goods obtained meet their family's consumption needs for that day. Overall, household cash incomes range from virtually nothing to about two hundred pesos per month.

At the present time, the *criollo* settlers are able to exploit a large pool of underemployed labor at extremely low wages. These employers further benefit because of the sporadic nature of the labor—they have no obligation whatsoever to provide work except when they need it, to provide more than a minimal wage, or to guarantee minimal working conditions. Most Wichí laborers accept this situation because they have no other alternatives, apart from migration, which is also a limited opportunity. Because the day wage provides access to desired goods—mostly food—it is preferred to traditional forms of subsistence, which are declining in viability at any rate. A case study of the Weenhayek, another Chaco people, has suggests that men's engagement in this uncertain labor market can be seen as an extension of strategies employed in hunting: "men went for uncertain the changas [day labor]; they could wait for hours, sometimes even days, at a street corner to get an uncertain job. . . . When and whenever they got something, they quickly transformed it into food and brought it home" (Alvarsson 1999, 32). In a case study of the Toba, Gastón Gordillo found that men prefer irregular wage work to foraging because the latter activity is associated with poverty and insecurity (2002, 271). This perception did not seem to be common among the Wichí in the region around Los Blancos, who place a high value on foraging, but may be more common in more urbanized areas.

When there is no wage labor available, the Wichí have several secondary sources of income, most of which are seasonal. Men may work cutting posts which are later sold to make fencing.[11] This work is typically done on order, through an intermediary, and the prices are very low. Intermediaries pay from one to five pesos per post, depending on the size and quality, and men can generally cut two or three a day. Women may gather wood or other products from the monte to sell to the *criollos* living nearby. Men may also sell wild products, especially honey and animal skins. Both men and women may produce craft products for sale, but the local market for such goods is extremely limited. Merchants occasionally and unpredictably travel through the area to purchase crafts, but give very low prices. The Catholic Church also occasionally purchases handicrafts, giving a better price, and some individuals produce craft items to sell when the opportunity arises. When none of these options are available, because of a limited market or the time of year, the use of hunted and gathered products becomes more important.

The material standard of living of the Wichí is much lower than elsewhere in the province or in the nation. None of the Wichí communities in the region near Los Blancos has electricity in the houses. In the Wichí community of Los Blancos, the carpentry workshop, built as a project by Fundapaz, has electricity; this is the only building in any of the communities with power. In comparison, most of the *criollo* houses in Los Blancos have power twenty-four hours a day, and the community of Page has a generator for three to four hours each evening.[12]

Public services such as health care and education are inadequate throughout the region, although there have been some signs of improvement in recent years. In some communities, the province employs a "health agent," a local resident who is minimally trained in basic public health and hygiene and who provides a link to more skilled medical professionals. Professional services, however, are often difficult to access. Hospitals are understaffed and doctors are responsible for a very large geographic area; medicines are often unavailable or expensive; and hospitals and clinics are often far away and transportation is difficult. The Wichí face further cultural and language barriers in accessing health care. Traditional Wichí healing practices are seldom used in this area, and knowledge about medicinal plants is in danger of becoming completely lost.[13]

Potable water is a problem endemic to the area, as much of the ground water is too salty to drink. During the rainy season, fresh water is cached in artificial ponds, but these rarely last through the dry season. The lack of fresh water, especially in August and September, is a health problem not just for the humans in the area, but also for domestic farm animals, many of whom perish during the dry season. There have been ongoing efforts by Fundapaz and other development agencies, including the government, to improve the reliability of the water supply, and the situation has improved in recent years, but water remains a significant problem in the region.

There are primary schools in or near the each of the Wichí communities near Los Blancos. Wichí children attend along with *criollo* children. Language is a major obstacle for the Wichí children, nearly all of whom do not speak any Spanish before they begin school. In the past few years, the schools have begun to employ Wichí adults as "bilingual assistants." In theory, these assistants are supposed to help the Wichí children gain literacy in their own language as well as act as a bridge to learning in Spanish. In practice, they function primarily as translators. While some teachers make efforts to teach the children literacy in Wichí, and to teach their *criollo* classmates some Wichí phrases, this is largely dependent on the individual teacher. In the communities near Los Blancos, there is no evidence of provincial support in the form of curriculum, materials, or emphasis on native-language skills. In fact, materials in Spanish are sadly lacking, and teachers face enormous obstacles in teaching even Spanish literacy and other basic skills at the primary level. A bilingual secondary school has recently opened in Los Blancos, drawing students from the surrounding Wichí communities; the first class will graduate this year. However, the majority of children do not complete primary school. Many adults are illiterate; in Page, for example, based on my survey, one third of adult women and ten percent of men are completely illiterate, and the functional literacy of most adults is minimal.

La Fundación para Desarrollo en Paz y Justicia (Fundapaz)

The principal NGO working in the Wichí villages near Los Blancos is the *Fundación para el Desarrollo en Paz y Justicia* (Foundation for Development in Peace and Justice), or Fundapaz. No other NGO has a significant presence in the area, although Fundapaz works closely with ENDEPA, a Catholic NGO that has field staff in Morillo, a town about 30 kilometers to the west. Government development agencies occasionally establish projects in the region, but these, like similar efforts in Iruya, have little long-term impact. None of these government agencies have field staff in the area, and such efforts are sporadic and have little follow-up.

History and Organization of Fundapaz

Since its foundation in 1973, Fundapaz, a private nonprofit organization, has worked in both indigenous and *criollo* communities in northern Argentina. While it is not officially affiliated with the Catholic Church, it sees itself as having "Christian inspiration" and maintains close ties with the Church. At times, Fundapaz has employed nuns and other religious personnel as part of its field staff. In Los Blancos, a small group of nuns were the most visible staff of Fundapaz for many years; although they retired a few years ago, many members of the Wichí community still refer to them when Fundapaz is mentioned.

Fundapaz works in several provinces throughout northern Argentina, with a variety of programs ranging from reforestation projects to a cheese factory. Besides Los Blancos, Fundapaz works in the provinces of Formosa, Santiago del Estero, Santa Fe, and Chaco. The regional programs are loosely affiliated and share a central administrative office which is located in the city of Buenos Aires. Its programs all share common goals: to increase the productive capacity of the small producers, farmers, and artisans in the communities in which it works, and to work to improve social organization in the communities. The organization portrays its work as that of a "bridge" between poor rural populations and the dominant society, a bridge which ideally functions in both directions.

Fundapaz was established with an endowment donated by the Franciscan order. Presently, most of its funding comes from nonprofit European development agencies, many of which are religious in nature.[14] Funding for some specific projects comes from government sources and large international agencies such as the World Bank.

In Los Blancos, the organization was founded to work with the Wichí, but it has gradually expanded its programs to work with the *criollo* communities as well. A small team of development workers establishes and maintains projects in both Wichí and *criollo* communities in the area. This team of six professional staff, plus the regional director, includes individuals with both technical and organizational skills. One member of the staff is a local *criollo* woman, middle aged, while the others are young college-educated individuals who have come from Salta and from Buenos Aires to work for the organization.

Fundapaz's staff divides their time fairly evenly between the Wichí and *criollo* communities, with some staff focusing on projects with each group. They run a variety of projects, from promoting the construction of family gardens to supervising the construction of community centers. The team also works to develop ecologically viable and sustainable agricultural techniques, using a demonstration farm to experiment with new crops and methods. Fundapaz promotes different kinds of projects in the Wichí and the *criollo* communities; as we will see, the reasons for this difference are complex.

Fundapaz's Projects in Los Blancos

Fundapaz's organizational philosophy and mission stress the importance of improving production and of organizing communities to enable them to better manage their own productive capacity. The work of improving local production tends to take "front-stage" in most projects, with the bulk of direct funds and attention going to implementing specific initiatives. The work of community organization occurs in the background, as the ongoing basis for all of the productive projects.

Most projects to improve production in the Wichí communities focus on building infrastructure to improve the ability of the Wichí to practice subsistence agriculture and herding. To this end, there have been projects to improve the water supply through the construction of wells and artificial ponds, to build enclosures for animals, to fence in garden plots, and to provide goats and other small animals to households. Other projects have been directed at non-agricultural production. In Los Blancos, Fundapaz implemented a project to build a carpentry workshop, buy tools, and train men in making furniture and other items. Another ongoing project has Fundapaz acting as an intermediary to purchase craft products. Men's crafts consist mainly of small wooden carvings of birds and religious figurines, a skill taught by the Anglican missionaries, while women produce woven bags and small household items made of *chaguar*.[15] Fundapaz collects these items and sells them to other agencies that market them, passing all of the proceeds directly to the producers. The men are paid directly in cash for the items they produce, while women are paid in cloth. The payment for women was originally arranged in this way because the sale of their crafts was part of a project to create sewing workshops. Although the workshop project has fallen by the wayside, payments have continued to be made in cloth, which is difficult for them to obtain locally.

The Fundapaz team holds regular meetings in all of the communities which provide a forum for participation in planning and for discussion of common problems. These meetings are generally well attended by both men and women. During a typical meeting, the Fundapaz staff discusses any ongoing projects and presents possible future projects. Such future projects are usually determined by the availability of funding, either from government agencies or other sources. The details of participation, the nitty-gritty of project implementation, and the discussion of problems that have arisen in ongoing projects are also on a typical meeting agenda. Recently, as with OCLADE, Fundapaz has begun to place more emphasis on participation, encouraging communities to take a more active role in developing projects that meet their specific needs. Ideally, this would mean that rather than gearing projects to meet the requirements of available funding, a community would decide what project it would like, and Fundapaz would then find funding sources for that project.

There is also a great deal of work that the Fundapaz team does in the communities that falls outside the scope of easily recognizable or funded "projects." Members of the team are involved, personally and professionally, with the lives of the communities in which they work, and perform a great deal of informal work in their relationships with the communities. This may range from acting as a source of information, to providing transportation, to mediating disputes. This informal work is an important component of the work of the development team.

Over the course of its history in the Los Blancos area, Fundapaz has undertaken numerous projects and programs. In the Wichí communities, many projects to improve local infrastructure have been completed or are planned, such as the construction of community centers, digging reservoirs for drinking water, and installing pumps. This concrete kind of project—building something—provides the clearest kinds of results. Agencies like Fundapaz, however, with a permanent presence in the community, have a distinct advantage over other organizations that enter the community to do similar things. Government agencies, in particular, are notorious for installing projects but providing no funding, training, or personnel for repairs, upkeep, or future materials. The long-term relationship of Fundapaz with the community ensures that there is adequate follow-up and maintenance of such installations—work that often falls into the "informal" part of the team's work.

Other projects are ongoing and provide less immediately visible results but are an essential part of the work that Fundapaz does in the region. These include educational programs, such as a course for women to explain how to care for goats, organizational efforts, such as encouraging communities to form their own organizations and working with these groups, and projects to encourage alternative production strategies, such as working with local artisans. These projects are more problematic in terms of the team's ability to evaluate their effectiveness and must be understood as long-term efforts. In the history of Fundapaz's work in the area, one of the most important causes it has undertaken has been an effort to help local communities gain legal rights to the land that they occupy, a struggle which took over fifteen years (this will be discussed in much greater depth in chapter 6). In this process, Fundapaz acted as mediator between Wichí and *criollo* communities, as lobby group in pressuring the government, and as technical advisor.

Conclusion

The Wichí communities near Los Blancos have undergone a process of tremendous cultural, social, and economic change over the last fifty years. The shift from nomadic hunting and gathering to settled dependence on wage labor and household agricultural production has not been a smooth transition but a complex and contested transformation. Along the way, many features of traditional culture have been perhaps irretrievably lost, while others have mutated beyond recognition. Still, a distinct and vibrant indigenous culture remains.

Change in Wichí ways of life has not been part of a simple evolution to capitalism or a market economy. The Wichí are not "moving toward" full participation or integration into global capitalism. Rather, they are integrated in this capitalism at the extreme margin. While subsistence production, primarily in the form of practices such as hunting and gathering, is still an important part of the Wichí economy, such production is shaped by local interaction with the dominant mode of commercial production and capitalist market relations. In these interactions, the Wichí are generally at a significant disadvantage vis-à-vis the dominant economy. Similar to a study of the Toba in Formosa, the hunter-gatherer economy of indigenous peoples in the Chaco is not merely a "survival" of past traditional practices, but a mode of production mediated and shaped by capitalist processes (Gordillo 1995, 107).

Hunting and gathering no longer provides the primary means of subsistence for these Wichí communities. Instead, it is either a subsistence of the last resort, when no work is available, or it is aimed at the market, when products that have some cash value are sold. The land available for hunting and gathering has been greatly diminished through its enclosure for ranching and its delineation as private property. The resources that remain have been reshaped, and greatly diminished, by their exploitation and degradation over the past sixty or more years. Because the land and natural resources available to the Wichí who live near Los Blancos are no longer adequate to meet their subsistence needs, they have had to participate in wage labor and market relations. Along the way, their own tastes and preferences have been shaped by their interactions with missionaries, with markets and, more recently, with the media. Under present conditions, there are few or no Wichí who would say that their community would or should "return" to traditional practices and complete independence from the dominant society, even if such a thing were possible.

In their interactions with the dominant market system, the Wichí, like the Toba of Gordillo's (1995) study, are disadvantaged in several specific ways. While Gordillo argues that this subordination is due, in an abstract way, to the labor requirements of capitalist agriculture, many of the disadvantages faced by both indigenous groups seem also to be the result of a remote location with poor transportation and poor soils and general high levels of poverty. In commercial relations, they are disadvantaged by distance to markets, by limitations of language, and by a low level of literacy. There are relatively few intermediaries who tend to have a monopoly and offer very low prices. Craft production of objects for sale has become one important source of cash, but buyers come to the communities only sporadically and pay extremely low prices for goods. Moreover, prices fluctuate with market demands, and a particular craft item or tradable hunting good (such as different kinds of skins, for example) may go out of style. Because prices that are received for any kind of commercial transaction are so low, involvement in such activities is kept to a minimal level, such that indigenous people generally only enter into commercial ventures as an alternative to wage labor (Gordillo 1995). On a positive note, Gordillo concludes that subsistence production, including hunting and gathering, remains important as a strategy to avoid exploitation in relations with the dominant economy (1995, 137). As long as indigenous households maintain the ability to glean their subsistence from hunting and gathering, they retain an "exit" from the dominant economy.

Within the arc of a single lifetime, the Wichí have seen tremendous changes in their lifestyle, their economy, and their cultural practices. No longer isolated hunters and gatherers, their daily lives encompass relationships with *criollo* settlers, the market economy, and the state. Yet there is no sense in the communities near Los Blancos that the Wichí are "less" Wichí, or that the *criollos* and *suele* (the Wichí word for those neither Wichí nor *criollo*) are less foreign. Discussions of their own culture are marked by a sense of crisis, a sense that the Wichí need to define as a people what is important to them and to creatively discover ways to maintain their cultural identity, language, and customs in the face of the market economy. They look to "development" as a tool to help them in this, and view Fundapaz and other NGOs as a tool and a resource in the constant process of defining and redefining the Wichí world.

Notes:

1. Quoted in Carrasco and Briones 1996, 68.
2. The term *criollo* is used in northern Argentina to refer to whites as well as those who elsewhere in Latin America might be termed *mestizos*. The term *mestizo* is not used locally.
3. The Wichí are often referred to in the ethnographic literature as Mataco (or Matako). This term has fallen out of use, and people where I worked used it only to refer to the language itself, preferring "Wichí, which means "people." Antonio Serrano noted that the use of the term *Wichí* originated as a general name for several groups with some linguistic differentiation, including Mataguayos, Matacos, Güisnay, Vejoces, and Noctenes (1947, 97).
4. This is common to many hunters and gatherers; see, for example, Lee 1993.
5. This is perhaps particularly true of ethnographic portrayals of hunters and gatherers; see Gupta and Ferguson 1992; Wilmsen 1989.
6. The part of the Chaco within the province of Salta.
7. Mostly of the *quebracho* tree, which was used for the wood for railroad cars and for tannin.
8. Such mobility is frequently encountered as an obstacle by NGO programs, which incorrectly assume, and often depend on, a high degree of stability of community membership.
9. There are numerous cautionary tales about caciques who abused their authority, usually by accepting gifts from white politicians, and were rejected by the community.
10. This information comes from Fundapaz's estimates. The best conditions are in the area to the north of Rt. 81, at one cow per 15 hectares. To the south, near Resistencia, this ratio increases to 30 hectares per cow, and in some areas it is as high as 40 hectares.
11. Cutting posts involves cutting whole trees, one tree per post. This is a significant contributor to environmental degradation, particularly since the tallest and straightest trees are most desirable.
12. The more remote *criollo* settlements do not have electricity.
13. The reasons for this loss are complex. In large part, traditional healing practices were discouraged by missionaries as well as health care professionals because they involved spiritual rituals. The Wichí themselves, from what I saw during my stay in the community, value Western medicine ("biomedicine") over herbal or other alternatives, although they continue to use some herbal remedies when they cannot obtain medical care. There is some evidence that other Wichí communities have retained more of their traditional knowledge and practices. This may be related to relative isolation from *criollo* communities, to the personal characteristics and prestige of shamans in some communities, or to a recent "indigenist" revival in some communities.
14. These include Bilance and Pan Para el Mundo, among others.
15. A spiny succulent, also called caraguata (*Bromelia argentina*).

Chapter 3: Development Discourse

The process and discourse of development has left few communities untouched. Throughout the contemporary world, agricultural communities can no longer be understood as "isolated" or "self-contained" in any significant sense. Rural villages, even the most remote, are affected by the policies and interests of the nation-state of which they are a part, by their involvement in international market systems, both as producers and consumers, and by mass media, which is increasingly accessible throughout the world. "Like their urban cousins, all rural people move within the densely interlinked world of high mobility, mixed-up intercultural traffic, and a fast-changing transnational political economy at the brink of the twenty-first century" (Starn 1992, 93). However, in most communities, the degree to which individuals are able to benefit from these external forces and transform them into sources of power and influence varies tremendously.

This chapter examines the construction of a development discourse on a broad scale, and then considers how such a dominant discourse shapes the work of smaller organizations. It situates the work of Fundapaz and OCLADE within this context in order to ground theoretical studies of the construction of a development discourse within the framework of local practice and to gain an understanding of how this discourse is deployed in the daily work of development projects. It discusses how larger ideas about development, poverty, and rural communities shape the daily practice of the NGOs considered in the two case studies. This chapter also considers some of the responses that emerge in the local communities to this multileveled discourse of development: the acceptance of and resistance to the idea of poverty, and how "development" is defined, encouraged, and rejected by would-be beneficiaries of NGO projects.

The Discourse of Development

Local NGOs operate within a global discourse of development; they are influenced by trends espoused by the larger development community. The education and training of their staff is based on theories of economic development and technical knowledge. They compete for funding from larger organizations that have well-defined ideas about what kinds of projects they are willing to support. At the same time, small NGOs create their own discourse to explain, justify, and understand their own philosophy and praxis. Such organizations frequently see themselves as quite distinct from larger development organizations in their goals, methodology, and relationship with local communities.

The distinctiveness of small NGOs is often predicated on a real or perceived strategy of active participation by the local culture in the development project. The question of how and to what extent local dynamics are situated in the larger context of globalization is often left unanswered. The process of capitalist penetration into rural areas is accelerating, with a tremendous impact on local relations of production. As systems of land tenure and the ways in which individuals may use productive and natural resources change, so do local social and political relations. The extent to which local people are able to take advantage of changing economic conditions depends on economic and political contexts. At the same time, we must take into consideration the multivocal and often conflicting political context of any rural community. NGOs provide both material and symbolic resources within this context. As agricultural communities are increasingly involved with and affected by the global capitalist economy, to what extent can NGOs act as mediators between local and dominant discourses of poverty and of equality? Are they successful at managing social and economic change?

A Global Development Discourse

What do we mean when we talk about "development"? The nature of social change can only be understood through an analysis of the relationship between large-scale processes and local contexts. Particularly in the last fifty years, the articulation of local economies into the global capitalist economic system has transformed societies throughout the world. In this process, the relationship between a dynamic economy, in terms of changing technologies, social relations of production, and relations between geographic regions, and what has been termed "human development," in terms of improved material conditions, significant life choices and chances, and individual expression, remains elusive. The human role in shaping social change can be imagined

> as a project that could be conceived of not only in economic terms but as a whole life project, in which the material aspects would not be the goal and the limit but a space of possibilities for broader individual and collective endeavors, culturally defined. (Escobar 1995, 83)

There is no question that change occurs continually; understanding this process of constant transformation allows us to direct it in ways that encourage local autonomy and empowerment and that improve "human development" in meaningful ways.

Goran Hyden posits that "economic history is largely the story of how to capture the peasants" (1980, 9). In the contemporary world, the relationship of rural communities to the state is often mediated through institutions, policies, and programs promoting economic growth. In some cases, development projects have brought improved standards of living, better health care or educational facilities, or other benefits to local communities; in many other cases, development projects have failed to bring about either anticipated or desirable results. Evaluating whether the changes such projects have on relations of productions and land tenure systems are beneficial depends on how the goals of development are defined.

"Development," whether human or economic, is not a politically neutral, technological process. At its very heart, it involves defining what is desired, what is possible, and what is to be eliminated as undesirable. The process of definition occurs in a highly contested realm of discourse. A dominant discourse is not like a cage, a restrictive and all-encompassing framework of fixed ideas and meaning. Rather, it is a way to understand the

> social and cultural processes that link together . . . disparate ideas, resources, rules, persons, and institutions in an open interactional field, constituting the field, defining the elements of the field, the range of accepted behavior as well as the modes of resistance, and emphasizing the reality of power in the construction of what is and can be known and done. (Shaw 1995, 20)

Along these lines, we can understand that "development" is not only as a process of economic change, but as a discourse, promoted by particular networks of agents, within which economic, political, and social change occur.

Arturo Escobar (1995) traces the emergence of a discourse of development since the end of World War II.[1] Development, he argues, must be seen as a historically produced discourse, in which "poverty" and "backwardness" are defined as the problems and "development" as the strategy for treating them (1995, 5-6). Development programs are presented as politically neutral and economically desirable, and as employing proven tools of science, planning, and administration. "Whether a development program's aim is to stem deforestation, boost agricultural productivity, or improve health conditions, development is posited as the solution. Distance, poverty, and the ignorance of villagers are the problems. . . ." (Pigg 1992, 506), at least according to development bureaucrats. As local conditions are translated through the development bureaucracy, they are conditioned by institutional knowledge and needs, so that projects do not account for local differences in practices or conditions (Escobar 1995, 111). In practice, the discourse of development avoids assigning responsibility for the problems it purports to treat, masking the inherently political process of access to resources as a neutral technological issue.

Developmental discourse defines "problems" in a way that does not necessarily suggest solutions; instead, it makes them amenable to the application of certain techniques. Inevitably, all development agencies and projects begin with the idea that the communities they are working in have certain "problems": poverty, low productivity, low standard of living, lack of organization, and so on. The definition of a problem justifies the goals of a project, the means used, and, ultimately, the existence of the development organization itself.

In a study of development projects in east Africa, for example, the failure of development projects to meet their stated goals is due to a disjuncture between the ideas of government and donor agencies on what constitutes "development" and the needs and concerns of local people. Peter Little (1992) describes a massive increase in development programs and money since the 1960s. These programs have been preoccupied with investing in irrigation and improved land management, and are often based on faulty assumptions about the local ecology and economy. Little characterizes various development projects introduced in the region by government and international agencies as misunderstanding the nature of the problem in such a way as to do, at best, no good, and at worst, to worsen the situation, as in the case of large irrigation projects (1992, 163-173). Little notes that there are often considerable discrepancies between the development concerns of local populations—that is, what local people consider their needs to be—and those of state and donor agencies, who may be more interested in macroeconomic indicators, large contracts, and visible projects, rather than in local conditions.

These differences, however, are attributable to more than incompetence or disinterest on the part of planners; they are directly related to notions of "modernity" and ideologies shaped by a dominant discourse that defines what sorts of "development" are most desirable. The ideology of development in this east African case is "antinomadic," focusing on settled agriculture as the solution, despite the concerns of a local population that highly values herding.[2] Development is equated by the state and its programs with settled agriculture, while herding is viewed as underdeveloped and "backwards." This leads to a bias in development policies and spending, favoring settled irrigated agriculture and the privatization of grazing lands. In east Africa, Little argues that investment in large-scale irrigation and the privatization of lands by the state has tended to favor wealthy absentee landowners, while failing to take into consideration the needs and interests of most of the people in the region.

While many international development institutions tend to act as though governments act as neutral creators and enforcers of rules, studies such as James Ferguson's (1990) demonstrate that the state itself has particular interests, both material and ideological (see also Evans 1979). Governments need both resources and legitimacy; they "exploit labor, compete for control of scarce resources, and take an active part in the allocation of resources among alternate users" (Berry 1988, 54-55). The apparent "depoliticization" that accompanied development in Lesotho in the 1980s is a case in point. In this study, Ferguson (1990) examines "development" as a mode of discourse and argues that while state-funded rural development projects largely fail in their ostensible goal of improving agricultural production, they are successful in the national project of extending government bureaucracy and control into formerly remote rural regions. The "anti-politics machine" of development projects allows the state to disguise a political agenda as a politically neutral, technocratic, and morally desirable program of "development."

In order for development agencies to function, they create a vision of a country's problems as fixable, as subject to apolitical, technical, bureaucratic intervention. Development projects divide the idea of politics from the highly political issues of access to wealth and resources. In the case of Lesotho, Ferguson (1990) demonstrates that this discourse obfuscates reality by creating a view of Lesotho that is wildly different from the actual situation there. The categories of development discourse are such that they frame reality in terms of ideal types, such as "subsistence farmers," and ignore actual relations of production that operate locally. For example, according to Ferguson, a 1966 World Bank Report asserted that Lesotho was essentially a subsistence economy, based on traditional peasant society. In fact, Ferguson argues, Lesotho was heavily involved in the regional economy, in which the majority of its people were not subsistence farmers but migrant wage laborers.

Timothy Mitchell (1995) makes a similar point in a case study of the discourse of development as it has been applied to Egypt. He systematically deconstructs "naturalized facts" which have been applied to Egypt by development agencies. The standard development discourse, pervasive in texts and analyses produced by such organizations as USAID, the World Bank, and the IMF, identifies overpopulation, a lack of arable land, and an inefficient market structure as the causes of poverty and hunger. This image of Egypt, Mitchell argues, is at odds with actual economic and productive conditions, which lead him to find that food shortages are the result of economic inequality and international policies that have led to much land being used to grow animals and their feed rather than food crops. The primary result of the development discourse in this case is to redefine problems as strictly environmental and demographic rather than political. They are thus made amenable to technological fixes rather than requiring a reorganization of economic production. This leads to the depoliticization of development issues by transforming questions of social inequality and powerlessness into issues of efficiency and control; however, as Mitchell notes, "it never need be asked at whose cost efficiencies are to be made or in whose hands control is to be strengthened" (1995, 146).

Understanding the ways in which a discourse of development operates to frame development practice offers a way to inquire into the ideas that "shape . . . the nature of development practice, the interpretive community of development agents, and the facts they emphasize" (Porter 1995, 84). Within any discourse, meaning is shaped at many levels. On a global scale, large agencies, the interests of donor governments, international conferences, economic theory, and measurable trends in the global economy are some of the factors that form a base for shared ideas about the nature of development. Some of these ideas may be implicit—formulations of human rights, economic growth—while others are more explicitly part of the goals of development, such as literacy and lower infant mortality rates. On a local level, meaning is negotiated using the ideas from this broader universe of thought and transforming them through the daily praxis of local organizations, communities, and individuals. The process by which this transformation occurs is multifaceted and multivocal. It encompasses the political, cultural, economic, and social interests of numerous actors. Meaning is negotiated not for its own sake, but to provide a rationale for the distribution of resources, both material and ideological, in an environment where such resources may be scarce.

The Discourse of Development and the Work of NGOs: Participation in Development

As an example of how a wider discourse is adopted by small organizations, local participation in development has been stressed by many development agencies in recent years. Yet critics maintain that most development programs continue to take a top-down, ethnocentric, and technocratic approach, where technical interventions are considered universally applicable (see, for example, Escobar 1995, 44). Despite a participatory rhetoric employed in the discourse of development, many programs and the individuals who work in them are paternalistic in their approach (Chambers 1983, 141). One study that compared the rhetoric of a development agency (in this case, a Swedish agency) to the practices and beliefs of individuals within the organization found that individuals at the highest administrative level expressed the greatest adherence to the idea of participation, while field workers generally had the lowest (Rosander 1992).

In a study of USAID development projects, Dolores Koenig attributes the problem of a lack of participation to the organizational structure of development projects:

> It often seems that the local population remains peripheral to decision making in projects even where participation is highly valued. This is not surprising when they also remain peripheral to the tight social group formed by project personnel. (1988, 355)

Because the staff of development organizations tends to be from "outside" the local culture or class, share a common language while lacking knowledge of the one spoken locally, and share similar cultural and class backgrounds, they exclude local people from participation in the informal parts of the decision-making process, which is where most ideas are actually worked out before they are presented in more formal contexts, such as reports and community meetings (Koenig 1988). The interests of paid staff and local community members who participate voluntarily greatly diverge.

In some cases, the rhetoric of participation functions to disguise a practice which disempowers the local people that it purports to include (Porter 1995). Adherence to principles of rational maximization as a means to improve agriculture, for instance, presumes that the farmer must also act "rationally"; often, however, "rationality" is defined by the constraints and goals of the program rather than negotiated with local people in a careful consideration of cultural practices and local conditions (Porter 1995, 78-80). Stephen Bunker's (1985) study of development programs in Uganda and the strategies adopted by local farmers indicated that where development programs play an important role in local agriculture, an individual's access to resources may depend on his or her willingness to comply with and adapt to haphazardly different policies. An individual's eagerness to conform to the rationales and methodologies defined by development programs as rational may be interpreted by bureaucrats as perhaps the most important "criterion of worthiness" to participate (Bunker 1985, 126).

Both Fundapaz and OCLADE have recently moved to include more local participation in their programs. This decision has been in response to trends in the larger development community. It has also emerged as a way to address local concerns, emanating from both within the NGOs and from the communities, about paternalism and dependency. Each organization has found the goal of incorporating *meaningful* participation to be both complex and difficult. Fundapaz sees local participation as a long-term goal as well as a short-term strategy, and looks for ways to increase the role of local communities in defining their development needs. OCLADE has moved to decentralize its administration, and has introduced "democratic" decision making into some of its projects, with mixed results, as we will see. The idea of participatory development is just one example of the ways in which small organizations are influenced by trends in a larger development discourse. In practice, this idea, like others, is transformed by the local context.

The Discourse of Development in Argentina

Organizations such as Fundapaz and OCLADE work within the specific context of state policies. Analyses such as Ferguson's and Mitchell's suggest that one of the consequences of the creation of a discourse of development is the seeming "depoliticization" of the actions and interests of the state in its rural territories and peoples. In both of their case studies, the state plays a central role as an actor in development initiatives. The relatively weak states described by Ferguson and Mitchell had interests in expanding their role in the national economy, in providing bureaucratic middle class jobs, and in strengthening political control over rural areas. In contemporary Argentina, the process of depoliticization has proceeded in a distinct way, through the withdrawal of the state rather than its active involvement in development projects. In this case, a strong state, one which had already had a period of expansion under Perón in the 1930s and 1940s, wanted to limit its spending and retract established government programs. The need to depoliticize and justify its actions was no less imperative, however. During the 1990s, the state discursively neutralized its withdrawal from social spending and development programs by employing a neoliberal rationale of privatization and decentralization. This legacy of smaller programs, combined with the fiscal crisis of the last few years, have combined to continue to keep social spending low.

Under the neoliberal government of Carlos Menem in the 1990s, policies were implemented in an effort to reduce government spending and debt, to control inflation, and to stabilize the national economy. This represented a dramatic change from the Peronist period, during which time there was tremendous social spending, and from policies of later totalitarian governments. The military regime, forced from office in 1983 after the debacle of the Falklands/Malvinas War, left a national debt of $39 billion, accompanied by four hundred fifty percent inflation (Andersen 1993, 306). The democratically elected government of Raul Alfonsín was unable to reverse this financial crisis, and in 1989, Carlos Menem, of the Justicialista party, was elected.[3] Menem's government instituted a program of economic reforms which included a currency revaluation and the freezing of prices, an increase in public utility rates (up to five hundred percent), and the aggressive promotion of foreign investment (Davis 1995, 140). In 1991, a program of further neoliberal reforms was introduced. These met with some success, and at the end of 1991, the economy was broadly deregulated. There was an increased emphasis on free trade, especially with the United States and within Mercosur.[4] Government-owned utilities, banks, military-controlled industries, and the national oil company were privatized, and the income used to meet government obligations. The national currency, the peso, was tied to the U.S. dollar in 1991. Consumer inflation fell from over twelve hundred percent in 1990-91 to just over seventeen percent in 1992-1993 (Felix 1994, 138) and has remained at manageable levels since, a major achievement. (However, when the peso was taken off the dollar standard in 2002, it plummeted, ending up at about a third of its former value.)

Economically and socially, the neoliberal discourse and policies of the 1990s came to a spectacular end at the end of 2001. By the late 1990s, high unemployment and growing dissatisfaction led to the election of an opposition government headed by Fernando de la Rua. By the end of 2001, a growing financial crisis and unpopular austerity measures led to a collapse of the government. Many analysts tie the economic crisis to unsustainable economic policies. The unpopularity of neoliberal reforms has been one of the driving trend in politics throughout South America for the last few years. As a result of strict spending limits, social spending was dramatically decreased. Critics frequently contend that Argentina's formerly large and prosperous middle class has been shrinking and that poverty has been increasing. Unemployment rose in the 1990s, reaching almost twenty percent nationally in January of 1997, and hovering at that level until the present time. Regional unemployment is much higher in some areas, including the north. In part, increased unemployment is directly due to privatization and government downsizing, as former state and parastatal industries have been taken over by private, often foreign, companies that rationalize the workforce.

The neoliberal discourse of development had complex results in Argentina. Nationally, it indeed resulted in the depoliticization of development in the sense described by Ferguson and Mitchell. The government's focus on macroeconomic indicators emphasized the success of its economic policies and justified the further withdrawal of social spending. According to neoliberal theory, as it was presented in the Argentine context, the government's role in development planning was minimized as responsibility shifted to the private sector. Development was depoliticized by removing it from the government's ostensible sphere of interest, or at least from its province of direct intervention. At the same time, government policies that determine the process of privatization, such as policies that encourage land speculation and the sale of lands formerly owned by the government to private interests, had direct and immediate political consequences.

The neoliberal discourse of development in Argentina was shaped by cultural as well as economic factors. At the national level, the government of Argentina seemed to have an overriding interest in presenting a self-image as a developed nation. Government representatives frequently made reference to Argentina as a "first world" nation. The European heritage of the nation's cities, culture, and the majority of the population was a common theme, and ties to the West, particularly to Europe, were emphasized over the fact (or accident) of Latin American geography. This self-image of a nation that is European and developed centered on Buenos Aires, and generally ignored differences of culture, ethnicity, and wealth within the country. The cultural identity of Argentina with Europe and the divisions between the capital and the provinces are not a new theme in Argentine politics, but have their roots in the nineteenth century, as the "guiding fictions" that define what it means to be "Argentine" were constructed, debated, and entered into the national mythology (Shumway 1991). The dominant national vision is liberal and elitist, centered in the upper classes of Buenos Aires. It tends to advocate the imitation of the United States and Western Europe as the path to success, to denigrate popular culture, and to look down on the ethnically mixed masses.

An anecdote may serve to illustrate the focus of the government on its international image. During the presidential election campaign in 1997, President Menem visited a poor city in the north of the province of Salta, where local unemployment topped thirty percent. In his speech, he introduced a plan to build an airport in Cordoba, a province to the south, to accommodate a supersonic jet to Japan. The teacher from Salta who told me about Menem's press conference went on to express her disbelief in the government's priorities:

> How can he possibly say such a thing, imagine such a thing, when the people don't have enough to eat? . . . That shows so much insensitivity, so much ignorance. Not just to want to make that plane, but to say that *there*? It would be one thing, if people weren't so poor, but here in the north, there are so many things that people need. . . . They want to pretend that Argentina is a first-world

> country. . . . This is not the first world. Now, I've never been to the first world. But I know that this is not the first world here. I have been to Peru, which is not the first world. I have been to Bolivia, which is not the first world either. And the south of Brazil, that is not the first world. And here it is the same, we are not part of the first world.

While the government focused on cultural and economic ties with developed countries, this speaker emphasizes the similarities between the north and its Latin American neighbors.

On a local level, the depoliticization of government involvement in development funding had a paradoxical effect, at least in the northern provinces. Locally, there has been an intense *politicization* of development, particularly in regard to projects that emanate from the provincial or federal governments. Funding, channeled through successive layers of government down to the municipal level, has become a reward for political support. Such a system is obviously rife with cronyism and corruption. As María Angela Aguilar (1993) points out, the idea of decentralization assumes the existence of local structures capable of managing resources equitably, when in fact these structures do not exist in many areas. Under such conditions, decentralization becomes a tool for local elites to strengthen a monopoly over incoming resources. Decentralization represents a *de facto* shift from a national to a local monopoly, one which is often corrupt and is no more likely to be responsive to the needs of the majority of the population.[5]

One example of such political manipulation of resources occurred in the interior villages near Iruya. A large meeting was being held one day by officials from the municipal government. Before the meeting, I asked one of the women there what the meeting was for. "The mayor is coming to give out work," she told me. The perception that the mayor, personally, was distributing work, was a common one in such projects. In fact, he had a great deal of discretion over who received work on the project, and who did not, and such work was generally awarded to his political supporters. She went on:

> It's completely political. He comes and gives out this work to people who will vote for [his party]. Since there's an election this year, they'll come around with all kinds of things. Well, I say that you have to make the most of it. But sometimes then people feel obligated. It's very political.

As the meeting unfolded, I learned that there was to be a project to build irrigation canals, funded by the provincial and federal governments. In discussing this project with another informant, I learned that the funding had originally been granted to assist with building a road. However, subsequent arguing about the placement of the road—which would have benefited a community which did not generally support the mayor's party—had led the local government to change its plans. Examples of such political favoritism were plentiful at the local level, as well as at the level of the provincial government. Government development resources act as a system of political rewards, and their distribution between regions, communities, and individuals is highly politicized. In such an environment, NGOs offer an alternative conduit for resources. Although the NGO sector may also be politicized in how it chooses to distribute resources, the criteria are different.

As the government withdrew much of its social spending, private organizations stepped in to fill the gaps. In effect, the work of development was itself "privatized" as the government sector took on a secondary role to charitable organizations. NGOs often implement projects that may formerly have been functions of government agencies, such as the work of building health posts undertaken by OCLADE. With ongoing debt issues and economic instability since 2000, Argentina's national government has continued to rely heavily on NGOs to provide local development programs. While the difficulties involved in government-sponsored development initiatives have been noted by many theorists, the large-scale privatization of development projects brings its own consequences. As numerous small organizations step into the void left by the withdrawal of the state, development planning becomes fractured, and schisms—geographical, methodological, and theoretical—arise in the cracks between different agencies. There is no comprehensive view of what "development" means. There is also a greater reliance on international organizations for financial support of development projects. Ironically, the successful promotion of the image of Argentina as a developed country on an international level resulted in the withdrawal of funds by many large organizations from projects in Argentina. Because of its macroeconomic success, it is deemed "developed" and of lower priority than other nations.[6]

Moreover, the reliance on external funding, rather than governmental planning of development, changes the scope and nature of development projects. One observer notes that "the decision on the distribution of resources and the design of policies . . . responds, in most cases, to the policies and programs designed by the international agencies responsible for their funding" (Aguilar 1993, 14). Government welfare policies, designed to create a general social well-being, are replaced by a more focused approach that identifies and defines people in situations of most extreme poverty. "The 'workers' or 'citizens' have already ceased to be those whom policies address. Now policies are directed at 'consumers,' 'users,' 'beneficiaries,' or 'trainees'" (Aguilar 1993, 15). Programs and spending are now directed at short-term projects with narrowly focused goals aimed at the poorest sectors of society, resulting at times in fragmented, ineffective programs which lack both long-term strategies and integration between different types of efforts.

Creating "Development": Studies from the Field

The ways in which an organization understands the idea of "development" are derived from its basic worldview, which itself is created and maintained according to a variety of interrelated factors. Conceptions of poverty, of economy, and of ethnicity inform project design and organizational structure. Views of the larger political economy and the role of local producers—actual and desired—also play a key role. In the case of both OCLADE and Fundapaz, their worldview is highly influenced by their religious roots, an issue which I will address in chapter 4.

Certainly, individuals within an NGO may hold divergent ideas and opinions. However, it is fair to consider an organizational conception and expression of the notion of development. We can trace the worldview of the organization through its concrete actions—the programs and projects it chooses to implement, the ways it does so, and its explicit statements about those actions and about its organizational philosophy and methodology—and through the implied meanings and understandings that underlie those explicit actions and statements.

"Development" as a practice is based on two premises. One is that there is something "wrong," some kind of a problem, inequality, or backwardness that needs to be, and can be, corrected. The other premise is an often implicit ideal situation, the final product of a "developed" condition. In between these two states lies a fuzzy realm of definition and explication: what are the causes of the problem and what needs to be done to fix it. In the daily world of small NGOs, problems may be well documented. Often they are inarguable—very few would claim that infant mortality is a cultural good. In this case, while the problem and the desired outcome may seem clear, the steps that one must take depend almost completely on how one defines the root cause of the problem and how this cause can be ameliorated. An understanding that infant mortality is based on lack of access to Western medicine will lead to far different programs than the idea that it is based on malnutrition or on indifferent parenting. Understanding the process of definitions—of problems, desired outcomes, and root causes—is significant precisely because these definitions, this discourse, shapes the concrete actions of the NGO, and also define its entire sphere of action—the problems that it sees as amenable to its solutions.

Both Fundapaz and OCLADE are significant conduits of material resources for the rural communities where they work. They operate in regions where such an influx of materials and opportunities are scarce, and their projects are thus welcomed by most local people. Each organization also plays a leading role in defining the problems of the local community, creating an image of "development" that shapes its agenda and delimits the domain of the local discourse of development. In this discursive role, each NGO brings resources that transcend the material. It mobilizes ideological and political resources. The NGO itself becomes a source of these kinds of resources, in addition to the material, for local people in their own quest to define and envision "development" in their community.

Making Peasants: Systems of Production and the Process of Development in Los Blancos

In a study of numerous NGOs that work in the Chaco region, Volker Von Bremen (1987) notes that nearly all development projects working with indigenous groups in the region have as a primary goal the creation of a productive economy. In his survey of past projects, he notes that this has generally taken one of two contrasting forms: the development of a small-scale market-oriented business, or the promotion of self-sufficient agricultural production (1987, 50-52). In either case, project models assume the need for creating a base of production. This assumption is made in the context of an indigenous economy that has traditionally been based primarily on the use of wild resources rather than on agricultural production or commerce. In fact, as I will discuss further below, many of the Wichí are not heavily invested in the idea of a self-sufficient productive economy, preferring an economic system that combines the use of natural resources with some form of paid wage labor. However, for a variety of cultural and technical reasons, NGOs such as Fundapaz continue to focus resources on developing some form of sustainable local production.

The goal of creating a more or less self-sufficient system of production in Wichí communities is explicitly and frequently stated in Fundapaz's literature and in informal communications. The current mission statement of Fundapaz defines its two primary objectives as (1) promoting and supporting community organization, and (2) developing productive systems. These two objectives are seen as interdependent, in a relationship in which community organization strengthens the possibilities for successful production and a strong base of production facilitates further community organization, in a cycle of positive feedback.

Although organization and production are presented as coequal objectives, the manner in which each is pursued differs tremendously. In daily practice, the work of promoting community organization is very much an underlying objective—there are no "projects" specifically aimed at improving organization as such. In procuring funding for projects, productive projects tend to have an advantage. Funding agencies seem willing to provide funds for projects that state a specific need, such as fences for gardens, and that produce, in a relatively short period of time, visible, measurable results. They are less enthusiastic about providing long-term support for the often vague goals of community organization. "Organization" falls into a shadowy, qualitative realm that does not easily lend itself to creating project proposals and applying funding to meet specific goals. However, it remains a conscious objective of Fundapaz staff, who informally use participation in meetings as a gauge of a community's organization and interest in productive projects. Organization, they suggest, is the base on which all projects can be built.

The NGO recognizes that hunting and gathering, exclusively, no longer can provide a viable source of subsistence for the indigenous communities of the region. The use of the monte by cattle and subsequent ecological degradation, an increased population, the sedentarization of the indigenous people, and private landownership have made this virtually impossible. However, Fundapaz clearly recognizes and supports of the importance of hunting and gathering in the communities. As one example, the director said,

> Sometimes the team worries too much about getting things done. They worry about finishing things. When they were building the community center in Misión San Patricio, for example, it was the beginning of December and they wanted to get it done so that they could say it was done by the end of the year. But everyone was hunting, going in the monte. I told them, wait, why push the project when there are things they can do in the monte? It is better to have the work from projects during other times of year, and the months when they can hunt, let them hunt.

However, the organization understands that most members of the Wichí communities, while they value hunting and gathering as both a way to preserve their culture and an important part of their subsistence strategy, do not desire to base their economy strictly on hunting and gathering. In a team meeting, the director warned against a romanticized view of an indigenous lifestyle of hunting and gathering: "We can't come in with completely new things, but we also can't present 'the indigenous package,' the idea that the Wichí should 'go back' to how they used to live." A team member agreed, "*They* don't want to go back." The considerable challenge to the NGO, then, is to create a development strategy that is ecologically and economically sustainable, in a region which is not suited to commercial agriculture, where employment is scarce, and where possibilities for commercial development are limited by a poor transportation infrastructure and a lack of access to markets. A focus on subsistence agriculture and herding has emerged as the primary focus of their efforts.

The great majority of projects promoted by Fundapaz in the several Wichí communities with which it works have focused on promoting small-scale agriculture and herding. The promotion of agriculture is highlighted by the fact that in the community that relies almost exclusively on wage labor, Los Blancos, there are many fewer projects ongoing than in the other communities. While Los Blancos has some land, located about 15 kilometers from the village, there are no families living there. When some families expressed a desire to move out to the landholding, the Fundapaz team enthusiastically encouraged them, and began to discuss what projects could then be started with those families. For those who wanted to live on the land, one team member said, there should be more support: "We need to think about how we can help the people who live out there."

Similarly, the community of Abregu is broken into two residential groupings, one which is located adjacent to Los Blancos and is reliant on day labor and another which has moved to "colonize" land claimed by the community. Fundapaz works almost entirely with the colonizing group, in an explicit effort to encourage this type of colonization. In a discussion in the "colony" about a project to purchase goats, a Fundapaz staff member, Marisol, said, "[You] have priority. All of the communities have presented this project [to the funding source] but since you have come to live out here on the land, when the project [money] comes, you will have priority." Priority in receiving project resources is offered as both an incentive and a reward to those who have chosen to make a commitment to subsistence agriculture.

Such a resettlement is not an easy strategy to promote in the more urbanized communities, however. A Fundapaz staff member from Buenos Aires, Vicente, admitted, "Most families don't want to move to the monte. They are from town, and they are more comfortable there. But they have to use this land, or they could lose it." Here, he is referring to one of the conditions of the land grant to the communities, which holds that the land must be occupied. Marisol noted,

> If people from the government come through and see that they aren't using it, that there is not even a little house, they will say, 'Why do you need this title, why do you even need this land?' And they'll take it away.

This concern is an important reason for Fundapaz's emphasis on promoting subsistence agriculture, but such self-sufficiency is also seen as one of the few viable and sustainable long-term development strategies available.

Many projects develop an infrastructure for household agriculture, such as digging wells and ponds, building pens for goats, and constructing fences around gardens. Despite nearly sixty years of settlement, most of the Wichí communities in the area lack such a basic infrastructure. Although various projects have periodically sponsored the construction of wells and fences, they need continual upkeep. The communities seldom have the resources or tools to maintain them, and they fall into disrepair and disuse quickly. The skeletons of such projects dot the landscape. In Misión San Patricio, a broken windmill looms above the community center. We were told that it had been installed to pump water from a well, but had broken in a gust of wind shortly after it was installed by university technicians, who never returned. In Los Blancos, an elaborate desalinization system had been installed by a government agency relatively recently but sat unused and abandoned. It had been there for over a year before my arrival, and no one seemed sure what the problem was; explanations that I was offered by people in the community ranged from a mechanical problem, to a lack of training in the community as to its operation, to a suggestion that the politician who was to have inaugurated it never came. Often, funding provides for the construction of a major construction project but not for its upkeep. In Misión San Patricio, for example, the community requested help from Fundapaz in repairing a pump for a well. The Fundapaz team scrambled to find "creative" funding that could be used to buy parts, since the original project had not provided any funds for maintenance.

Fundapaz views an adequate infrastructure as essential to the success of household agriculture. In particular, fencing and potable water are seen as the most important preconditions for household agricultural production. In a discussion of a project to build fences, for example, the regional director of Fundapaz declared that "fencing the land is the base of production" in the Chaco. In agriculture, fencing serves primarily to keep domestic herd animals from eating the plants. Without such protection, cattle and goats quickly find and destroy any crops that are planted.[7] Even small gardens located near the house must be fenced since animals are typically set loose to forage daily. Not all fences are created equal: fences made of posts and wire are preferred to fences made of branches and thorny plants that are often used when other materials are too expensive. One team member explained to me that such natural barriers, although cheaper and easier to build, are "terrible." They provide shelter for insects and snakes and are more easily penetrated by herd animals, especially goats.

Water is the other factor that constrains production. The region is very dry, and much of the ground water contains salt and other minerals in concentrations too high to be potable.[8] Wells must be dug, often a hundred meters or more, to reach this ground water. The amount of salt in the water varies locally. A government water technician said that while water considered potable contains up to 1,500 milligrams of salts per liter, the water from the town well in Los Blancos contains 3,000 milligrams per liter, and in Page the ground water contains 6,000 milligrams per liter. Despite the salinity, people in Los Blancos, both *criollo* and Wichí, drink the well water when fresh water (called "sweet water") is not available; in Page, it is considered too salty to drink even by local residents.[9]

Garden crops are grown only during the rainy season, when sufficient fresh water is available. Animals, however, like people, require a source of fresh water all year. In most of the communities, large artificial ponds have been constructed as part of recent projects. These ponds, usually only a few feet deep so that they do not hit sand, collect water during the rainy season for use through the dry season. Like gardens, they must be fenced in, so that herd animals do not overuse the supply. This water often runs out, through use and evaporation, two to three months before the beginning of the rainy season, depending on the weather any given year and the size and location of the pond.

According to these two priorities, fencing and water supplies, Fundapaz plans, seeks funding for, and implements projects designed to improve conditions for small-scale agriculture and herding. Subsistence production is the implicit goal of nearly all of the projects which are undertaken. In order to enable subsistence production, the NGO invests in developing infrastructure, subsidizes the purchase of inputs such as animals, and offers instruction on basic agricultural techniques.

It is crucial to note here that very few of the Wichí households in the region derive most of their subsistence from subsistence agriculture. Instead, the great majority of households rely on a combination of irregular day labor and the use and sale of gathered and hunted wild products, supplemented by the use of agricultural products. This subsistence strategy, which maximizes available labor and local resources, both wild and commercial, is seen by Fundapaz as inherently risky compared to agriculture and herding, which provides most of the *criollo* families in the region with a marginal but reliable base of subsistence.

Because most Wichí households are not oriented towards subsistence agricultural production, Fundapaz undertakes the more formidable effort needed to promote the idea of smallholding and inculcate the values associated with subsistence agriculture along with the concrete tasks of building infrastructure. Subsistence agriculture and herding are promoted as "more reliable" sources of income than irregular day labor. This value system is promoted despite a considerable divergence with the attitudes expressed in the communities. The Wichí do not tend to see agriculture as any more reliable than day labor or hunting. As one community elder noted in a discussion of gardening, "If God blesses them, the plants will grow. If not, pests will come and destroy them. The same as [happens] with us."

In order to make household agriculture successful, the development team argues, Wichí households have to dedicate more of their labor to constructing and maintaining basic infrastructure. They claim that the Wichí have to learn that over the long term, labor thus invested will yield greater rewards than day labor, which typically only earns enough for one day's food. Members of the team privately acknowledge that this is an uphill battle, as most families cannot spare the income from a day's work in order to make such a long-term investment. However, projects promoting subsistence agriculture continue to be the focus of Fundapaz's development efforts. Over the long term, team members agreed, there have been improvements. When asked what Fundapaz has accomplished, they cited the fact that the Wichí "have more," in terms of their material circumstances. But, equally important, they noted that members of the communities "are more conscious of what they have," and that they "take better care of what they have." These last two points reflect not the material success of development projects, but progress towards instilling the values of a peasant farmer.

The importance of preserving and caring for property is the ideological backbone of nearly every agricultural project. In a project that was to distribute goats to families who did not have them, for example, a development worker carefully explained the purpose of the goats and the project to assembled families a few weeks before the goats themselves arrived:

> The goats are being given to you so that your family has them to eat. They are not to sell. The goats aren't to sell, they are to use and have more. Maybe you can sell the young males, if there are a lot, but not the females.

She went on to explain the rudimentary infrastructure necessary to raise goats:

> You have to have a garden, to grow food for the animals too. Now there is food for them to eat [in the monte], but when it gets bad, what will they eat? First you have to make a pen, so that when the goats come you will have a place to put them. First you have to worry about this. And in your garden, you have to think about planting something for the goats, for when there is nothing in the monte.

Instructions along these lines were repeated many times in the weeks before the goats were brought to the community. While many families had some experience with keeping goats, only about a third of the families had goats at the time of the project (see table 4).

Table 4: Livestock Ownership in Selected Wichí Communities

Kayip
Number of nuclear families: 17
Families with goats and/or sheep: 6 (35%)
Average number of animals*: 12

Misión San Patricio
Number of nuclear families: 35
Families with goats and/or sheep: 11 (31%)
Average number of animals*: 14

* In those households that have animals.
Based on survey data, August 1997.

The fear of the Fundapaz team was that the young goats would quickly be sold off to meet more immediate subsistence needs of the families. Fundapaz, like other organizations working with the Wichí, frequently expresses the idea that the Wichí do not save, or store, agricultural products. However, there is considerable evidence that in the period pre-dating white settlement, the Wichí did stockpile wild products such as algarroba as well as cultivated produce. The current failure of the Wichí to store goods is not located in some feature inherent to the culture, but in the prevailing economic situation in which most families find themselves. Households live so close to the margin that saving is often not possible. This margin is combined with a social organization that promotes, values, and requires sharing, rather than accumulation. If a household has a surplus, it is soon redistributed through kin networks.

Interestingly, much of Fundapaz's training on goat-keeping was directed primarily at women. Women were assumed to be the ones who would bear most of the responsibility for raising the animals. Several training sessions on veterinary health and household remedies for goat illnesses were conducted which were attended exclusively by women. Within the communities, the Fundapaz team focused on assisting women with caring for the goats. This is largely due to the fact that in the surrounding *criollo* communities, goats are "women's animals" while cattle are "men's animals." When I asked one *criollo* woman about this division, I was told, "Some men know a lot about goats. But they don't admit it." Since the Wichí do not have the same history of animal-keeping, a similar gendered division of labor does not fully structure their work with the goats. Wichí men are not embarrassed, as their *criollo* neighbors would be, to be seen herding goats.[10] However, as women are trained instead of men, they are beginning to take on more of the daily tasks associated with the animals. This is further encouraged by the existing differences between men and women's work in the communities. While men are frequently involved in day labor that removes them from the village, women are usually in the village, and their trips into the monte for wood and water coincide with tasks involved in caring for the goats.

Despite the idea that women are the primary caretakers of goats, men were most often the ones who entered formally into the project that distributed goats. In Misión San Patricio, out of twenty-one households participating in this project, only two women were listed, both of whom were widows.[11] Men are more likely to formally enter into projects than women in part because of their higher literacy—many of the women in the community cannot sign their names—and fluency in Spanish. But they are also presumed by a gender-biased development system to be the "head of household." In most projects, men represent the household; the only exception is a project that collects women's craft projects to sell for cloth. As Fundapaz has begun to design projects that work with the Wichí kinship system of extended families, most men are affiliated with their wives' kin group but continue to represent the nuclear household.

Efforts by Fundapaz to encourage subsistence agriculture carry implications beyond just a shift in the emphasis of a household subsistence strategy. They imply a larger process of cultural change. A project to encourage families to construct garden plots, for example, met with only a lukewarm response. The project encouraged the use of vegetables such as radishes and carrots which grow well in the region, but which the Wichí do not consume as part of their regular diet. Because they are easily grown, the *criollos* tended to grow their own and were not interested in purchasing the surplus. As one of the staff members of Fundapaz noted,

> We have to look at what they [Wichí families] will use, or what they can sell. Otherwise, unless they see a specific reason like use or sale, they will not bother doing it. . . . If the Wichí don't do something, it is because they are not interested in it.

Something as apparently straightforward as building gardens is working at the level of wholesale cultural change, despite the number of years that the Wichí have been living in relatively settled communities here. It involves changing not only patterns of work, but also habits of consumption.

Development Strategies: Ethnic Development Planning

The underlying dynamic at work in the promotion of subsistence farming in the Wichí communities becomes more apparent when compared with the strategies and goals that Fundapaz has for development projects in neighboring *criollo* communities. The *criollos*, like the Wichí, have a diversified subsistence strategy, relying on a combination of sources. They differ in that the *criollos* employ the much more familiar strategies of peasant agriculture. This familiarity allows Fundapaz to more easily concentrate on projects aimed at improving their productive capacity. Because the ecological conditions are the same, some of the infrastructural projects are the same as those enacted in the Wichí communities. The ideas and discourse that surround these projects, however, have a different starting point, and are played out in distinct ways.

The great majority of *criollo* families in the region can be described as smallholders, combining agriculture and animal husbandry to eke out a marginal but predictable subsistence. Generally, most households raise some produce, mostly fresh vegetables for their own use and fodder for their own animals. Goats are raised, nearly always by women, for household consumption. Cattle are raised in small numbers; most families have thirty to fifty head of cattle, while the largest herd in the region numbers perhaps two hundred fifty. Cattle are raised primarily by men, and are treated as a way to store household capital. They are sometimes slaughtered for household consumption, but most often are sold, a few head a season, to markets in the city.

Some of the projects that Fundapaz undertakes with the *criollo* communities are the same as those in the Wichí villages—building fencing, digging wells, and offering education on agricultural techniques to improve production. Other projects focus on improving the possibilities for commercialization, especially of cattle, and on developing agricultural systems that make better use of the natural environment. One project, for example, was directed at reforestation of areas that had been left barren by erosion caused primarily by cattle. A new project, just recently begun, will provide stipends and materials to families willing to develop small plots that experiment with using both wild and domesticated crops in the same area, for example, intercropping food crops with trees.

These projects are undertaken solely with *criollo* households. In part, this is because these households are generally better off than the Wichí households, and thus can afford to take some small risks and invest labor in long-term projects. More importantly, however, it is because the *criollo* families of the region are already well-established as smallholders. Most families work primarily on their own land, with few individuals participating in wage labor. Gathering of wild products is almost never practiced; while some wild products are used, such as firewood or some kinds of fruit, they are usually purchased cheaply from Wichí neighbors, and do not form a significant part of *criollo* households' overall subsistence strategy. While hunting and fishing sometimes contribute to household subsistence, they are undertaken primarily as leisure activities. Only a few select wild items are used, and both knowledge and use of the products of the monte are much more limited than with the Wichí.

Even where the goals of development projects are the same, the project design and methodology may be different in significant ways. For one, projects that involve individual cash credit have been introduced with the *criollo* communities, but not with the Wichí. In a project to build ponds, for example, the *criollo* communities set up a rotating credit fund, using an initial grant that allowed each family to borrow from the fund to build a pond and allowed them to set a flexible repayment schedule. As the fund is repaid, other families borrow from the fund and are able to build. The monies are used to pay the tractor driver, to purchase fuel for the tractor and contribute a small amount to an amortization fund for the tractor, and to purchase any hardware that might be needed, including materials for fencing.[12] The families, in a meeting, worked out the repayment schedules and terms and most families agreed that they could repay the fund within six months to a year.

Projects involving credit have been used in the Wichí communities, but to a much smaller extent. These projects usually involve a symbolic repayment in kind rather than a cash outlay that actually contributes to the goal of the project itself. For example, a project to build gardens, initiated with government funding, required that each family contribute some of their produce to either the school or the infant feeding program. The project began with a grant of one thousand eight hundred pesos, half of which had to be "repaid" in kind. In Kayip, nine families were participating in this project, each receiving about 200 pesos to spend on tools, fencing, and seeds. The "repayment" period was over the next seven years, bringing it to the year 2005. In practice, the "repayment" of the grant probably received little follow-up attention, and the length of time involved virtually ensured that the full amount would never be reached. Another "repayment" project initiated by Fundapaz involved goats: families received a number of goats and had to "repay" with their offspring. In this case, the offspring were to go to other members of the community, usually within the recipient's immediate or extended family. Here, the direct involvement of other family members and the invocation of kinship ties and use of local patterns of redistribution make it much more likely that the "repayment" transaction will actually occur. In both projects, the symbolic repayment is conceived of as a way to "accustom" the project's clients to the idea of credit and repayment, rather than as a way to recoup the financial outlay of the project itself. This formulation springs from the funding source's project design, with Fundapaz acting as the intermediary. In this way, ideas that are current in the thinking and discourse of large development agencies—in this case, microcredit—are enacted in the local context.

Another significant difference between projects in *criollo* and Wichí communities is that projects with the *criollos* are far more likely to be on a household basis, while with the Wichí they are more often "communal." In building water sources, for example, each *criollo* household is presumed to need its own pond or well, where the Wichí "need" only one or two in the community. In part, this is due to residence patterns and the ways in which each group uses the resources available to it. The *criollos* live on dispersed homesteads, some of which may be several hours walk from any other. The Wichí, in contrast, live in concentrated villages. For most *criollo* households to share water sources is thus impracticable. The *criollos* also own far more animals, in general, than do the Wichí—in fact, many *criollo* households own more animals than all of the families in a single Wichí village. They thus require more water, and more dispersed water sources so that the immediate surroundings are not completely denuded.

These residential patterns are based on the underlying subsistence strategies of each group. The *criollos*, who make extensive use of unfenced grazing areas in the monte, rely on their large herds for much of their subsistence. Because the animals are generally turned loose to graze, and may roam through quite a large area in search of food, households must be scattered in order to allow the animals some area to graze in. Frequently, they are not grazing on land actually "owned" by the household (see chapter 6), but the dispersion of households does contribute to some degree of sustainability, although the long-term effects of such grazing are deleterious, and in some localized areas even disastrous. The Wichí, in contrast, own few animals, which also are allowed to graze freely. With the exception of a single household in Los Blancos, Wichí households own only small livestock, not cattle; these smaller animals require less grazing area and eat a greater variety of plants.

The *criollo* households that survive on smallholdings in the region rely substantially on cattle as a reliable source of income. Because of ecological concerns about the long-term sustainability of the monte as a grazing area, however, Fundapaz does not actively promote the acquisition of cattle by Wichí households. At the same time, it does encourage subsistence agriculture in the Wichí communities as its primary long-term development strategy. However, given the marginal environmental conditions and the lack of cattle which have a great deal more value than small livestock, even a complete transition on the part of the Wichí to subsistence farming would probably result in considerable material poverty, as well as a degree of cultural impoverishment.

Changes in Methodology

Recently, Fundapaz has made a conscious shift in methodology, trying to move from a situation in which projects were often presented as givens to one which advocates a more proactive relationship between the communities and the organization. The director described this new approach: "We talk to the clan, to see all of their needs. Then we go looking for projects. We have to knock on different doors, to find the projects that can meet these needs." This shift in methodology represents a change in the relationship of the organization with the community. As one staff member commented, "Before, Fundapaz did everything—we had the idea, we made the projects, we came in with the resources, and everyone signed up. People recognize that this has changed."

Once a relationship between a community and an NGO develops, a cycle of dependence may build gradually over time. As an example, Volker Von Bremen considers a case study of a situation in which an indigenous community became highly dependent on an external organization (1987, 47). With increased dependency, there were increased expectations of the organization (in this case, a mission) by the community. The community tried to solve its most immediate problems by looking for aid from the mission, based on a history of such aid. The organization, in turn, was paternalistic, expecting "passivity and a position of unilateral and passive waiting on the part of the indigenous community" (1987, 48).

The dependence that the NGO perceives as a problem may also represent a kind of cultural adaptation by the Wichí to the presence of development projects. In a study of missionaries among the Enxet people of the Chaco, Stephen Kidd (1999) argues that the Enxet extend their own cultural values about the role of a leader to Anglican missionaries who work in the area. "Since love and gift giving are conceptually linked, the Enxet feel that it is entirely legitimate for them to receive material goods from the missionaries" (Kidd 1999, 52). Similarly, the Wichí expect leaders to act as generous providers, and extend their own notions of "goodwill" (Palmer 1997) to Fundapaz.

In Los Blancos, a dependence on the NGO has developed that is difficult to change. This dependence is due in part to a top-down methodology which assumed that the "developers" knew better than the indigenous people what was in their best interests. It has also developed in this particular region because of the lack of options and fonts of resources available to the communities. Fundapaz is, in fact, the only significant NGO operating in the region around Los Blancos. In contrast to other parts of the world, where an array of NGOs and projects may allow local people to pick and choose between programs, the Wichí have only had the choice between accepting projects created by Fundapaz or having no outside aid whatsoever.

A shift to a participatory methodology creates challenges in communication. Even those Wichí who have a long involvement with development projects have only a vague idea of what the process of obtaining funding for any given project entails. A more common view, frequently expressed, is that Fundapaz has a large warehouse somewhere, and chooses to parcel out materials according to its own whims. This kind of idea underscores the importance of clarity in the process of development projects. It demonstrates that many people in the communities do not understand the process, and feel that it is beyond their control or influence. They often feel as though resources are being withheld from them based on caprice, stinginess, or even malice.

Participation, at least in the form envisaged by the NGO, is not always easy to come by. This is recognized by Fundapaz; as the director stated, "We have our discourse, and our practice. The problem is putting the discourse into practice, of keeping the theory in the day-to-day activities." Fundapaz would like to see a situation in which members of the community suggest ideas for projects that would meet their needs, and then work with the team in order to obtain funding and complete these projects. To this end, Fundapaz holds regular meetings in all of the communities, large open meetings which everyone is invited to join and which are generally well attended. Despite such formal participation, however, the agenda is usually set by the NGO staff, who propose projects based on their knowledge of what funding is available. The Wichí, in turn, often wait and see what options may be available to them, rather than suggesting projects. Wichí leaders have limited knowledge of the possibilities to acquire funding for projects, apart from those which are presented to them by Fundapaz.

Despite occasional conflicts with Fundapaz, the Wichí communities maintain a strong relationship with the organization. Contrary to one possible explanation of this attitude as rooted in passivity, I would argue that it in fact represents a strategy to maximize use of a resource, in this case the NGO. The Wichí communities frequently are able to adapt the goals and interests of projects to meet their own interests, transforming development aid into a resource that is employed in their diversified subsistence strategy. Development projects, like the monte, goats, and cutting lumber, become one source of income among many. The "failures" of development projects to produce their stated goals, whatever they may be, are only viewed as a failure by the Wichí if the project itself never materializes. The short-term benefits of projects, such as income during construction, are seen as an end in themselves, and even valued more than the project itself.

A project to construct a community center in the Abregu colony, for example, where there are only six households, was welcomed by the community. The center itself, like those in other communities, is rarely used—community centers are most often employed by Fundapaz to hold meetings or by outside visitors like the doctor or an anthropologist. However, the construction of the center represented a steady source of employment and income for several months. As Fundapaz struggles to encourage "participation" in conceiving projects, the response the team most often receives is, "we need more work." To the communities, the form that this work takes is in large part immaterial—if there is funding available to build a center, then they would like to build a center. If there is funding for something else, that would be equally acceptable. For the NGO, the idea is that aid from a project should help indigenous people to live without the project. For the indigenous people, the importance of the project is located in its present benefits.

Refashioning "Development"

The discourse of development is neither monolithic nor totalizing. "Development, for all its power to speak and to control the terms of speaking, has never been impervious to challenge and resistance, to reformulation and change" (Crush 1995, 8). One form of challenge may come from local communities, who adapt, change, and use both the concepts and the resources brought to them by development programs. As with any universalizing discourse, development plays "into local forms and conditions in unexpected ways, changing known structures into strange hybrids . . . as non-Western peoples . . . fashioned their own visions of modernity" (Comaroff and Comaroff 1992, 5). In one case study of such a hybridization of development concepts, for example, Don Kulik (1992) discusses how villagers in one remote Papua New Guinea community see "development" as an almost miraculous material transformation of society but resist the individualization of property (for similar studies, see Dahl and Rabo 1992).

The role of Fundapaz goes beyond simply acting as a conduit for resources. Fundapaz is in a unique relationship with these communities, one which is not matched, under the current situation, by government projects or other outside projects. The Wichí communities have generally accepted Fundapaz as a mediator between themselves and the dominant society. This process of mediation, as it is understood in the communities, certainly includes the procurement of resources, but also extends to accepting Fundapaz as an intermediary in political situations, the most important of which has been the legal battle to obtain land titles (see chapter 6).

The acceptance of this role for the NGO does not imply that there is no conflict between members of the community and the development team. Instead, this relationship is negotiated through daily interactions. As we saw above, the Wichí transform development projects to meet their own ends, employing Fundapaz as another resource in a diversified subsistence strategy. Wichí "resistance" is not to the projects themselves, but to the concept of production that the projects bring. In fact, the projects themselves are cheerfully accepted and even demanded by the community, even as the Wichí generally refuse to accept the shift to subsistence agriculture promoted by those projects.

The Wichí concept of "development" bears little resemblance to the NGO ideal of a productive economy based on household agriculture and herding. Attitudes towards development within the Wichí communities are complex, multivocal, and often contradictory. There is no single "Wichí vision" of development. Nevertheless, there are certain shared assumptions, a degree of consensus, and expressions by local Wichí leaders that suggest Wichí ideas about "development." One community leader from Los Blancos neatly summed up what he saw as the development goals of his people: "There are three things that are important: the land, rights, and work. That is all we want."

At a meeting in July of 1997,[11] one community leader outlined his goals for the Wichí and some of the challenges that they face as a people:

> We need to teach our children, so that they also learn. We are entering secondary school, college, but they do not teach the things of our culture. We are looking for this path, which is the land, legal status for our communities, health, education. Our organization, to be Wichí, must be organized according to our own culture. The national constitution talks about the different cultures. They are asking now what we want, what [form of] organization, what customs, so that these are not lost. For these reasons we must talk to our young people, so that they learn from our path.

As this speaker expressed, in many ways the immediate goals of development proposals—health, education, production—are secondary to deeper concerns. The real issue for most Wichí is not the number of goats that a family receives as part of a husbandry project, but maintaining a sense of cultural identity and a sense of control. While young people need formal education in order to help themselves and to help their communities, they also need roots in those communities and a sense of their own heritage. Organizations and processes which are imposed from the outside do not contribute to "being Wichí."

Another community leader, speaking during the same meeting, was less optimistic:

> There are programs, there is help, but they do not reach here. Justice does not reach indigenous people. . . . The indigenous people will always be poor until they die.

Here, outside involvement is not seen to offer any hope for the Wichí. Generations of broken promises, misunderstandings, and unfulfilled expectations have left a significant part of the Wichí community with a sense of fatalism, cynicism, and even despair.

The goals and methods of larger development projects often appear to have little relevance to the daily lives of people in these rural communities. One Wichí leader from the Pilcomayo region, speaking at an international NGO conference in Europe, said,

> We listen to the European Commission and other organizations that give money, speaking of large projects with large amounts of money, and we are dying of hunger. . . . They come from the World Bank, from BID, they come from Holland, from the European Commission, with so much money. And we are dying of hunger. For this I said, we don't understand anything about these organizations. And for the same reason, we want to develop projects that come from the community itself, to say what it is that we need here and that we are

going to give a project to an organization that comes from our own initiative, to be able to manage it, to be able to understand it. If it is a project designed here in Europe, we don't understand it. . . . We want to develop projects in the region with the approval of our people. Because if we continue as we have been, we will never understand, instead it will continue to become worse. (Francisco Perez, Wichí cacique of Comunidad Cañaveral, Pilcomayo, at an international conference in Germany, January 1996, cited in Carrasco and Briones 1996, 247)

On a general level, the goals of many of the Wichí are straightforward. In meetings, interviews, and discussions, one theme that emerges time and again is respect. In its broadest sense, respect signifies consideration for indigenous culture and for the rights of indigenous people. On a more personal level, people speak of their desire for respect in their daily interactions with *criollos* and whites, at work, in public services, and in dealings with their neighbors. Another prominent theme that emerges is the need that many Wichí feel for education and training. Knowledge is a highly valued cultural good. In traditional culture, skills were passed down by example from adults to children, and what a person knew and could do was an essential marker of his or her status in the community. Now, members of the community see the process of learning as multidimensional—they focus not just on what they can learn from NGO projects and trainings, but on what they can learn from one another, and what outsiders can learn from them. The willingness of outsiders to learn from the Wichí—to learn their language, for example—is seen as one marker of respect.

Economically, the main themes that echo in the communities are security and flexibility, as well as being treated fairly in interactions with the capitalist market. The Wichí continue to use the natural resources of the area as a significant part of their subsistence base, but they are also heavily involved in wage labor and see employment as a desirable end. "What we need is more work," I was told on many occasions. In fact, few members of the Wichí communities in the villages near Los Blancos have steady employment—the few who do work either as assistants in the schools or in the health posts. Most men, and many women, find work as irregular, unskilled day laborers. The problems with such a system are obvious: as workers, the Wichí are highly exploited. They are frequently forced to accept much less than the prevailing daily wage (eight to ten pesos), often accepting payment in kind that may value only a few pesos. Because work is scarce, they accept such conditions. Short-term construction projects or other such efforts are welcomed as a source of employment, even if the project itself is of dubious merit or if the source of such employment is obviously politically motivated. Many of the Wichí would like to see development strategies that create more sources of employment and increase the equitability of labor conditions.

At times, specific ideas presented by Wichí communities about projects that they would like seem impractical or counterproductive to NGO staff. One example of this kind of conflict occurred in one of the Wichí communities in which I was working. A group of families consistently asked for funding to start a herd of cattle. The NGO staff, on the other hand, felt that cattle are too ecologically destructive to introduce them in communities which did not already have them. Despite the explanations that the staff offered the community, some individuals felt increasingly frustrated, as though their requests were not being taken seriously. In this case, it is not only the cows, but what they represent, that may be at the crux of the Wichí request. In the *criollo* culture of the region, cattle are a symbol of wealth and prosperity. The value attached to owning cattle goes far beyond the monetary value of the cows themselves. What the Wichí were requesting may have been some of the status that is associated with cattle, a way to gain more respect from their *criollo* neighbors. On a more practical level, the value of a cow, in cash, is far greater than that of a sheep or goat and they are easier to sell. During the dry season, when cash, work, and food are all scarce, the sale of a cow would provide a large income to a family. Cattle thus represent a source of status and economic security.

The arguments of the NGO staff that cattle are ecologically destructive had a hypocritical ring in the ears of the community, since their *criollo* neighbors possess cattle—in far greater numbers—that graze on lands the Wichí claim as their own. Projects were underway to help the *criollos* manage their livestock in more ecologically sustainable ways, and the Wichí felt that they understood the damage that cattle cause and could learn to minimize it, with similar aid. Finally, the request for this project was not just for cattle, but for materials for fencing, tools, and "assistance"—in the form of food—for the time that the families invested in constructing fencing. Such direct aid is common in projects and is, in itself, highly valued by the Wichí no matter what the project is. As a relatively large-scale project, the assistance itself would represent several weeks of subsistence during the dry season when other forms of income are scarce.

In Los Blancos, the NGO and the local communities offer distinct views of development. Wichí leaders emphasize the need for work and for education, within a context that allows them to preserve their culture. Fundapaz is also highly concerned with, and sensitive to, the need to preserve Wichí culture. Economically, however, it continues to offer projects to institutionalize subsistence agriculture without cattle. The debate over the desirability of subsistence agriculture takes on a different form in the highlands, where culture and agriculture are also inseparably connected in a discourse of development.

"Moving Forward": Creating Development in Iruya

Throughout the highlands in northern Argentina, the phrase used to describe the process of development by local people and NGOs alike is "*seguir adelante*," to move or continue forward. The idea of "progress" pervades local political speeches, community meetings, literature produced by the NGO, and the speech of local people themselves when they discuss their futures. Despite the apparently linear, progressive statement embedded in this shared metaphor, the path "forward" is anything but clear. To a certain degree, the actors involved in "moving forward" agree on the basic outlines of the problems. In the *departamento* of Iruya, the underlying causes of the problems of economic and human development are long term and structural: a low level of agricultural productivity, poor access to markets, a lack of paid employment, and an impoverished infrastructure. The region suffers from social, economic, geographic, and cultural isolation. Where there is much less consensus is in an understanding of potential solutions to these problems, which are, in fact, rarely addressed in the praxis of development projects in the region.

There are several development programs active in Iruya, but of these, OCLADE is the most important and most active. The few other programs working in the area are sponsored by the federal or provincial governments. OCLADE's relatively long-term presence in the area and its relationship with the Church contribute to a sense of trust on the part of the population, which is generally skeptical of outside organizations. Many government programs, in contrast, are short term, and often suffer short life spans as the result of policy changes. Other more permanent agencies, such as INAI,[14] are not very active in the region.

Unlike Fundapaz, which has relatively narrowly defined objectives and spheres of programming, OCLADE has taken a broad, inclusive approach to the development problems of the region. Its programs encompass health care, education, production, community organization, investments in infrastructure, social issues such as domestic violence, and efforts at promoting regional organization between communities. Perhaps as a consequence of this breadth of scope, its programs are often opportunistic, taking advantage of available funding, and/or crisis-driven, in response to immediate short-term needs. Historically, OCLADE has been most active in areas of health and education in Iruya, in part due to the personal skills and interests of some of the people who were key to founding the organization, and also as a response to historic needs of the community. Like Fundapaz, OCLADE has acted as an important conduit of material resources into the region: projects have provided materials to construct systems for drinking water and for irrigation and to build health posts, among other things. Also like Fundapaz, the role that OCLADE plays in the community goes well beyond acting simply as a source of material resources, as ideas about "development" shape its work with the community and the response of individuals to its programs.

Developing Women

One of the most prominent projects of OCLADE in Iruya during the period of this research was the administration of a network of infant and child feeding centers, which were combined with a preschool program. Another important program, slightly less active, focused on organizing women's groups in each community. A third program, which was just getting started when I was in the community, was an adult literacy program aimed exclusively at women. These three projects, taken together, represented the great bulk of the actual work that was being done by OCLADE in Iruya, receiving the overwhelming majority of staff time and the focus of community attention. They reflect the long-term interest of OCLADE in projects that promote health and education. Significantly, they are all aimed primarily at women.

Issues of health, education, and family are all flagged almost automatically as "women's issues" by OCLADE, as is perhaps the case with many small organizations working in the field of human development. Women have often been absent from mainstream development efforts (see, for example, Boserup 1990), but a growing number of programs are aimed at women as integral participants in the process of development. Small NGOs may be particularly active in designing projects to benefit what they see as women's specific needs. Some researchers have pointed to the inclusion of women as a significant feature of such projects, arguing that this represents not just a shift in priorities but a change of methodology and an increase in meaningful grassroots participation.

While the incorporation of women into development projects is surely a positive step and one which should be encouraged, it is still crucial to look at the extent to which their inclusion differs from that of men. In the case of OCLADE, women seem to constitute a different kind of "participant" with more narrowly and specifically defined interests. As this discourse is mobilized, the needs of women are portrayed as distinct. An OCLADE publication introduced an article on women in this way:

> The women of the Puna and Andean valleys have spent many years quietly working in the house and in the fields with the animals and the harvest. Many times alone through everything, with our babies, suffering from solitude, from a lack of communication. Alone with our pain and fatigue and also with our joys. (*Yareta* 1997, 4)

Women's specific needs are strongly linked to health and education, rather than to production. The programs that OCLADE directs at "women's concerns" focus on nutrition, literacy, child raising, and consciousness raising in the form of women's groups. In the past, materials for infrastructural construction projects have been channeled through the women's groups as well, but these were primarily for materials to improve housing, and later to contribute to building health posts and buildings to house preschools. Projects to build irrigation and water supply canals were implemented through other forms of community organizations.

Divisions of Labor

The strong association of women's needs with projects in health and education occurs despite the fact that women play an integral role in the household economy, contributing significant amounts of labor to agricultural production. Many women own their own land and contribute to household decisions regarding agriculture.[15] Because fifteen to twenty percent of men migrate seasonally to work on agricultural plantations, many women are left alone for as long as six months each year to do all of the household and agricultural labor. Women perform much agricultural labor, including weeding, harvesting, and cutting fodder for animals. Plowing is one of the few tasks reserved exclusively for men, while women follow behind the plow to plant seeds. Heavy labor, such as building houses and retaining walls, is also regarded as male work, and a single woman will generally hire labor or call on her male kin to do such tasks. Women are completely responsible for most domestic chores, including cooking and washing clothes, tasks which men almost never do. Women do have primary responsibility for raising children, although men sometimes help with basic childrearing duties. One major chore in the region is gathering wood for cooking fuel, a task which women often combine with herding animals.

In the rural communities in the department of Iruya, there is little class stratification (see chapter 1).[16] There are virtually no landless households, and differences in wealth are small, marked primarily by the number of animals a household possesses, the amount of land that it has, and, in some of the communities, by markers of wealth and status such as a pickup truck. The difference between the families with the most land and animals and those with the least are small, and may often be related to age and the family cycle; young households control fewer resources than older households. In the NGO's discourse, however, women are homogenized to a greater extent than their male counterparts, becoming, in effect, an underclass within the rural community. Women are depicted as "suffering more" from poverty. In an interview, the bishop of the prelature said,

> In the Assembly [of the prelature] the most notable causes of women's suffering were seen: the lack of education, of training, the economic situation and the alcoholism of men. They work from when they are very small, they are taken out of school early, which is why they are less trained. The consequences of the economic situation fall on women, men take off, they close themselves in with drink, or they leave the situation. But women stay. . . . [When women are included in programs,] it is as if they were revitalized, they feel happy. The fact of recognizing this function, of giving them space to participate and learn, makes them happy, because they are taken into consideration for something important like the education of their children and bringing the programs forward. In fact, when the programs have been evaluated the women ask that they be continued. (Bishop P. Olmedo, *Yareta* 1997, 9-10)

Here, as in much of OCLADE's discourse, men are considered as one factor in the oppression of women. Alcoholism, regarded as a problem exclusively of men, is frequently blamed as a cause of family problems.[17] Men are also frequently blamed for abandoning a family, usually by migrating to the city. Interestingly, a 1995 survey conducted by OCLADE asked respondents to identify the "main causes of women's suffering."[18] The problems most frequently chosen were a lack of education (fifty-six percent) and illness (fifty-five percent). Poverty was identified by thirty-five percent of respondents, while thirty-two percent replied "being a woman." Alcoholism and abuse were each identified by less than four percent of respondents.

To a certain extent, OCLADE introduces ideas derived from Western feminism and the experiences and training of the urban women who make up much of the NGO's paid staff. At times, this means that the programs introduced in the communities fail to meet what local women see as their most urgent needs—increasing production and access to markets. In many ways, however, local women who participate in OCLADE's projects are able to adopt the programs to meet their own needs and priorities and are generally positive about the overall impact of the organization in their lives. A closer examination of some of these projects reveals the role that they play in these communities and the ways in which OCLADE's discourse shapes its daily praxis.

In the following pages, I examine a few of OCLADE's projects, how they function, and their impact on the communities. This is not an exhaustive review of past or present projects, but an analysis of some of the projects that were most active during the time in which I conducted my research, in the communities in which I worked (San Isidro, Río Grande, Campo Carreras, and Colanzulí). As we will see, the kinds of programs that OCLADE establishes are based on OCLADE's ideas of "development" and the needs of the community. The response of the community, in turn, is based on a sense of needs and a desire for "progress" that does not entirely coincide.

Women's Groups

One of OCLADE's major programs has been to work with women of the communities in the form of women's groups. Gender relations in the community are complex, and of course are part of a system of cultural beliefs and practices. Women's and men's roles are shaped by both traditional cultural practices, that is to say, originating in the Kolla culture, and by exposure to the gender roles and models of the dominant mestizo culture. Although OCLADE tends to emphasize the suffering of local women, the Kolla culture is much more egalitarian than the dominant Argentine society. In fact, it would appear that one of the chief spheres of local gender inequality occurs at the intersection of the two cultures, as Kolla women have less access to education, wage labor, and political influence than do men.

Women sometimes complain that their work leaves them little time for attending meetings and participating in organizations. A young member of the women's group in San Isidro said to me,

> It can be hard to have meetings. There is always something to do: watching the sheep, harvesting, cleaning. It is difficult to have meetings. For example, yesterday when you came I had to go down to the river to wash the clothes. There is always work to do.

A middle-aged woman with several children concurred, explaining that this is part of what makes it difficult to organize the group: "Now the group is not great. The women have a lot of work now. We have to work on the land if we want to eat. Here, there is little employment. We live from the land, from agriculture." The tremendous demands placed on women by their daily work present a challenge which must be taken into consideration by OCLADE and its programs.

Women's responsibilities also make it difficult for them to attend training sessions or meetings outside of the community. Because OCLADE serves a large area, through two provinces in the northwest of the country, meetings and training sessions are generally held in regional centers. For any woman in a rural community, traveling to such events usually involves several hours' walk to Iruya, a three-hour bus ride to Humahuaca, and then often another bus ride, of at least several hours, to wherever the meeting is being held. There are also concerns about financial costs:

> When we go [to outside meetings], we always have to pay for something, for food. For some of the women, this is very hard. They might have to pay someone to watch their children, or their animals. There is one woman who has sheep, and she has to pay someone to watch them for her when she goes. We always have to spend money, for different things like this. It is hard.

Childcare can also pose difficulties. One young woman said,

> It's hard to arrange things, to go to these meetings. This time, I am going to leave the baby with my mother. She is too much of a bother at the meetings, she makes a lot of noise. The travel is a lot for her too.

Sometimes the difficulties involved prevent women from participating: "Sometimes people want to get training but they can't go. They lose four or five days of work, or they can't leave the house, the children."

Despite the difficulties involved, women who participate in the group place a high value on their experiences. One woman in Río Grande who has worked for many years with OCLADE said, "The most important thing that OCLADE has done, for me, is to provide training." Such training and education allow a woman to broaden her own experience, to share with other rural women, and to gain new skills and knowledge. A young woman described her experiences at a recent training:

> I like to be with the other women. I go to learn, and I learn a lot. I learn the most from the women from other places. Their problems are different from ours, since their lives are different, but it is surprising how we are the same in so many ways. We have many things in common. . . . The people from here are timid. They are afraid of talking. But when you go to the courses, you lose this. When I went at first, I didn't want to talk. I was afraid to say anything. But now I like it.

According to women who have participated in the women's groups, the program has contributed, over the number of years that it has been in place, to the increased participation of women in community activities and meetings. The Kolla culture tends to include a high degree of equality within the household.[19] Men and women, in most families, make major decisions together. Women control household resources, including land, independently from their husbands. Again, migrant labor means that women may be alone, running the household independently, for much of the year.

However, in the public sphere, women, particularly young women, while they are not excluded, may take a secondary position. "Here, there is a saying: Men are for the streets, women are for the house." When the women's groups first started, as one woman recounts, men were resistant to the idea:

> Before, the husbands didn't let the women come to meetings. Everyone has had this problem. The men say, why are you going, what can you get from this? There were a lot of men who said, you are losing time, what are they teaching you? But now the women say, I'm going anyway. The men are more used to it now, and they don't complain as much.

Not only do women participate in the women's groups, I was told, but this has also led to women being more active and more willing to speak out in other public gatherings. "Before, they didn't want to say anything. Now they do more. Before, women have suffered a lot. They were always in the house. Now they go out more."

This comment suggests that the women's groups have contributed to breaking down barriers of isolation that are part of rural life in the community. Households are relatively dispersed in most of the area, and women do not often have the opportunity to visit with neighbors or family. Moreover, many women spend a great deal of time pasturing their animals, a solitary task. The women's groups have provided a forum for women to socialize and meet together on a regular basis. Other projects, such as the preschool program, have served the same function. One of the *mamas cuidadoras* said,

> There are many benefits for those who work in the program. For example, I myself went to school, but there are other women [who work] who haven't had any school at all. It has been good for these women. They are much more open

now. Before, they were very quiet, shy. They were much more timid before. They were afraid. Now they go to meetings, they do more things.

In the past, both San Isidro and Río Grande have had active women's groups.[20] Over the past several years, both of these groups, while they still exist, have become considerably less active. This inactivity is generally seen by the community, at least in part, as a result of the withdrawal of certain activities and support by OCLADE. One male community leader told me, "[The women's group] worked very well at first. But then OCLADE left it, and after that it didn't function well." I would argue that the sense by many former participants that OCLADE has "abandoned" the women's group is due to changing program goals and methods by OCLADE, a theme I will consider at greater length below.

The women's groups once were used by OCLADE as a direct conduit for channeling material resources and development projects into the communities. For the women in the group, membership provided a means to direct material assistance which was highly valued. One member, explaining the history of the group in San Isidro, said,

> Before, there was a group that went well, three or four years ago. They [OCLADE] gave us roofing materials and cement to fix up our houses. They also gave materials for the church. There was some good help. . . . The women fixed up their houses. . . . They aren't doing much now.

Another woman echoed this sentiment,

> In the last few years, they haven't done much here, they haven't been very active. When they started [in 1987], they did a lot. They used to give the women things to help them build their houses. They gave them roofs, materials for construction.

The women's groups also were the conduit for local building projects, providing the local base to organize materials, labor, and support. As the groups' importance as a conduit for obtaining resources has diminished or disappeared completely, the groups themselves have become significantly less active.

Child Nutrition and Education

One of OCLADE's biggest and most visible programs in Iruya is called Yachay, which runs the system of infant and child feeding centers and preschools. Yachay was started several years ago to combat high levels of infant and child malnutrition and to better prepare rural children to begin school. A recent survey (March 1997) by local health care workers measured infant malnutrition at twenty-four percent in the *departamento* as a whole, and malnutrition in children ages one to five at sixteen percent.[21] The measure of malnutrition used in this study is a simple measure of weight for size and age, and does not include any factors such as vitamins, protein, or other dietary deficiencies. As the promoter for Yachay told me:

> Malnutrition is very bad in the interior, especially for children and babies. People have food here, but they really have very little. Most people only eat once a day, and they might have a soup or a *guiso* [stew], which is mostly liquid. Then they might have some tea with a little bread, and that's it until the next day. Here in town, people eat meat, but in the interior they eat very little meat. They eat mostly corn, and potatoes. The children, especially, don't get enough to eat.

The Yachay feeding program is run with government funding and is aimed at children under the age of six, pregnant women, and lactating mothers. In some communities, elderly people without family support as well as disabled individuals have also been allowed to attend. Food is distributed through a collective cafeteria; meals are prepared and participating mothers must bring their children to the center for lunch. All of the children in the community are eligible to attend, although not all families participate.[22] The preschool program is generally held right after lunch and is open to children ages two to five. Usually, fewer children participate in the preschool than in the lunch program.

All of the communities in which I worked participate in the Yachay program.[23] San Isidro and Campo Carreras have buildings that were constructed for the program that act as day care centers and cafeterias, while in Río Grande and Colanzulí, the program operates in borrowed rooms of someone's house. The facilities in all of the communities are limited to a small kitchen (several just have a woodstove), a storage space with a few toys and other supplies, and another room equipped with child-sized tables and chairs. In the centers I visited, the walls were cheerfully hung with paper garlands and art projects by the children.

Yachay trains and pays local women to work in the lunch program and the preschool. Usually, there are three women who work at any given time: the cook and two "*mamas cuidadoras*" who work with the children in the preschool. The women are each paid a stipend of seventy-five pesos monthly and work fifteen to twenty-five hours a week. In most of the communities, this work rotates among a group of six to eight women, so that most of them work only every other month or even every third month, splitting the stipend accordingly.

The preschool and feeding programs are supervised by promoters who are trained in the fields of child development and education; in fact, both of the women who work as promoters for the Yachay program in Iruya have a background as elementary school teachers. The preschool is intended to prepare children to enter school by teaching them basic social and learning skills. The daily activities typically include songs, games, short walks, art projects, and unstructured play time. The program is about three years old. According to one of the *mamas cuidadoras* who has worked in the program since its inception, "When we first started, the children didn't want to participate. They would hide. Now they love to come. . . . When I went to school for the first time [as a child], I didn't even know how to hold a pencil. But these children know how to draw, they know what a pencil is, everything. They can learn more quickly [when they start school]."

Nearly all of the other women who work as *mamas cuidadoras* are equally as enthusiastic about the benefits that the children gain from attending:

• "They learn a lot. They learn to write, to draw, to sing. They also invent a lot of things themselves, games and stories. They are very curious, and ask about everything. The other things that can be done here aren't as important as the preschool. The children love it. They invent a lot of things. The children know a lot about the customs and traditions here, by themselves. For example, one of them will pretend he is riding a horse, or they will sing, like coplas [local songs]. And they're still little. Then, when they go to school, they already know a lot of things. They don't know how to read, but we put labels on things, names, like the door, and they know that there is a word that you can write that says that."

• "The preschool has a lot of benefits for the community. Before, when the children went to school, they went to first grade without knowing anything. Now they know more. They can use a pencil, they can use their hands more. It is good for the community, and good for the children. They also have relationships with other children, little friends. Before, they used to cry. When they first come to the preschool sometimes they cry, to leave their mothers, but then they like it afterwards. It is good for everyone."

• "The preschool helps the children a lot. When they go to school, they are better able to learn."

Interestingly, however, mothers who bring their children to the program who do not work as *mamas cuidadoras* see the lunch program as much more of a benefit than the preschool:

• "The lunch program has been a benefit for the children, and a lot of help for us. In the house, sometimes there isn't enough food. There, they are always fed well, and there is more in the house for the older children."

• "This is a good program—the children here lack vegetables and good things to eat. My little one, he used to go there [before he started school]. This has been good for the community."

• "It's good for the children. They feed them well. It's good when they stay in the preschool, too. They learn a lot."

• "We lack a lot of things to support our children. This helps us a lot. This way, I don't have to cook lunch. I don't have as much food to give the children, the things that they need. I have potatoes to give them, but I don't have vegetables."

The child feeding program has acted to ameliorate the problem of malnutrition to a certain extent but not completely. There are many families who do not bring their children to lunch or the preschool. In part, this is a problem of organization and program design. For some families, particularly those who live further from the village center, having the time to bring a child to the program is difficult at best. In San Isidro, where the houses are spread up and down a narrow valley, community members see this as a clear problem which limits participation: "It is very far for the women to bring the children. The mamas can't leave their work to bring them, and again to bring them home. You have seen how far some people live. It only serves those who live nearby, right here in the center." Women who have other children or family members at home may have to stay home to cook and serve a meal at that hour; although school-aged children receive lunch at school, women may have to feed older children, husbands, or other family members (such as parents). Even in families with scarce resources, it may be easier to stretch a meal a bit to feed a small child along with the rest of the family than to spend one or two hours bringing them to the program.

Among the children who do attend the program, there remain a few who are malnourished (again, by the standard of low weight for age and size). In one of the communities where several children who regularly attended were underweight, one of the preschool workers said, "Malnutrition is a big problem. We don't know what we can do. The children come every day and eat, and they don't gain weight. We have changed the menu, trying to give them different things, but they still don't put on weight." One of the *mamas cuidadoras* blamed this on a poor water supply and frequent illnesses in the children. A promoter, however, told me of her suspicions that the children still just weren't getting the food: "It's hard to get the women to prepare things properly, and then to give it to the infants. No matter how many times we tell them that what we are giving them is for the children, they eat it themselves. They are so hungry themselves that they make something, and they give the baby one bite, and then they eat six, and it goes like that, so the children aren't getting enough nutrition." Another worker told me that she believed that the lunch that children received at the program was their only meal of the day.

The Yachay program inevitably raises questions of cultural child-rearing practices. One of the promoters acknowledged that the child-rearing practices of the local culture are quite different from those of the mainstream society: "People are very different with their children here. Sometimes it's hard to watch. They push them away, keep them away. I suppose they are preparing them, teaching them that things are hard. They love them, I know, but they don't show it at all. They are not affectionate with their babies or small children. I guess it's because of how life is here." As is evident in this statement, when such differences are recognized, they often appear somewhat shocking or "improper" to those from Argentine culture.[24]

Often, however, basic cultural differences are overlooked or overwhelmed by the programmatic concerns of the program administrators and promoters. Issues of "proper" child education and development, that is, those that pertain to the dominant culture and current trends and beliefs in the field of child psychology, are generally treated as the overriding concern of the program. In fact, the program, particularly the preschool, seems to have been established, at least in part, to directly counter the general patterns that outsiders saw in local child-rearing practices. As one community leader in San Isidro told me, apologetically, "Here, it is part of our culture, that they don't give a lot of importance to children. OCLADE has been working with this, with the preschool and the lunch program. We tend to leave the children a little to one side. It's a small part of our culture."

On the local level, however, the fact that local women work as the primary day care workers counters this to some extent, as they adapt and transform both local practices and what they are told in trainings and meetings. The daily praxis of the preschool blends both customary and Western child-rearing beliefs and practices, in a microcosm of local reality.

Changing Objectives

Recently, OCLADE has shifted its attention from programs of direct assistance to issues of education and community organization. There is a sense that the needs of the community have changed, that direct assistance is no longer as crucial as it was ten years ago. There has also been an ideological shift by the organization, which I would argue is a reflection of feelings in the wider NGO community, away from programs supplying material resources in favor of more organizationally oriented projects. One of OCLADE's directors explained that the organization feels that people in the communities were growing overly dependent on OCLADE as a source of material resources. She suggested that this dependence makes people slow to request help from other sectors, particularly the government, even where they are entitled to services, because they rely on OCLADE. The organization has thus changed its emphasis to providing support for projects organized locally, providing training, and managing educational programs, such as the preschools.

Community leaders recognize and understand this shift in emphasis. In San Isidro I was told, "OCLADE wants us to organize ourselves more, alone. They want the people to work more together, to formulate projects that benefit many people." However, the speaker continued, this has presented the community with some difficulties: "Sometimes people get together and present something, but then by the time that the time comes to do the work together, there are few people left." As may be the case with the women's groups, the withdrawal of direct support has left something of a vacuum which community organizations have found themselves unable to fill. However, I believe that this vacuum is not an enormous obstacle to the kind of shift that OCLADE is trying to promote, a shift to self-reliance in the communities. Rather, it would suggest a need for direct training on issues of community organization and conflict resolution, and a need to change the kinds of services that the organization offers to focus more on technical and administrative support.

There are some members of the community who strongly support this kind of a shift in focus. A community leader in Río Grande, for example, said:

> To me, OCLADE was formed to work with the problem of malnutrition and infant mortality. But afterwards, they kept going on to do the same things. They think that things don't change, that people here need the same things as when they started, ten or fifteen years ago. They gave things, before, to improve the life of the people. The community center, the health post, the school, the preschool. Then last year, there was a big meeting [the assembly of the prelature] and we saw that we need irrigation canals and the commercialization of our production. A lot of these things now, they see that the government has to do them. OCLADE can generate things that will allow us to grow. The most important thing OCLADE can do is to act as an intermediary for resources. In general, their presence here is positive. But there needs to be more active participation by the community. We need more technical assistance, more help with concrete. things. But they are open, they have always kept their doors open.

OCLADE's shift in emphasis from programs of direct assistance to a strategy of organizational support is not unique among such organizations. In fact, Cristobal Wallis, an anthropologist working in northern Argentina, finds that this is a typical pattern for religious development agencies (Wallis, personal communication). What does this process imply for the future of OCLADE's involvement in the region, and for the prospects of improving the conditions of life of the people of Iruya in a culturally appropriate way? OCLADE is involved in a deliberate process of encouraging communities to look for other sources of support, money, and projects. The main source for this support is generally the government. The ramifications of a shift to increased community dependence on government funding are complex.

In a recent paper, María Angela Aguilar (1993) discusses the process of decentralization that has been a strategy of the neoliberal state in the last few years. This process, she suggests, has included a *greater* role for NGOs for the implementation of projects that may formerly have been functions of government agencies. What this tends to imply in practice is that NGOs increasingly act, in effect, as subcontracted agencies, responsible for the administration of programs that are run mainly on government funds. In fact, OCLADE has indeed taken on this role in some of its projects, most notably the child feeding program. However, we must consider that this role is in many ways contradictory with the goals and strategies of OCLADE itself, those of reducing dependence on the agency while helping people to become more able to develop their own strategies for improving their communities. Instead, it sometimes puts the NGO in the rather uncomfortable position of being required to implement policies that are not its own in order to continue to ensure program funding. For example, it is certainly possible to envision ways in which the child feeding program could be administered in a more effective, culturally appropriate manner; however, the restrictions on funding dictate the manner in which this money must be used.

Moreover, the neoliberal Argentine state, recently under attack for its lack of attention to social issues, has tended to replace welfare policies designed to create general well-being with a more focused approach that defines and identifies people in situations of most extreme poverty. Programs and spending are now much more likely to be directed at short-term projects with narrowly focused goals aimed at the poorest sectors of society, resulting in ineffective programs which lack long-term strategies and links between different types of efforts. This does not coincide well with the long-term strategies that an NGO such as OCLADE, which does have an ongoing relationship with the community, may see as more effective.

Conclusion

How can we understand the role of organizations such as NGOs in the process of local development? "Local development" is a complex process of resistance and accommodation, of accepting some outside interventions while rejecting others, and of political negotiations at the level of daily interactions. The examples cited in this chapter serve to illustrate how a discourse of development is deployed and changed through interaction with local cultures and practices. Despite such a process of change and accommodation, such a discourse serves to define the spheres of interaction and the arenas in which "development" is presumed to occur.

By defining nutrition as a "woman's issue" and presuming that it is based on an absolute lack of food combined with a culture that is not child-centered, for example, OCLADE then directs its programs towards nutrition and child development. It is possible to envision how an alternate discourse, suggesting that the same problem was based on poverty due to a lack of commercial opportunities or paid employment, would suggest an entirely different approach to implementing solutions. These cases serve to illustrate how NGOs tend to define problems in a way that make them amenable to technocratic solutions. Changing relations of production in a given region is a far more formidable task than improving quantifiable measurements of poverty.

The choices made by small NGOs in defining and claiming a realm of discourse may go beyond the technocratic, however. As some theorists have suggested, small NGOs and grassroots movements do represent an alternative to large more bureaucratic organizations and the state. In the next chapter, I will consider Fundapaz and OCLADE as religious organizations, and the extent to which an alternative discourse of development has been shaped and motivated by concerns that have emerged out of this religious background.

Notes:

1. Other theorists, for example, Cowen and Shenton (1995) and Watts (1995), argue that one can trace the emergence of a discourse of development back to the nineteenth century.
2. Along these lines, Shaw (1995, 27) argues that the Kikuyu and Maasai were represented as different kinds of colonial subjects, which influenced land and labor policies towards them and conditioned their responses to colonialism.
3. Although the Justicialista party is considered the heir to the former Peronist party, and is built upon the same coalitions as the Peronists, its current policies are widely considered to be a sweeping departure from traditional Peronist economic and social strategies that entailed generous social spending, a strong alliance with organized labor, the control of key industries by the state, and populist programs.
4. A free trade bloc, similar to NAFTA, which includes Brazil, Argentina, Uruguay, and Paraguay.
5. In fact, such problems are not limited to the local level. Menem's government has been plagued by a recent series of scandals involving corruption in the privatization process at the highest levels of government.
6. Argentina has ranks relatively well on many indices human development: literacy, infant mortality, potable water, and so on. This is a reflection, in part, of the concentration of the national population in the area around Buenos Aires, where services are good. It also reflects years of generous government spending. However, there are persistent pockets of poverty, especially in rural areas and in the north.
7. Rabbits and other small wild animals also eat crops, but generally cause far less damage than large herd animals.
8. In some areas, the ground water contains arsenic.
9. Like most outsiders, I found the water in Los Blancos too salty and bitter tasting to be palatable.
10. The fact that Wichí men do handle goats may contribute to racial discrimination and a construction of Wichí men as a "feminized" Other by local *criollos*.
11. There were two other households whose participation was not definite, and who I am not counting here. Both would have been women entering into the project—one a young woman who had not separated from her parents' household, the other a widow.
12. The tractor itself is owned by Fundapaz.
13. This meeting was a regional meeting to discuss the *Participación de los Pueblos Indígenas*, or PPI. This was a process, accompanied by ENDEPA, to encourage indigenous communities to make recommendations to the national legislature on laws that directly affect indigenous peoples. The final document was presented to the national legislature in August 1997.

14. *Instituto Nacional de Asuntos Indígenas*, the agency of the federal government responsible for indigenous affairs since 1985.
15. Many households or individuals in the region have no legal title to their land. However, there are well-established rules of usufruct rights, which are held by women as well as men.
16. Excluding the village of Iruya itself, where there is slightly more economic variation between households.
17. Women only drink in public at festivals and other public rituals, and then it is still considerably less conspicuous than male drinking. In my time in Iruya, I only once heard gossip about a female alcoholic, while male alcoholism was fairly common.
18. The survey did not ask about "men's suffering" or about suffering more generally.
19. However, this is not to imply that there are not cases where women are abused or mistreated by male family members. As in any society, there are problems of family violence and abuse.
20. There have been other groups in the department. I am looking at these two communities as examples, as they are the cases I am most familiar with.
21. This data comes from a household census taken by health care workers (*agentes sanitarios*) every three months, going door-to-door to all of the dwellings in the department. The data used here come from the census dated March 14, 1997. I am grateful to Armando Tacacho and the hospital in Iruya for sharing the data from this census with me.
22. The only official requirement for attendance is a DNI, the Argentine equivalent of a social security number; however, there are some children who attend without such a document.
23. However, the program in San Isidro was suspended by OCLADE while I was there due to a number of problems, including consistently low participation.
24. In fact, based on my observations, I would say that children, particularly infants and very small children, are treated with a great deal of affection, including physical contact with their mothers; babies, in fact, are rarely put down. Of course, things like "affection" and how children are treated varies a great deal between individuals and families in Iruya as anywhere else.

Chapter 4: Religious Idioms of Development

> To continue to move forward, we especially need religion.
>
> Elena, Iruya

Like their secular counterparts, religious NGOs range from barely organized charity efforts to global institutions. As one might expect, the extent to which any organization has an explicit theory of development underlying its initiatives also varies. Some may not even regard themselves as "doing development," while others have a highly complex economic and social agenda.

Fundapaz and OCLADE both originate as religious organizations. They draw on a religious philosophy that is progressive and political, emerging from the tide of liberation theology that swept Latin America after the mid-1960s. In order to understand the ways in which these NGOs make use of this religious philosophy, both implicitly and explicitly, I begin this chapter with a look at liberation theology. As we will see in the second part of the chapter, OCLADE has much stronger institutional and philosophical ties to the Catholic Church, and draws much more heavily, if uncritically, from the ideas and style of liberation theology. Fundapaz, by contrast, is less enmeshed in a religious discourse, but bases all of its work on the ideas of "social justice" that emerge from its religious background. In the final part of the chapter, I consider how missionization has affected the Wichí, and how the religious context of the Chaco forms a complex backdrop for the work of Fundapaz.

The Discourse of Liberation Theology

Religious development organizations operate within particular ideological frameworks when creating and developing development programs. These frameworks may be different, in important and significant ways, from those of mainstream, nonreligious NGOs. As Van Kessel and Droogers (1988) suggest, as long as development is seen as a technical, economic problem, the focus of development efforts will be on economic, technological fixes. They imply that a specifically religious idiom of development, in contrast, will be more focused on ends rather than means (1988, 54), and suggest that religion is "being used creatively to promote emancipation and social change" (1988, 58). Religious organizations "see the individual as a sacred being with the right to a life of dignity and worth. When religion informs social change, the effects of development transcend the physical and material by reaching what is important to people" (Mayotte 1998, 67).

During the last twenty-five years, Christian religious discourse and praxis in Latin America, as well as globally, has changed considerably. Both Catholic and Protestant churches have become increasingly involved in development projects as one way to attract followers. In some parts of Argentina, for example, Catholics, Pentecostals, Jehovah's Witnesses, Mormons, Baptists, Congregationalists, and Seventh Day Adventists, to name a few, compete with one another through their charity work (Ruggiero 1988, 80-84). The nature of religious work has itself changed: missionary work by most denominations has shifted its ideological focus, reframing its efforts to attempt dialogue rather than conversion, offering "an" answer instead of "the" answer (Tennekes 1988, 39).[1] Churches also enter into development work for ideological reasons as a way to enact ideas of social justice. Here, I am interested especially in the Catholic Church and the ways that it has engaged in development work in Salta.

From the colonial period until the beginning of this century, the Catholic Church was a major political player and landowner in Latin America. It also provided a unifying moral framework that legitimized the actions of governments and sanctioned the continuing power of the elite classes. Until the Vatican II conference in the mid-1960s, the Latin American Church consistently identified itself with ruling groups. Its attention to social and political issues focused on promoting "traditional values of family, property, and God" (Benavides 1987, 112), while ignoring social problems. Internally, the Church had a strong tradition of rigid hierarchy and authoritarianism.

However, as Ivan Vallier points out, the Catholic Church is not an integrated, monolithic efficient superstructure; rather, it has been, and continues to be, ideologically divided, organizationally segmented, and often uncoordinated. Organizationally, the Catholic Church is a conglomerate of relatively isolated bureaucratic units (Vallier 1970, 24). In Latin America, this lack of central coordination has been exacerbated by the need to cover large areas with limited personnel and by the control of Church officials by local authorities and elites. As a result, the Church has played an ambiguous and often contradictory role in political life. Since the middle of the twentieth century, the Church has become even more fragmented, as several different renewal movements, including liberation theology and charismatic Catholicism, have challenged its traditional hierarchical organization.

Both liberation theology and charismatic renewal movements can be seen, according to David Stoll, as efforts by the Church to counter competition from Protestantism (1990, 27). They have been effective in channeling new energy into Catholic beliefs, but have also challenged the authority of traditional hierarchical structures. The charismatic renewal movement can be understood as a sort of Catholic Pentecostalism, an emotional, mystical form of worship that has attracted segments of the middle class, especially in Europe (Stoll 1990, 29-30).

Liberation theology has been one of the most significant religious movements in Latin America in the last thirty years. It arose during the 1960s as a growing concern with the problems facing the poor on the part of the priests who worked most closely with impoverished communities (Berryman 1987, 13). Its leading exponents, including Gustavo Gutierrez, Juan Luis Segundo, Hugo Assman, Enrique Dussel, and others, have made a deliberate attempt to interpret their Christian faith from the experiences of the poor, and at the same time to help the poor reinterpret their own faith (Berryman 1987). For both its adherents and the Church as a whole, it has redefined not only theology, but what it means to be a good Catholic living in the modern world (Lehmann 1990, 118). Since its inception, the term "liberation theology" has been generalized, and must now be understood to reflect a wide range of beliefs and practices depending on local conditions and individual interpretations, but still sharing some common features (Norget 1995, 3).

Liberation theology has at its core the politicization of religious faith. It is based on a political reading of the Bible, one that assumes that every action is a political action. Influential authors like Gutierrez emphasized the historical roots of the early Christian community, and based their understanding of faith on the principles of marginality, dissent, and self-sacrifice. Implicitly, and often explicitly, liberation theologians have been critical of the role of the Church in maintaining oppressive social systems. While liberation theology is not a unitary doctrine, several tenets are central: (1) the idea that indifference to politics is a political choice, and that all theology is political; (2) churches are frequent collaborators in the status quo of exploitation; (3) religion is inherently concerned with human fulfillment; (4) exploitation hinders fulfillment; (5) the political world, including exploitation and poverty, is an important part of theology; (6) the Church and individual Christians should work to alter the conditions of exploitation (Robertson 1986, 74-75). Drawing on both Marxist and dependency theories, liberation theologians generally posit that the conditions of poverty in modern Latin America are rooted in the structures of capitalism.

Liberation theology developed over a number of years, beginning in Europe after World War II. As a response to a growing sentiment that the Church needed to liberalize some of its doctrines, Pope John XXIII called for the first council since Vatican I (1869-1870) early in 1959. Vatican II began in 1962 and continued until 1965, with an agenda set by progressive European and North American bishops. The ideas accepted in Vatican II, while they may not seem terribly radical from a lay perspective, set a tone of liberalization and change of the rigid authoritarian structures of the Church. Most significantly, the bishops accepted the idea that the Church was not infallible, but was a "pilgrim," like everyone else, in a spiritual quest, and the idea of "human progress" as evidence of God working in human history, and condoned a shift to the use of vernacular language instead of Latin for the Mass (Berryman 1987, 16-17). The most important consequence of Vatican II was the acceptance of the idea of discussion and debate which should include lay members of the Church. As a result of Vatican II, "the Church rediscovered the people and the world in which they live" (Van Kessel and Droogers 1988, 61).

From a Third World point of view, there was increased openness to criticism of structural poverty and oppression (Berryman 1987, 20). In 1968, one hundred thirty Latin American bishops[2] met to discuss applying Vatican II to Latin America. This gathering represented an attempt to make a conscious break from European theology, to recognize that Latin America had specific social and cultural contexts. The bishops took as their key question the relevance of Christianity in the struggle for a more just world (Berryman 1987, 25-26). Taking a more radical tone than Vatican II, they called for the Church to be involved in the transformation of society, advocated radical, democratic, nonviolent change, defended human rights, and called for consciousness-raising evangelization (Berryman 1987, 22-23). The Medellín conference concluded that Latin America was in a "state of sin" through oppression, institutionalized violence, and structural poverty (Robertson 1986, 78). The commitment and ideas of Medellín were reinforced and reiterated at a 1979 conference in Puebla, Mexico, which had as a theme creating the Church as a "preferential option for the poor" (Berryman 1987, 42-44).

Liberation theology has focused on the meaning of poverty and the struggle for a more just society. Its proponents adopted a methodology developed by Paulo Freire (1970), principles of popular education which assume that the poor and illiterate are intelligent adults. While Freire himself was not a theologian, his approach to education, drawing on the experiences of learners to develop a politically active community, has been highly influential.[3] Freire's model of *concientizaçao* (conscientization) was derived from a variety of disparate sources and provided a non-Marxist language of mass political agitation (Lehmann 1990, 96-99). Liberation theologians have adopted this method of facilitative leadership, designed as a nonpaternalistic approach to help a community "come together, articulate its needs, and become organized" (Berryman 1987, 35-37).

Liberation theologians have suggested an economic model of radical change, including land reform, the nationalization of key industries, educational reform, an independent foreign policy, and an end to discrimination against indigenous groups. They advocate a grassroots democracy with the participation of entire population in the nation's political, cultural, and economic life, based on the teachings of Christ (Benavides 1987, 129). Economically, liberation theology borrows heavily from the concepts of dependency theory that were popular in academic circles during the 1960s. However, unlike dependency theorists, liberation theologians stressed the importance of religion in promoting equitable development (Van Kessel and Droogers 1988, 66). Theologically, liberation theology attempts to demystify Catholicism and reject the idea of worldly suffering. The traditional Catholic idea that there is a "radical dichotomy between a spiritual and a worldly salvation" is attacked and reframed as "an ideological construction rather than a constitutive element of Christianity" (Benavides 1987, 127). The distinction between spiritual and material spheres is not Biblical, they argue, but in the interest of the status quo.

The use of Marxist concepts by many of the most prominent liberation theologians has been a target of attacks by conservative opponents throughout Latin America. Colombian Archbishop Alfonso López Trujillo, for example, has been a vocal critic of the socioeconomic analysis of liberation theologians. Trujillo (1977) argues that liberation should be defined in spiritual rather than political terms, advocating the political neutrality of the Church; the Church should be seen as a "mother, and not a midwife for revolution," he claims (1977, 71). He denounces the idea of class struggle, and roundly criticizes Gutierrez and Bigo in particular, arguing that they misinterpret Medellín and substitute Marx for Christ (1977, 45).

Since the early 1990s, the liberationist element of the Latin American Church has continued to face challenges, including pressure from the Vatican to rein in its more radical elements. The national churches have emerged as a site of struggle between the international Church and local hierarchies, and the terms of debate within the national churches have been increasingly influenced by Vatican conservatism (Stewart-Gambino 1992). Pope John Paul II worked to restore the authority and moral doctrines of the pre-Vatican II era; he filled the majority of vacancies with conservatives and traditionalists, while many progressives were removed from teaching duties or reprimanded (Stewart-Gambino 1992, 8). Trujillo, for example, is now a Cardinal appointed by John Paul II. Religiously, John Paul II worked to encourage saint cults and the cult of the Virgin, while strengthening the role of the priest as a religious intermediary. Such cults, according to David Stoll, represent "traditional Catholic piety" and distance the Church from Protestant styles of worship that focus on a more "personal" relationship with God (1990, 40).

On a local level, liberation theology has proved problematic for some of those it wanted most to reach: the poor and politically oppressed. The active resistance to oppression advocated by many liberation theologians proved suicidal for poor people in some regions, most notably perhaps in Guatemala, where guerrilla fighters eagerly embraced revolutionary Catholicism and endangered many peasants. The politicization of the Church caused the military government to add "Christians" to its list of enemies. The "traditional function of religion as a sanctuary from oppression" (Stoll 1990, 313) was undermined, which led many followers to withdraw from the Catholic Church.

As a whole, the Catholic Church faces other challenges, including the impact of political redemocratization and Protestantism and Pentecostal growth. The Church itself remains divided, with radical liberation theologians continuing to advocate fundamental religious and political change; progressives, who stress grassroots activism; and conservatives, tacitly or explicitly supporting the political right (Stewart-Gambino 1992, 5). The recent redemocratization through most of Latin America threatens the traditionalist authority structures by encouraging democratic principles of dissent, while the emergence of civil organizations diminishes the central role of the Catholic Church (Stewart-Gambino 1992, 8-11). Meanwhile, the increase in Protestantism that has been a continual trend in recent years is considered a threat by both conservatives and progressives within the Church (Stewart-Gambino 1992, 13-14).

While the influence of liberation theology is significant throughout Latin America, each national Church took a distinct political stand in response to tumultuous Latin American politics during the 1970s and 1980s. The Peruvian Church, led by Gustavo Gutierrez, remained one of the most progressive (Benavides 1987, 122). The Chilean Church has allied with a full range of governments, including socialist and authoritarian, taking a generally centrist position that accommodates political reality. After 1976, when the Church itself was threatened, it distanced itself from Pinochet, and became a center of opposition to the regime (Benavides 1987, 123-124). In Argentina, the Catholic Church hierarchy has generally remained one of the more conservative of the Latin American churches.

In the 1960s, there was significant support for the liberation theology movement in Argentina. In 1967, the *Movimiento de Sacerdotes para el Tercer Mundo* (Movement of Priests for the Third World) was founded, advocating revolutionary, nationalist, humanist socialism. This organization included over eight hundred out of five thousand Argentine priests, and played a role "out of proportion to its numbers" since its members had more direct contact with the poor than nonmembers (Berryman 1987, 21). However, most of those involved were "relatively marginal to the church hierarchy" (Jelin 1994, 42). The movement was also strongly tied to the Peronist left, and lost much of its support after Perón returned in 1972 and failed to carry out the leftist political agenda (Snow and Manzetti 1993, 155-156).

The military regime viewed liberation theology as a Marxist threat, and moved quickly against its advocates. The highest members of the Church hierarchy cooperated with the regime. They defined the military's campaign against the guerrillas and the accompanying social repression as a "holy war" needed to defend morality. Dissenters were quickly silenced: there were more than forty deaths and one hundred disappearances of clergy, including two bishops, and active laymen, and some churches were bombed. These attacks were directed at liberation theologians, those working with the poor, and those who criticized the regime. The Church hierarchy did not protest any of these occurrences, and this lack of institutional support demobilized lower levels of resistance (Andersen 1993, 184-192).

The military itself had a strong Catholic identity, and incorporated this into their concept of Argentine nationalism ("Nunca Más" 1986, 338). It linked religious faith with political orthodoxy, and stressed that support for the military was necessary for the survival of traditional Catholic values. At times, non-Catholic religious groups came under suspicion by the military regime because they "opposed the military, aided refugees and the persecuted, and worked for human rights" (Ruggiero 1988, 82). Others came under suspicion merely for being non-Catholic; all non-Catholic religious groups were required to register with the Ministry for Foreign Affairs. Any sect could be banned if the government believed it posed a threat to "order" or "morality"; the Jehovah's Witnesses, for example, were banned from 1976 to 1977 (Ruggiero 1988, 82).

While the explicit tenets of liberation theology have not been widely espoused by the Argentine Church, certain segments of the Church have quite recently begun to act as a focus of opposition to neoliberal economic reforms. As unemployment has risen and social spending has been cut, several prominent bishops have openly criticized government policies, arguing that macroeconomic priorities and deep cuts in social spending ignore the needs of the poor and damage the middle class, many of whom have lost employment as the government sector has been reduced. Such statements have been voiced by prominent clergymen at the national level, as well as by less visible bishops and leaders working in poor areas. Church opposition to neoliberalism is uneven, depending in large part on the interests and political leanings of individual bishops and priests. However, Catholic criticisms of neoliberal policies in Argentina echo Church sentiment worldwide. Even conservative Church agents, including the Pope, have denounced neoliberalism as promoting an ethos of secularism (Norget, personal communication). However, this emergent role as a national social conscience marks a radical departure from the former conservatism and the active suppression of leftist critics within the Argentine Church.

Catholicism in Iruya

The Catholic Church in the prelature of Humahuaca, which spans much of the province of Jujuy and the northwestern part of the province of Salta, is one of the segments of the Church that is quite outspoken in its criticisms of neoliberal policies. Because the prelature is administered by a religious order, it is somewhat insulated from the Argentine Catholic hierarchy. Most of the clergy of the prelature are foreign, the great majority from Spain, although in recent years a few local priests have been ordained.

Officials in the prelature, including the bishop Pedro Olmedo and his brother Jesús, a priest in the far north of Jujuy, have been actively involved in social protests and political movements in the region. At times, this involvement has provoked an angry response from government officials. The governor of

Jujuy, in an attack on Jesús Olmedo, referred to him in a statement as a "madman" (*energúmeno*) (*Animadores* 1997, 1), after the priest participated in demonstrations against high unemployment. The governor went on to accuse Church leaders of inciting the protests and encouraging violence. In response, the Church quickly mobilized support from its adherents, from labor unions, and from opposition politicians in defense of the actions and statements of the bishop and Church leaders. This incident serves to illustrate the role that the regional Church has taken on as a social critic and activist. While the governor's remarks may have overstepped the bounds of acceptable political discourse, the fact that he felt a need to attempt to undercut the authority of religious leaders points to the moral authority and power that the Church is perceived to have and its ability to mobilize its followers against political policy. The subsequent ability of the Church to garner support from various sectors of a rather disorganized opposition is a sign that the Church is in fact making inroads as a legitimate voice of opposition.[4]

To a large extent, however, the role of the Church in the political and social sphere is defined by prominent individuals, such as bishops. This fact is generally recognized by politically active members of the Church. A social worker from Salta noted that the bishop of Humahuaca is much more politically active than other religious leaders in the north:

> The bishop in Oran [for example] is much more implicated in politics, in the system, you know what I mean. He doesn't fight for the people the way the bishop here does. . . . The bishop of Salta is very paternalistic. But you know, he never goes out to the poor barrios, or to the countryside. None of them do. They have no idea of what the life is like.

A Catholic missionary from Buenos Aires echoed this sentiment, noting that Olmedo has been known to work in the fields with the people, and contrasted him to urban bishops who live "as though they were rich."

In Iruya, social and political relations are heavily tempered by *personalismo,* an emphasis on a relationship with a powerful individual who tends to exemplify or signify an organization, is strongly identified with it, and may in fact hold a good deal of concentrated organizational power. Within such a context, it is important to note that Olmedo was the parish priest in Iruya for a number of years before he was appointed bishop. He also played a central role in the foundation of OCLADE and is closely associated with the organization in the minds of many locals. His personality, and his political positions, thus carry great importance locally, even more than they would coming from a religious head without such local ties. His long-term residence in the community established numerous personal ties, and his willingness to share in the activities of daily life is commented on and appreciated by locals as it was by the missionary noted above. A Kolla woman complimented the bishop on his solidarity with local residents:

> He has done a lot for the people here. He never stops, he is always going somewhere, to all of the little towns. If they are eating potatoes, he eats potatoes. If they are eating soup, he eats soup. It doesn't matter to him if that is what he is used to eating. He sits right down with the people. There aren't many other priests like that.

Until the Claretians took over the administration of the prelature, the area was served sporadically by Franciscan missionaries. According to local residents, a priest would visit Iruya once or twice a year, but almost never would visit the smaller centers of the interior. According to some local Catholics, the weak presence of the Catholic Church encouraged the "invasion" of evangelical churches, which have established a strong foothold in the region (see below). The arrival of the Claretians established a more stable Catholic presence, and the Church's activities quickly expanded to include programs to train local lay leaders in the interior and efforts at social development, which led to the creation of OCLADE (see chapter 1).

The Church in Iruya is clearly strongly influenced by the tenets of liberation theology. The political activism of its leadership stems from a belief that

> the essence of [the Church's] mission is to do a bit of what Jesus did, to have a special calling for the poor. . . . The Church is a space of participation found by the poor. . . . The Church [is] increasingly involved with these groups of those who are excluded [by the current economic system], groups which are increasingly large and have distinct characteristics. On the other hand, from this situation of extreme poverty in which they live emerge initiatives, concerns, from the poor themselves which the Church must support. (Bishop Olmedo, interview in *Yareta* 1997, 9)

The focus on the Church as a "space" for the poor is a common theme in the work of liberation theologians, one which finds its echo locally. Other themes which emerge prominently in local religious discourse are the oppression of women and children, the need to develop and strengthen community organizations and structures in order to work collectively to ameliorate conditions of poverty, and, to a lesser extent, the importance of expressing and defending traditional local culture.

The emphasis on the ideas of liberation theology by the leaders of the prelature and by local priests has not received an entirely positive response in the community. Members of the local elite, in particular, are quick to criticize what they view as the leftist and unnecessarily political teaching of the Church. A middle-aged woman who has been involved in the community for many years said that although she likes the local priests on a personal level, the Claretians are "radicals" and "communists." One landowner said that she has been "shocked" by the sermons and "the things the Church was teaching about rights and politics, instead of just teaching the Bible and religion. Religion should have nothing to do with politics." She was particularly offended, she continued, by what they had been teaching about property:

> that private property is bad, and that people are naturally entitled to the land here. I went to them and told the priests that they couldn't teach this, that private property is the law of the country and they can't teach anything contrary to the law. . . . After I complained, things changed. Now they focus more on teaching the Word of God, and the sermons are much better, explaining the Bible lesson and what it means. . . . It is easy for [the Claretians] to be socialists. Look, they have all these resources, that great big house in Salta. Why don't they give that away? I went to one of the sermons, and the priest was going on about how the poor would go to heaven, the crippled, the marginalized, on and on. And I asked him, I asked him, what about the rest of us, the beautiful, the intelligent, those who work hard. Where do we go? . . . One of them told me that I had too much land here, why didn't I give it to the people? Well, I was so mad. I am trying to do so much here, to show them how they could live better. Doesn't the Bible say, not to give a man a fish but to teach him to fish? But this is their attitude, they want the people to be dependent on them.

However, such criticism of the liberal teachings of the local Church represents the exception rather than the rule. Large landowners are few. Most Iruyan farmers, with no legal title to the land that they work, would seem to identify themselves with the oppressed of the sermons.

The Church remains one of the most important and central local institutions. Because of the odd natural geography of the village, it is not laid out according to the traditional Spanish colonial design of a central plaza ringed by church and government offices. Instead, spatially, the church building itself stands at the gateway to the town, the first structure that one sees as one enters Iruya via the main (and only) road. The great majority of the local population, about eighty percent, is at least nominally Catholic. While daily mass in Iruya draws only a handful of worshippers, mostly women, Sunday mass is reliably attended by sixty to eighty people. On holidays and festivals, the small church is packed to overflowing, with attendees filling the space at the rear of the church and often spilling out the door. There has been an effort to reach out to young people, and the church has an active youth group. Some Catholic ceremonies and rites are adhered to more faithfully than others: many couples do not have a religious (or civil) marriage ceremony, for example, but most children are baptized and receive their first communion.[5]

The general acceptance of the liberal theology of the local Church is due at least in part to the traditional authority of the Catholic Church and a certain "cultural Catholicism" that makes people willing to accept Church teachings uncritically. Because there was not a strong Catholic presence before the arrival of the Claretians, there is little in the way of an immediate point of comparison for local church-goers; they are unlikely to feel that recent teachings contradict something they were told by a former priest. Moreover, the priests themselves, as educated men and as foreigners, are accorded status even beyond that which they would receive as clergy.[6]

However, the tenets of liberation theology resonate with many local people in ways that go beyond an unquestioned acceptance of doctrine. The ideas of sacrifice and oppression are rooted in local culture as well as in the Catholic faith. Sacrifice, in particular, is seen as a natural characteristic of local life. One woman said, "We have to work the land to be able to eat. Here, there are no jobs. We live by working the land. . . . Here, there is no money. But the land is good. But [only] with the sacrifice of oneself." Another woman, describing her daily routine, summed it up by saying, "This is how I sacrifice myself." The Church, as one of the few viable local institutions, is seen as an ally in this daily struggle.

In the villages of the interior, there is considerable participation in local Church activities, a testament to the success of the Claretians and their approach to religious faith. In response to the problem of the difficulties of reaching the numerous small villages and settlements in the region, the prelature has developed a large network of local lay leaders who conduct worship services and teach catechism in the absence of a regular priest. At the level of the prelature, there are over a thousand such volunteer leaders. In the *departamento* of Iruya, each of the smaller villages has several lay leaders, mostly men. They conduct weekly prayers and catechism classes in small chapels, a crucial function in a region where the priests make visits through the interior only once or twice a year. Lay leaders, said one man, "have a lot of respect here. But the Church doesn't use them as resources as much as it could." One of the lay leaders of Campo Carreras concurred,

> We still don't know how to take advantage of the courses that the priests give us. But as they say, the reign of God is small, and we have come a long way. . . . We started with only fifteen families [active in the Church] in 1986 and now this year there are fifty. . . . At this point, we have about sixty percent [of the families in the village]. . . . It's very good, the prelature helps us very much, with our land, with our school, with our chapel. For a lot of things, where others have only opposed us. And it's a lot. . . . I think that the Church has given us a lot, it has sent us many things to work on.

Such lay leaders, like the rest of the community, recognize that the Church under the Claretians serves not only as a center of religious faith, but as a source of both political leadership and material resources, in a region where both are scarce.

OCLADE: Enacting a Religious Discourse

By the late 1970s in progressive Catholic circles, there was a growing awareness of inadequacy of mainstream development efforts (Berryman 1987, 34). Liberation theologians were critical of what many termed *desarrollismo* ("developmentalism"), used in a pejorative sense for reforms that failed to address issues of power and politics. Many argued that *desarrollismo* emphasized "planned social change" without a consideration of society as such, creating a development model in which "people have to overcome bothersome obstacles" like culture and religion (Van Kessel and Droogers 1988, 55). Liberation theology, by contrast, suggested a model of radical change. In this vein, many new Catholic organizations were established and old ones revitalized to promote the Church as a "preferential option for the poor."[7] Many of the particular reforms proposed by liberation theologians have fallen out of favor in recent years, because of failed land reform efforts in many regions (see Dorner 1992) and a recent trend towards privatization of inefficient state industries. However, the strategies and methodologies suggested by liberation theology, such as *concientización* (Freire 1970), have had a lasting impact on proponents of alternative development.

OCLADE was founded in 1983 as an effort by the prelature to increase its work in development. A prominent Claretian priest working in the region outlined the order's interest in development work:

> One of the fundamental concerns of the Claretians in the prelature of Humahuaca has been, beyond any doubt, human development and integrated development for the people. The social and economic conditions of the Humahuaca Canyon and the Puna . . . demanded that the Church and the [Claretian] missionaries take this position and [make] a clear answer. (Olmedo Rivera 1990, 277)

As an organized development agency, OCLADE supplanted traditional charity-oriented approaches and piecemeal efforts by individuals within the Church working to introduce projects to the communities in the region. Administratively, it is directly linked to the religious administration of the prelature, with several priests involved in its direction. It relies heavily on the Claretian order for much of its funding, receiving other funding from both religious and non-religious sources (see chapter 1). Philosophically, it is also tied to this religious base: its mission is to support the communities of the prelature in their efforts to improve conditions of human development. The Church's involvement in human development itself is portrayed as a "religious manifestation," rather than as an evangelical outreach program or a way to garner support in the communities.

In keeping with the ideas of liberation theology, economic development is promoted not as an end in itself, but as a means to the ultimate end of achieving greater human dignity. According to OCLADE's general coordinator, in a short article that appeared in a provincial development newsletter:

> The '90s decade introduces new challenges to the work of Integrated Human Promotion [*Promoción Humana Integrada*] and part of the evangelical announcement: The KINGDOM [of God] is not a promise for after death. It is an OBLIGATION of HERE and NOW. The organization of small groups and local associations for political participation. So that increasingly, our people need less from OCLADE and can start to TAKE THE WORD and decide their destiny. (Ruiz 1993, 23; emphasis in original)

Ruiz goes on to emphasize the distinctions between OCLADE and other development agencies. He criticizes the "technical workers [*técnicos*] who only know the Development of their offices" (1993, 23). He positions OCLADE, in contrast, outside of the "development establishment," locating it "with the people in their daily work" (1993, 23).

In this daily work, OCLADE administers a broad range of programs, from promoting literacy to improving animal health to feeding small children. It emphasizes projects in health and education, at times at the expense of projects promoting commercialization and increasing production. The villagers around Iruya rely on subsistence agriculture, supplemented by occasional wage labor and very small incomes from selling produce. There are several ways that this economic base could be expanded, but the one mentioned most often by local people is the possibility for increasing the commercialization of their produce. However, OCLADE has shown little interest in working in the area of commercialization.

A number of years ago, OCLADE supported efforts at developing a cooperative to market craft products, in this case woven goods, and a "growers' association," organized much like a cooperative, for marketing produce. Both organizations operated for a few years and then "fell apart," according to local accounts. One former participant explained,

> Everyone started fighting, about stupid things, personal things. This one had all the ponchos, this one had the money. There was too much individualism, people couldn't work together. Some people wanted to sell ponchos outside of the cooperative, and you can't do that. There was a lot of tension. People just were fighting and couldn't work together.

OCLADE staff tended to explain the failure of the cooperatives the same way, attributing problems to "infighting" and individualism:

> It's how the culture is here. For many years, people have been living separated, in houses that are far from each other. They have worked their own land, and haven't had to work with other people. And if you look, there are a lot of cooperatives in the city that fail. And if we can't do it, and the thing is more a part of our culture, how can we expect people here to be able to do it?

After its attempts to establish cooperatives failed, there have been no further projects to promote commercialization. In part, this may be because OCLADE's religious philosophy eschews the values associated with capitalism. Cooperatives represented a philosophically acceptable alternative, based on ideals of cooperativism and collective action. A market-oriented approach, based on individual participation, is not amenable to these values. In fact, according to at least one informant, part of the reason the growers' association failed was a lack of attention to and understanding of the realities of commercialization and business:

> There were more problems than we expected. We bought a truck, and we thought that we could just take the products to the market, but it was more complicated than that. We didn't have a regular buyer there, so that was a problem. Then, we had some problems with administration, managing the funds and keeping records.

While OCLADE was supporting the association, there was not sufficient support or training in administration, and problems arose between producers about bookkeeping and payments. At the same time, the association faced competition from the existing buyer. This intermediary came to the villages at the time of the harvest, bought their produce, and sold manufactured goods and foods at grossly inflated prices. He extended credit to households, with the predictable result that the income from the sale of their produce often fell just short of their expenditures, leaving them in debt to the intermediary the following year. This system had been in place for many years, and when the growers' association was initiated, the intermediary attempted to bolster his position as the sole market outlet. The same informant, who was closely involved in the association, explained that the intermediary raised the price that he paid for produce, temporarily, in order to drive the association out of the local market:

> The intermediary had a monopoly here before. He had a lot of capital, and could compete better than we could. . . . With the commercialization, it was our fault that it didn't work. The people had a long relationship with the intermediary, fifteen years or more. We didn't think about that. They thought of him as a patron, as the person who gave them their daily bread. He gave them credit, he bought their things and sold them things. We didn't think of this, that we were setting ourselves up to be in competition with him.

The obstacles to promoting the commercialization and marketing of local products thus stemmed from several sources: a lack of commitment to such a collective effort on the part of participants; inadequate administrative support; high transaction costs; competition from existing market intermediaries; and a lack of knowledge about regional markets. Still, OCLADE focuses its attention on the tensions and arguments that arose within the community, and blames the failure of commercialization not on market conditions but on local culture and a "lack of community." In other cases as well, OCLADE has had a tendency to pull out quickly from projects when there is internal dissent or conflict between participants.

OCLADE's religious philosophy shapes how it deals with political problems within its programs. When there is seen to be "too much fighting," the organization tends to pull the project out, to suspend the program, or to stop working in a community. This is often justified by saying that there are other communities that "really want" a project, and if the first community cannot work together, there are others who could benefit. OCLADE has a very strong ideology of community, of cooperation, and of collectivism that shape its programming decisions and its daily operations. Solidarity is among the values that the NGO associates with the strength and nobility of local culture. In an editorial, the director of OCLADE wrote:

> The world of poverty of our region has enormous potential, unknown even by its own inhabitants, denied and at times rejected by the Argentine society. Survival in very extreme conditions of poverty is possible thanks to the development of a group of values and actions, among which solidarity stands out. The thousands of experiences of communal work, of mutual assistance, reflect the capacity to *salir adelante* [move forward] by ourselves in spite of the difficulties.
>
> The lack of material goods does not imply the absence of projects of life, of culture, of decency, of morality. The faith of the poor, their religious dimension, that permits them to maintain their traditions, ancestral customs of respect for nature, for work in solidarity, of openness to others, knowledge often forgotten, are riches for the world that the poor offer to a society which is bleeding for having lost these values. (Torres, in *Yareta* 1996/7, 1)

The idea that people should work together to improve things for the collective, a very strong idea of Christian communism in the primitive sense, derived from OCLADE's religious background, makes issues of conflict and conflict resolution particularly problematic. When people don't get along, it is seen as a moral failure, one which people themselves should overcome for their own good, rather than as a structural problem that needs to be figured on and planned for.

Similarly, commercialization itself may conflict, ethically and morally, with the religious values that underlie OCLADE's programming. An idealized form of subsistence production, one based on strong nuclear families and extended kin groups that lend mutual aid, is more palatable to this worldview than small farmers competing in a regional market, which would nearly inevitably lead to increased differentiation between households locally, as those that control more labor and land would be able to capitalize on their advantages. Because the real poverty of the region is striking to those from outside the local area, as are most of OCLADE's staff, the NGO works, piecemeal fashion, to alleviate the worst symptoms of this poverty, such as child mortality and malnutrition, illiteracy, and a lack of access to basic health and educational services. Creating substantive change in local relations of production, however, goes beyond the scope both of what may be technically possible and morally desirable to the NGO.

The weakness of OCLADE's commercialization efforts was not only an underlying ideological opposition to capitalist or market values, but an ideological reductionism. Cooperativism itself was highly idealized. There was no serious effort to theorize collectivism, to anticipate and prevent problems that could arise, or to mediate disputes. In its actual interaction with the market economy, there was no consideration given to bridging the distance between that system and the local community; the two were conceptually separate and apart. When the project failed there was little effort to critique its approach.

At the same time, OCLADE's entry into the market through the cooperative, while rejecting the value system associated with the market, was an effort to reap the profits that the market economy offers. There was no awareness of the contradiction embodied within the cooperative project. In an ideological "cut-and-paste" approach, OCLADE attempted to keep the best ideals and values of both collectivism and the market while ignoring the pitfalls of each.

Even though they eschewed capitalism, the market itself was not blamed for the failure of the cooperative. "Relations of production" were not understood as the underlying problem; the local economy was not theorized in terms of its relationship with that of the region or the province. The project's failure was attributed to the "failure" of the local culture, which was characterized as not being community-minded enough in its pursuit of a piece of the capitalist pie. Instead of an economic analysis of the project and the local context, the NGO framed its explanation of the difficulties that were encountered in moral terms.

Organization and Participation

Organizationally, OCLADE has been able to mobilize the social and ideological resources of the Church to create its own base of support and a network of households who work most closely with the program. The network of lay leaders trained by the Church to conduct religious services also disseminate information about development projects and act as a point of contact between the most isolated rural communities and OCLADE. The director of OCLADE characterized this network as "our most important support. If it weren't for them, we wouldn't be able to do anything." The use of this network by OCLADE strengthens the link between the Church and the organization in the minds of local residents as well. Projects initiated by OCLADE are frequently said to be sponsored by the Church or the priest. Many people, including those involved in projects, do not differentiate between the NGO and the Church itself.

The Church has served as a point of entry for many of those who work most closely with the organization. The network of volunteers on which OCLADE depends is drawn from the ranks of those who are involved with the Church in other capacities. One woman active in both Church and NGO described her experience:

> I started to work in this struggle, in one way or another, twenty-four years ago. We formed a youth group, as part of the Church. Afterwards, we did other things. I was involved in this, in the Church. It was very important for me. I learned a lot.

The Church provides the basic network from which OCLADE draws its participants.

However, Iruya, like many contemporary Latin American communities, is no longer homogeneously Catholic. Over the last decade, especially, the region has seen the rise of evangelical churches that have drawn a significant proportion of the population.[8] Iruya is home to at least three small evangelical churches, which between them can count about ten percent of the population of the department as adherents. One of these churches is Baptist and the other two are small denominations, one reputedly linked to a group from Philadelphia and the other to a church in Sweden. Aside from occasional visits from missionaries or pastors from outside the region, all three churches are fairly independent of these larger ties.[9]

While the evangelical movement has made great strides locally, ecumenicism has not. The conflicts between the Catholic majority and the evangelical minority are deep-seated, and these conflicts shape the work of OCLADE. Few members of evangelical churches participate in OCLADE's programs. The only exception to this is in the village of Colanzulí, where most of the residents belong to an evangelical church. OCLADE maintains that it serves the entire population, regardless of religion. However, the general relationship between evangelicals and Catholics is tense, and the participation of one group often means the *de facto* exclusion of the other. The promoter recounted one incident where she was asked by Catholic members of the community to close one of the infant feeding programs because "mostly evangelicals were using it. That's the kind of tension, that they didn't want to feed those children." Members of the evangelical churches criticize the Catholics for drinking and the worship of saints, which they regard as paganism, and often stage protest marches on fiesta days. The Catholics, in turn, condemn the evangelicals for being "closed" to the rest of the community and for being intolerant of local customs. Personal relationships between individuals in the two groups exist, but often are cool. A Catholic community leader explained that relations are generally good, except "when there are conflicts. Then religion arises as an issue. . . . Things become more personal."

Syncretism and Religious Discourse

In practice, Catholicism in Iruya and the surrounding towns is a creative, syncretic pastiche of Catholic and non-Christian local practices. At some occasions, the blending of the two traditions is nearly seamless, as local elements are brought into the fold of "Catholic" ceremonies. At other times, the line for the outside observer is more clearly demarcated, as the rich symbolism of saints accommodates the supplication of agrarian spirits in practices that may not be questioned as syncretic by local participants. Finally, there survive numerous non-Christian practices, some of which are encouraged by the Church itself as colorful "local traditions" and others which are practiced more clandestinely.

The worship of the *pachamama* (loosely translatable as Mother Earth), practiced throughout the Andean region, contains a complex of signification in Iruya, with shades of meaning, belief, and practice coexisting within a single symbol. Locally, *pachamama* worship is invoked at several junctures. It is tied to the agricultural cycle, with offerings made to safeguard the earth's fertility. The *pachamama* is also symbolically linked to an array of practices with connotations of birth and fertility, new beginnings, or travel. Worship practices may range from the very simple, such as a small offering of liquid poured on the ground, to a very elaborate ceremony of offering alcohol and cigarettes, burning incense, and burying symbolic items.

Pachamama beliefs may be more openly expressed in neighboring communities of the *puna* than they are in Iruya itself. In towns such as Humahuaca and Tilcara, for example, *pachamama* ceremonies are common at the beginning of festivals and public rituals. While these are sometimes aimed at tourists, they are also part of a resurgence of Kolla identity that is more common in these larger towns. In other centers, such as Iturbe, *pachamama* rituals have been part of public ceremonies that are mainly for the local population, attracting few tourists. At a festival in Iturbe, for example, which drew participants from neighboring villages and towns, including Iruya, the day's festivities began with an elaborate *pachamama* ritual. Two older men began to dig a hole, one using a pick to loosen the dirt and the other scooping it out with a shovel. Once it was maybe a meter deep, and about a meter on a side, they started the offering. A big kettle full of hot coals was placed next to the hole, and herbs were placed on top of it to burn. The invited politician (a provincial representative) was given the honor of beginning the ritual, coached by several men who stood behind her. She knelt down in front of the hole, crossed herself, then made a sign of a cross over the hole. They handed her things, one by one. First was beer, which she poured into the hole, before crossing herself again and finishing the cup. This was repeated with hot tea, then with *chicha* (a mildly alcoholic drink made from fermented corn or peanuts), wine, soda, and pure alcohol. She ended by pouring in some ashes mixed with confetti, crossed herself again, then one of the men poured some ashes on her head while a woman wrapped strands of colored paper around her neck like a garland. As she rose, the ritual was repeated a number of times by the organizers and participants in the day's festival, which was a song (*copla*) competition.[10] The whole ritual took well over an hour. Much of the audience stood and watched quietly, while cups of *chicha* were passed around by women from the host community. A similar festival in Iruya only a few weeks later began with the national anthem, with no reference to the *pachamama*.

However, *pachamama* beliefs persist in Iruya, especially in the interior. A lay leader in San Isidro described local beliefs:

> The *pachamama* [worship] people do here is to give things back to the earth, which is like our mother. When they start to work in agriculture, in October, they give some food to the earth. And in the mountains, there are particular places where one prays to God, everyone who goes by. They build a little shrine, and the people leave offerings there, and pray for a safe passage.

Here, this speaker equates the *pachamama* with the worship of the Christian God, a syncretic conflation which is common in the region. To the outsider, however, *pachamama* worship has both symbolic and affective dimensions that mark it as separate from Christian worship. In fact, in Iruya, *pachamama* worship is generally not part of public ritual, but is kept within families and in the private sphere. Although it is a quiet belief, many informants admit that it is an important part of both agricultural and life cycles, and say that it is one of the most important of local traditions. While some Iruyans dismiss such practices as superstitious, at least publicly, the piles of offerings one can see at such shrines is silent testimony to continuing practice.

Interestingly, the Catholic Church is an active participant in the revival of the practice of *pachamama* worship. There is an interest on the part of the liberationist Church in promoting the "indigenization" of worship, incorporating local beliefs and practices into religious praxis. Jesús Olmedo, a Claretian priest, defends *pachamama* worship as a manifestation of the relationship that the Kolla people have with the land, calling it "a profound reality, religious and transcendent. . . ." and criticizing those who argue that it is "paganism, superstition or pantheism" (Olmedo Rivera 1990, 177).[11] The *pachamama* ceremony, as an example, is taken as a visible sign of local culture and is encouraged as an expression of ethnic identity. One nun described an upcoming fiesta: "We want to have the music, to do the *pachamama*, to have displays of craft products. This will help people re-value their own ways of doing things, their own culture."

The Church's attention to *pachamama* ceremonies such as the one described above seems to value it as a visible cultural symbol, but not as a genuine religious practice. *Pachamama* worship represents a syncretic belief, where the *pacha* is accepted as a representation of the Christian god. To some degree, despite Olmedo's assertions to the contrary, this reinforces the idea of the *pachamama* as a quaint local superstition, one which may be embraced as a marker of cultural difference, but which may trivialize the actual practice. The Church, in this case, may be embracing the form of the practice, but one which is carefully devoid of its original symbolic content.

Practices such as the *pachamama* in Iruya illustrate the larger, more complex and multifaceted issue of indigenous identity. While people are proud to express their "local" culture and "local" roots, they do not generally identify themselves as "indigenous" or even as "Kolla." In recent years, the Church has played a significant role in promoting a resurgence of interest in an identity as Kolla and indigenous.

The prelature in general, and OCLADE by extension, encourages a local identity that is specifically Kolla and indigenous. Another NGO run by the Church, ENDEPA/EPREPA, has been particularly active in promoting a local sense of indigenous identity, as well as promoting indigenous rights and supporting land claims. While there is a genuine concern with the rights of local people, to a certain extent the particular indigenous identity that the Church encourages is based on visible, colorful, "folkloric" aspects of culture rather than a more complete, "authentic" culture. As with *pachamama* rituals, the promotion of indigenous culture finds its focus in visible recognizable symbols of Kolla culture, but stops short of understanding and promoting indigenous ways of knowing and doing.

To a certain extent, the ways in which OCLADE and the prelature define indigenous is closely linked to ideas of suffering, poverty, and oppression. It is a politicization of identity, in a way that seeks to make people more aware of and interested in their own condition and to see it as a ramification of larger political choices made by the state. It is clearly linked to the ideas of liberation theology: the indigenous peoples of Latin America, the people of Iruya among them, have been oppressed and exploited by centuries of dominance, and the solution lies in raising the people's consciousness of their own oppressed condition.[12] Again, Jesús Olmedo supplies a revealing account of the Claretian order's point of view:

> [The Claretian missionaries] found a profoundly religious and receptive people, open to transcendence and ready for the evangelical message. Their simplicity and utter poverty prepared them to understand the . . . life of Jesus of Nazareth. The Claretians rapidly caught the condition of an oppressed people and the urgent need for liberation. (Olmedo Rivera 1990, 274)

There is a problematic relationship between the emphasis on the poverty of local people and the belief that subsistence production represents an important aspect of local identity, to be valued for its own sake. Subsistence production is ennobled, linked to a particular ethnic past. At the same time, such production fails to create what development specialists, Church leaders, and often (but not always) local people themselves regard as an acceptable standard of living. Subsistence production is defined as "less developed" in terms of material standards, but as intrinsically part of the local culture. This contradictory relationship creates a tension that contributes to the ambivalence of OCLADE's administration in its productive programs. While subsistence production is defined as inadequate by the NGO, it also represents a more noble, ethnically appropriate means of production than the major alternatives, production for a market or wage labor. This conflict, unaddressed and unresolved, underlies OCLADE's failure to consider transformative strategies of local development.

Fundapaz: Secularization

As a Catholic organization, OCLADE works with a predominantly Catholic clientele. Its close relationship with the Catholic Church allows it to draw on some advantageous resources: a large body of Church members who are willing to participate in its programs and act as local leadership; a steady source of financial support; and a sense of moral authority that underlies its projects. Fundapaz, which shares some Catholic roots, lacks most of these advantages in its work with the Wichí. Fundapaz does not have a direct relationship with any particular parish or religious order and is unable to depend on financial or other kinds of support from the Church. Moreover, the large majority of the Wichí are not Catholic at all, but Anglican. In this section, I will explore the ways in which Fundapaz has chosen to de-emphasize a religious message in favor of a more technical mission. While not abandoning a commitment to ideals of social justice that inform its work, the NGO operates in a much more complex and interconnected Catholic-Protestant interplay than is found in the *departamento* of Iruya. The religious difference between the Anglican Wichí and the Catholic *criollos,* with whom Fundapaz also operates a number of projects, provides another marker of the ethnic divide in the region. Their Anglican faith is a central part of how the Wichí understand their communities and their culture, and I explore the significance of Anglican missionization in understanding how development is defined and understood, and its impact on the relationship between Fundapaz and the Wichí.

Catholicism and Fundapaz

Fundapaz was founded as a Catholic development organization in 1973. Administratively, it was never part of the Catholic Church hierarchy, but its roots, both personal and financial, were closely tied to the Church. Like OCLADE, but somewhat earlier, it emerged as the creation of several social activists who were involved in rural communities and who perceived a need for more services and opportunities for those communities. As the organization matured, its discourse and praxis moved away from this religious foundation to be based on a more secular, technical approach to development. From its foundation until the present time, the organization was gradually professionalized, and its discourse also shifted from one based on a religious appeal to social justice to one more focused on concerns of economic efficiency and political empowerment.

Despite its shift to a secular, technical discourse, Fundapaz is still perceived by the Wichí and by many others in the region as a Catholic organization. This is due in part to the formerly close association between the organization and the Church. When Fundapaz first began to work in Los Blancos, the organization's staff in the region included several nuns who lived and worked in the community. These women worked extensively in the Wichí communities for a number of years, until 1988. Often, their approach seems to have been based less on ideas of "economic development" and more on traditional charity. Rather than implement "projects," the nuns used their own available labor and the resources available to them through the Church to meet what they saw as some of the needs of the communities. Much of the work that they did in the communities was based on close personal relationships that developed over time. Members of the Wichí communities, when asked about the work of these women, include accounts of coming to their house to share a *mate* (a type of tea) and talk. For the Wichí, who were generally treated with a degree of racial discrimination that precluded such social interactions with their white neighbors, the warm personal relationships that they developed with the nuns formed the basis for an ongoing relationship with Fundapaz as an organization. At times, these talks evolved into informal meetings that provided a vehicle to share information among the Wichí themselves. One Wichí leader, who as a young man participated in many of these discussions, explained,

> When Sister Melita used to be here, there were meetings all of the time. One elder would teach one youth. That way, everyone continued to learn. . . . Because the elders have a lot of wisdom. They know more about the things of the past. The young people learned a lot from them.

Much of the work of the nuns was informal and noninstitutionalized. Acting as an intermediary between Wichí individuals and the government was one central role. One of the nuns frequently assisted people in acquiring government documents such as birth certificates and identification documents (required of all Argentine citizens), as well as completing the paperwork needed for the elderly to receive a small government pension. These processes involve the negotiation of bureaucratic hurdles that require fluency in Spanish as well as travel to the provincial capital, obstacles that frequently precluded people in the communities from obtaining them. Another of the nuns taught women in the communities to sew clothes for themselves and their families. She established a system of exchanging crafts produced by the women for cloth and materials to make clothes, a system of exchange that Fundapaz continues to this day (see chapter 2). These two aspects of the nuns' work, help with bureaucratic processes and instruction in sewing, are what are most frequently mentioned by the Wichí as the ways in which they helped the communities.

The informal approach of the nuns, while it created strong bonds between the communities and Fundapaz, has left a legacy that is at times problematic for the work of the NGO as it shifts to a more professional, systematic methodology. The regional director suggested that the efforts of the nuns to meet every need of the community created a degree of dependency that has been difficult to undo. The nuns were very responsive to complaints from the communities and would use their own funds to purchase food, clothing, or other items that were in short supply. At times now, the communities continue to request aid from Fundapaz in the form of charity, rather than in the form of more formal development projects that Fundapaz now sees as its primary focus.

Along with the involvement of the nuns, much of Fundapaz's staff was drawn from laypeople who were actively involved in the Church and had an interest in the kind of social and economic activities promoted by the NGO. Field reports and other literature from this period often specifically referred to themes of social justice and linked this explicitly to Biblical and/or Vatican teachings, much as we have already seen in the case of OCLADE. Such literature justified programs primarily on their moral and ethical merits, rather than relying on technical or economic grounds. In this way, the discourse employed in this literature was distinct from the technocratic discourse of development discussed in the previous chapter.

Over the last decade, Fundapaz has undergone a process of professionalization of its field staff. The laypeople and religious workers who formerly provided the bulk of the organization's staff have gradually been replaced by a team of professional specialists, individuals with training and education in agriculture, natural resource management, and community organizing. At the same time, there has been a corresponding shift to a more technocratic development discourse. While the organization has not completely abandoned a religious discourse, it employs it more selectively and at different levels of the NGO as a whole. Recent field reports focus on the concrete needs of the communities, measured in quantitative terms, and on the technical merits of proposed projects. A religious idiom is still employed at higher levels of the organization, especially in newsletters sent to donors, many of whom are members of the Catholic Church or Catholic funding organizations. Even here, the language used is less specifically religious, tending to employ abstract concepts of democratization, social justice, and equality rather than explicit references to religious sources.

This shift from an explicitly religious idiom of development to one which is more technically oriented occurred gradually and incidentally, not as a conscious strategy so much as the result of a process of adaptation. As the organization became more established, its work was tempered by the realization that more technically skilled advice was needed to devise strategies for sustainable development initiatives. At the same time, the process of obtaining funding was becoming more competitive, as even religiously based funding organizations began to demand more technologically oriented strategies and concrete results. Some researchers have suggested that this amounted to "donor fatigue," as agencies came to feel that they were seeing little progress after a number of years of providing generous funding.

As a result, Fundapaz has shifted to an almost completely technical discourse of development. At a recent meeting, an organizational consultant emphasized that the NGO needs to examine every project in terms of its efficient use of funding, its efficacy in meeting goals, and its effective results. Such a results-oriented discourse represents a dramatic shift from the more global concern with community well-being that stemmed from a discourse based on the tenets of liberation theology. While such concerns may still serve in a limited capacity to help the organization design and describe its mission in the region in which it works, they have little relevance to, or impact on, its daily praxis.

The Wichí and the Anglican Church

Since the first half of this century, most of the Wichí have joined the Anglican church. Prior to that time, there were few Catholic missionary efforts in the region (see Makower 1989). Over the course of the last fifty years, the Anglican church has had a tremendous impact on the region, promoting a sedentary lifestyle for the Wichí, implementing its own development programs, and transforming the religious worldview of an entire people. In the oral histories of the Wichí, the arrival of the Anglican missionaries is a central theme, and marks the most significant event in living memory. The elders of the communities are part of the first generation to have been converted and settled, and in their accounts of Wichí culture there is a clear break between "before" the Anglicans came and "after."

Such an oral history was recounted by Guillermo, a young community leader in Kayip:

> You know that the people here care a great deal for the Anglicans. It's because they were the ones to come and teach us, to teach the Wichí. Back in those times, it was very difficult. In 1905, there was a big war here. Then the missionaries came, from England, and they asked the government to allow them to have four years, to teach the Wichí. The whites [blancos] here then didn't want to bother with the Wichí. The people were all afraid, because of the war. So the Anglicans asked to be allowed to work for four years, and the government allowed them.
>
> So the Anglicans set up the first mission. . . . They came all the way from England, when the whites here didn't want to bother with the Wichí. They had to travel a long time, first by boat, and then by foot, or by horse. It took three months, the trip by boat! Can you imagine? . . .
>
> The four years that the government had said they could have had gone by, but they let them stay more, because they were teaching the Wichí about the Bible. Before, there was the war. And there was a lot of fighting, between the Wichí and the whites and between the Wichí. But when the missionaries came and taught about the Bible, the Wichí learned that people are all brothers, and they stopped. It is for this that the Wichí love the Anglicans so much. If they

hadn't come, there would have been an even bigger war, and the Wichí might all have been killed.

Some of the whites here then, they didn't want the missions. Because then, only the whites had guns, and the Wichí only had bows and arrows. They didn't want the Anglicans to give the Wichí guns. If there was fighting, they didn't want the Wichí to have guns. But the government said the missionaries could come, so they did. They did give the Wichí some guns. There were a lot of problems at first. . . .

The people came from all over here to go to the mission, to learn what the missionaries were teaching, about the Bible. They came from all over this area. They came to live at San Patricio. Then many of them went back where they came from. Before, you know, the people didn't live like this, in villages. They moved around, all of the time. But then they came to stay in the mission. Before, there was no road here, no train. Then the whites started to come to live. But before there were only Wichí, in all of this land.

In Los Blancos and the surrounding communities, the Anglican faith has supplanted traditional spiritual beliefs.[13] The eldest generation, in particular, condemns many traditional practices as "witchcraft," following the condemnation of the early missionaries of customary healing, religious ritual, and other spiritual traditions. One older pastor described the religion of the Wichí before missionization:

They were not believers. They didn't believe in God. They believed only in the sun and the earth. They didn't believe in God. The traditional culture is not good. There was a dance [the *pin-pin*], and there was witchcraft. The culture changes each year. There are good people, and the culture changes. And now there are people, pastors, that want to teach the people the word of God. And it should be this way. It is a sacred thing, the word of God.

Just as Don Enrique described how the Anglican faith has changed the Wichí culture, the Wichí have transformed the nature of Anglican worship. Services incorporate exuberant music and enthusiastic prayer, bearing little resemblance to staid Anglican services found elsewhere. Similarly, the understanding of basic religious tenets comes through a cultural filter that emphasizes the aspects of the Christian faith that harmonize with the worldview of the Wichí. An Anglican missionary indicated that the particular interpretation that the Wichí congregations have of Christianity is

in some ways . . . a more sophisticated spiritual understanding of the Bible than [we have in] our own culture. Wichí concepts of property, for example, are much more in keeping with Biblical teachings than those of England. We [British] tend to skip over those parts of the Bible that talk about property. We read them, but they are not as important to us—we pass them over and focus on things that are more culturally comfortable. But the Wichí focus on those parts, about poverty, about sharing.

In the Wichí communities near Los Blancos, the Anglican church is tremendously successful despite the minimal physical presence of missionaries or white church leaders at the current moment. While there are occasional visits by outside clergy or missionaries, Kayip has never had a permanent missionary and Misión San Patricio has not had one since the early 1980s.[14] Instead, each community has a pastor, one of the Wichí elders, chosen by the congregation. The Anglican church has encouraged literacy in the communities, and especially among the pastors; many of the elders in the communities are literate thanks to Anglican literacy campaigns. The Anglican church has also made efforts to promote literacy in the Wichí language, and have produced a Bible and other materials in Wichí.[15] There is active participation in the church and services by both women and men, who profess deeply held religious beliefs. This stands in marked contrast to the difficulties of getting people to participate in NGO activities, for example, or other kinds of meetings. While there have been Anglican-sponsored development initiatives in the past, the Anglican church does not currently provide the community with any material help or have any development projects that reach this far.

In the 1970s, the Anglican church sponsored several large-scale development projects. A ten-year plan, called Iniciativa Cristiana (Christian Initiative), was developed, the objective of which was

> to identify with the Indian communities in their attempt to adapt to a situation of massive change, helping them to understand and share positively in the new culture . . . relating it to the old culture without despising that culture's traditional values. (Makower 1989, 161)

The IC sponsored a series of agricultural projects, with the goal of increasing the production of cash crops (tomatoes and peppers) using irrigation. There was also a program of "industrial" development that provided machines for a carpentry project. Two of these failed (in La Paz and Misión El Toba), due to the distance of the communities from a market. At Misión Chaqueña, Carboncitos was established as a development community. The project provided housing, education, health care, and employment. This project also failed, however, due to inflation and the onset of the Falklands/Malvinas War (Makower 1989, 163). Many families from the region around Los Blancos migrated to participate in the Carboncitos project, returning after a year or more when the project was terminated.

After the failure of these large development projects, which came at a time when the Anglican church was in turmoil in the aftermath of the Falklands/Malvinas War, the Anglican church largely withdrew from economic development. Missionaries and those closely involved with the Anglican church feel that it is unlikely to return to such large-scale projects in the foreseeable future. One missionary explained,

> Since then, development has followed certain global trends. The church also follows these trends in development. The danger is that we swing from one thing to the next thing, with no continuity. . . . The thinking [of religious funding agencies] is largely in line with secular thinking. Now they want short-term projects, things that have to be funded for three years or so and then turned over to the community. . . . It just isn't realistic. . . . The problem is that the church's efforts at development are in line with these global trends.

The Anglican church, like many other religious organizations involved in development, is moving away from a religiously motivated discourse or idiom of development to one which is more consonant with mainstream development discourse.

Away from Dependence

The Wichí, as members of the Anglican church, have stopped looking to that organization for projects in the communities. While many members of the communities can be forthright in their criticisms of organizations that they feel are not doing enough for them, there are few such complaints voiced about the Anglican church's withdrawal from development projects. There are two factors at work in the relationship between the Wichí in the Los Blancos communities and the larger Anglican church that contribute to shaping this lack of negativity.

The first element in the acceptance by the Wichí of the Anglican's lack of involvement in development is physical distance. Since the earliest mission efforts in San Patricio, there have not been Anglican missionaries living in the communities. There has also not been a permanent Anglican development team visiting on any regular basis. The communities have thus never been accustomed to having a steady influx of material resources coming from the Anglican church. The projects that were pursued by the Anglicans were relatively large-scale, located in distant communities to which the Wichí of Los Blancos had to travel if they wanted to participate. Many did choose to do so. But the element of distance meant that no expectations grew about having the Anglican church deliver development to the Wichí doorstep, so to speak. This is in clear contrast to the relationship that evolved with Fundapaz.

From its inception, Fundapaz worked in the communities, establishing small-scale projects that increased the material wealth of the Wichí. In retrospect, and given current trends in theories of development, this approach has certain advantages over large-scale projects such as the agricultural plantations created by the Anglican church. The relationship that developed between Fundapaz and the Wichí communities, however, was based on a degree of dependence that has ultimately come to make the organization uncomfortable. The Anglican church was able to avoid this dependence, albeit perhaps unintentionally, by keeping its projects one step removed from the daily lives of those in the communities near Los Blancos.[16]

The second factor in the Wichís' acceptance of the inactivity of the Anglican church in development is the active role that they themselves take in church administration and leadership. The Anglican church, since its earliest involvement in the communities, has cultivated Wichí leadership. Although not all members of the community are equally active in the church, those who are most active tend to be the leaders of the community. In some of the communities, the pastor is also the cacique (leader or headman). The convergence of political and religious leadership conforms to traditional cultural expectations that those with spiritual knowledge and power are most able to lead the group in other matters. In other communities, the cacique and pastor are different, a situation which has sometimes led to tension when they have different views. Either way, the Anglican church has become a powerful institution in the Wichí communities, an institution in which the leaders of the community are actively and centrally involved. The Wichí do not see the Anglican church as an "outside" organization but as something of which they are an integral part. There is thus no expectation that "they"—the Anglicans—will deliver something to the communities. The Anglican church has successfully cultivated a sense of ownership and membership of the church to the extent that it is seen as an integral part of the community rather than something which emanates from the outside. The Wichí do not rely on the church for development initiatives because the conception of the church is that it is within the community.

Catholics and Protestants

Locally, the division between Catholics and Protestants is sharply drawn on ethnic lines: the *criollos* are Catholic, and the Wichí are Anglican. In Los Blancos and the surrounding *criollo* communities, other evangelical churches have not made significant inroads. The religious divide between the Wichí and *criollos* merely serves to accentuate and amplify other divisions between the two groups. Guillermo, from Kayip, described this division:

> Even though all of the *criollos* were Catholics, they had never done anything, to teach the Wichí about the Bible. Only recently have they done anything, with ENDEPA, with Fundapaz. They thought the Wichí couldn't learn. But the Anglicans thought they could.

While the vast majority of *criollos* are Catholic, the presence of the Church is not very strong locally. There is a small chapel in Los Blancos but no resident priest. The nearest priest is located in Morillo, some 25 kilometers away. Although Los Blancos and the more remote *criollo* settlements are within his parish, he seldom visits them.[17] Local lay leaders preside over a small Bible study group, but for most Catholics, Church attendance is limited to a few life-cycle rituals and occasional holiday Masses. Church participation is weak, but an identity as Catholic persists and serves as an important ethnic marker.

Although it has an identity as a Catholic organization, Fundapaz has not evinced any interest in acting as a missionary agent among the Wichí. This is in contrast to another Catholic organization, ENDEPA, based in Morillo. ENDEPA is primarily a religious organization, but it does initiate and sponsor development projects in the Wichí communities near Morillo. ENDEPA's staff, all of whom come from urban areas, clearly see themselves as missionaries, with a progressive, liberationist theology and methodology. Although they describe missionization as their first goal, they are deeply respectful of the Anglican faith of the Wichí with whom they work; at one meeting, for instance, an elderly Wichí pastor was invited to lead the group in prayer. Development, in keeping with a liberationist methodology, is seen as a means to an end. One of its workers described the organization's development work: "For us sometimes it means that helping someone with 'development' is taking them to the hospital, or helping them through a personal crisis. It's not just building wells." As a Catholic organization, development work provides a way to reach the Wichí. The Wichí, in turn, seem to accept ENDEPA's development assistance but have largely turned down the possibility of religious conversion. Development has not proven a way to win converts, but a strong religious identity has not weakened ENDEPA in its efforts to reach the Wichí communities in other ways.[18]

In contrast, Fundapaz does not actively identify itself as religious at all in its daily work with both *criollos* and Wichí but focuses its attention on the details of projects, funding, and local organization. Fundapaz is familiar with ENDEPA's work, so this decision is not because of a fear of losing support or alienating the Wichí on religious grounds, but rather is based on an institutional culture that is invested in the technical aspects of creating successful development projects. The underlying justification and motivation for Fundapaz's work comes from a vision of social justice and the values underpinning liberation theology, but this vision is at a remove from its daily work.

Conclusion

Development projects affect a community on several distinct levels. Most obviously, development programs seek to change the material conditions of production, primarily through reallocating resources (for example, land, technology, information, access to markets, or credit). This reallocation of various resources may change the social relations of production: by expanding access to the means of production, by changing the productive roles of women, or by changing the strategies that may be employed within or outside the community, such as seeking more education for children. On another level, development organizations may play a central role in changing the symbolic relations of production—the beliefs that people hold about the "rightness" or justice in the distribution of resources. In this chapter and the one that preceded it, I have suggested that organizations such as NGOs may have an important role in negotiating between the "local" and the "global" visions of "development," in the definition of poverty, the strategies chosen, and the cultural (sub)text of local projects. This negotiation occurs between international and local NGOs as well as between NGOs and local people.

As these case studies have illustrated, the ways in which "poverty" is defined by a development organization has clear ramifications for the kinds of programs it implements, its own methodology, and, just as importantly, the arenas of local life that it defines as outside the scope of its interests. Such definitions are not always fully articulated, but nevertheless inform the program's actions and philosophy. They are created in a process of dialogue with ideas of development gleaned from larger institutions and trends in global development, from an organization's own ideological background, in this case based on a liberal Christianity, and from conversations with local people, who are also involved in a separate but interrelated process of definition and discourse.

We have seen that an evolutionary framework informs many aspects of defining and understanding "development." There is a clear hierarchy of economies implicit in the work of these programs. In Los Blancos, poverty was defined as a lack of subsistence farming, which was clearly preferred to an economic system based on the extraction of fugitive natural resources. In Iruya, subsistence farming was defined as poverty, as the local economy was understood to provide insufficient access to technology, health care, and education.

In both cases, however, the organization and its staff retain a degree of ambivalence about the degree to which "development," based on such an evolutionary model, is either practical or desirable. While the introduction of new systems of production, medicine, or education, or an increase in their availability, is one of the frequently unstated goals of development organizations, the "traditional" lifestyle of an indigenous community often serves as a point of comparison. As we have seen, many religious NGOs were created as a direct response to the challenges posed by liberation theology. Liberation theology did not merely pose theological or ecclesiastical questions, but offered a far-reaching social and political critique of Western society, capitalism, and the marginalization of the poor. As individuals and organizations armed with such critiques began to extend the work of development into indigenous communities, these very communities offered an alternative model to the dominant society. Indigenous peoples were not simply a subset of "poor" people. Rather, they constituted a distinct population, one whose intrinsic values and interests were seen and portrayed as not just genuinely different but often as morally superior. Still, given the very real conditions of poverty and discrimination that structured such peoples' daily lives, religiously motivated development organizations felt the need to become involved, to mediate the relationship between isolated communities and the dominant society, to improve the physical conditions of those communities and their access to the centers of power. The project of development thus involved a considerable ambivalence.

Notes:

1. See also Kozak 1994 for a discussion of Catholic missionary discourse among native Americans in the United States.
2. Out of a total of over six hundred Latin American bishops.
3. Freire's books were at the top of the banned book list in Argentina under the military regime (Ruggiero 1988, 119).
4. It may be worth noting that provincial politics in the province of Jujuy are rather more confrontational and dynamic than in Salta, where an entrenched landowning class maintains a firm grip on much of the political power in the province, and the Catholic hierarchy remains conservative and traditional. The prelature of Humahuaca spans parts of both provinces.
5. When marriages are performed, it is most often after a couple has established a household and often has several children. The Catholic Church has been encouraging formal marriage, in some cases pressuring parents to be married before their children are baptized. Still, according to my survey data, only about half of couples are formally married. Many live together in common-law arrangements. Separation is relatively uncommon once a couple has one or more children, although it is socially accepted in cases of domestic violence, alcoholism, and other such cases. In some cases, a couple may not form a household together, despite the birth of children. Generally, the child stays with the mother, and there is little stigma attached to single motherhood. Most often, a child born in such circumstances is accepted by the mother's eventual partner, or, more rarely, raised by grandparents.
6. My husband and I were accorded similar status on the basis of being educated and foreign, an experience that is surely similar to that of many anthropologists but which, nevertheless, causes moments of embarrassment and awkwardness.
7. This phrase originated as a slogan of the Latin American Catholic Church at the Medellín conference of bishops in 1968.
8. Here I use "evangelical" in the way that it is generally employed in Latin America, as referring to any Protestant denomination. In North America, "evangelical" generally refers only to a small subgroup of Protestant churches. In Iruya, these distinct usages happen to more or less coincide, as the particular Protestant churches active in the village are denominations which would probably be considered "evangelical" in North America.
9. While I was in residence in Iruya, there were no visits by foreign evangelical missionaries, and the last such visit was reported to have been "many years ago." There were visits by Argentine pastors from outside the region.
10. *Coplas* are a type of song, often accompanied by a small drum and, occasionally, a flute. Locally, they are highly stylized, with each community having its own distinct tonality.
11. He also notes that Kollas do not equate the *pachamama* with the Virgin Mary, as has occurred elsewhere in the Andes. The Kolla see the *pachamama* as "violent and vengeful if she does not receive her due worship," while the Virgin is understood as unfailingly tender and merciful (Olmedo Rivera 1990, 172).

12. There is a certain coincidental irony in the fact that the prelature is led by Spanish missionaries, seeking to reform a system created and supported by their own spiritual ancestors.
13. There is some evidence that traditional practices are more persistent in the area near the Pilcomayo; see, for example, Makower (1989).
14. Most of the Anglican missionaries and clergy were expelled from the country or fled during the Falklands/Malvinas war.
15. The current translation was produced many years ago by Anglican missionaries. The Anglican church is currently working on a new translation, using a team of Wichí and non-Wichí translators.
16. A rather different relationship seems to exist in Wichí communities that still have the presence of an outside Anglican missionary, which is also where the large projects were situated. There, a much closer and more dependent relationship persists between the Wichí and the Anglican church.
17. In fact, during the time when I lived in the community, the priest never came, including for a fiesta when he was expected but failed to turn up.
18. Despite religious differences, in fact, the Wichí have shown a deep respect and regard for the ENDEPA staff. The director of the local ENDEPA team was chosen by the Wichí as the NGO representative whom they wanted to work with during meetings at the national level to revise the constitution. The choice, according to my informant, came down to the ENDEPA director and the director of Fundapaz, both of whom are well-liked and trusted.

Chapter 5: Land and Its Uses

> The indigenous person has a very broad concept [of land] that is not based on the occupation of a plot of land. Rather, it is a vital space of life, of subsistence. That is the profound concept that he has of land.
>
> Orlando Sanchez (Toba) (ENDEPA 1992, 5)

Land claims were a dynamic issue of contention in both Iruya and Los Blancos during the period of my fieldwork (1996-97). These communities were able to make claims on land, under Argentine law and national policies, because of their status as indigenous communities. The unique relationship that is presumed to exist between an indigenous culture and its territory is the context of the policies and the claims themselves.

In both cases, the NGOs who worked there played an important role in initiating and pursuing land claims made by local residents. In this chapter, I will explore the ways in which the relationship between indigenous peoples and their land has been invoked, created, and reinvigorated by the communities and by the NGOs. Then, in chapter 6, I will discuss the specific land claims cases, the role of the NGOs, and the consequences of land reclamation for the local communities.

Indigenous Cultures and the Natural Environment

The relationship of indigenous cultures and the natural environment has been a topic of interest to anthropologists, and more broadly to those interested in both ecological conservation and indigenous rights, since at least the late 1970s. An essay by Gregory Bateson (1979) argued that there are patterns of connection between all living creatures, a view which modern science, at least since Lamarck and Darwin, has lost in favor of particularisms and defining a thing in terms of what it "is" rather than the role it plays in a given context. Bateson developed the idea that ecosystems include not only biological organisms, but cultural understandings of the physical environment as well.

Reichel-Dolmatoff (1976) offers a more specific case study that considers the relationship between cosmology and ecology in an indigenous culture, in this case the Eastern Tukano of the northwest Amazon. He argues that the fragile ecosystem of the Amazon requires a society to develop not only adaptive behavioral rules but also a coherent belief system "which would make endurable the problems of man's existence in an unpredictable world" (1976, 308). The cosmology and rituals of such a society represent a set of ecological principles, which function to maintain a balance between resources and social needs. In this cosmological system, "nature" is not untouched or pristine; rather, the natural environment is seen as having been transformed and structured by the ancestors who have imbued it with symbolic meaning (1976, 309). In Reichel-Dolmatoff's view, the Tukano have little interest in maximizing their use of resources (1976, 310-311). Instead, their model is one of equilibrium, emphasizing the interrelatedness of all things, much as described by Bateson.

The Tukano believe that humans neither dominate nor live in harmony with nature, but rather that they form a fundamental component of nature itself. Reichel-Dolmatoff finds that the Tukano understand that their adaptive rules are necessary as a regulatory mechanism to ensure individual and collective well-being (1976, 312). They place ritual restrictions on the use of resources such as animals and plants. Shamans are particularly knowledgeable, and control access to resources in a more or less conscious way depending on the individual.

E. N. Anderson (1996) looks more specifically at the issue of indigenous ecological knowledge. His discussion is geared to the contemporary debate on environmentalism, and he uses indigenous relations with the natural world as a point of comparison for the West. He contends that environmental problems are a mixture of reason and passion, and that the solutions must also be such a mix (1996, 9). Anderson explores indigenous ecological beliefs, tending to represent them as "irrational" but at the same time arguing that they may serve rational ecological ends, noting that the "errors" are not in the observations of indigenous peoples but in their inferences. He observes that native peoples often represent ecological management in spiritual terms, through specific social codes and institutions, and that conservation in traditional systems is part of a religiously sanctioned ethical code (1996, 10-11).

While Anderson represents indigenous representations and management of the environment as rather accidentally or incidentally successful, Colin Scott (1996) uses a case study of the James Bay Cree to develop a concept of culturally specific science. Every culture draws deductive inferences, tests them through experience, and adjusts its models to conform to the observed world. Scott employs the idea of the "root metaphor" to describe that which is understood as the causal force by a culture.[1] "Root metaphors" represent paradigms of culturally specific science. The root metaphor of each culture's science is distinct, and in this, modern science is just one among many, although it chooses to characterize others as "unscientific" (1996, 69, 85). Scott notes that when structural or functional connections between indigenous cosmology and ecological management are constructed by an outside observer, it often appears as though a modern scientific method "has captured what remained unconscious or invisible to native subjects" (1996, 71), while the intellectual process, from the actors' point of view, remains obscure. Instead, in Scott's analysis, the central root metaphors of a cosmology are better understood as practical social and environmental knowledge than as mystical precepts (1996, 72). In this relationship between knowledge and cosmology, "the difference between myth and science is not structural but procedural" (1996, 74). Root metaphors are creatively used to interpret events and experiences. The root metaphor itself becomes implicit over time, and is often unconscious in empirical description, while myths come to represent "condensed expressions" of the root metaphor.

These authors, as well as others, have persuasively argued several themes: that indigenous systems of ecological management can be environmentally sustainable; that they are based on careful observation of the natural environment and represent an empirically informed understanding of resource use and a philosophy of conservation; and that they are intimately linked with indigenous cosmology (see also Picchi 2000; Niezen 1998). The understanding of the natural environment as an ecosystem of which humans form an integral part is typical of egalitarian societies. Indigenous knowledge of the natural environment may be inscribed in myths, which serve as a powerful teaching and learning tool. It may also be manifest in social codes and institutions. Even language reflects notions of place and creates representations of the material and spiritual world (Basso 1996).

The link between ecological rules of use and cosmology is what enables these systems to function over long periods of time, giving them emotional value, widespread obedience and adherence, and a coherence that is lacking in the modern scientific approach. Bateson describes this coherence as a "metapattern," while Scott attributes it to differing "root metaphors." This is a more sophisticated approach than a strictly functionalist or materialist perspective might be, one which could argue that myths arise as a consequence of the need to justify particular necessary behaviors. Instead, these authors argue that cosmology provides a framework for understanding, not just a rationalization for behavior. Within this framework, individuals creatively employ symbols and concepts to continually reinterpret the world.

In this chapter, my goal is not to argue that the Wichí and the Kolla enjoy any sort of prototypic idyllic relationship with the natural environment. I wish to avoid the stereotype that these indigenous peoples live "in harmony" with nature. The ways in which contemporary Kolla and Wichí people and communities use their land has been shaped and determined not just by indigenous systems of land management, but also by colonial systems and relationships with the modern state, by external groups and their practices, by conditions of poverty, and by their relationships with the market. Instead, I wish to explore how, in each of these communities, the natural environment is understood, conceptualized, and incorporated into practice—how culture and landscape interact. These conceptions, which underlie cultural practices, are challenged and often transformed in the process of land tenure disputes, which is the subject of chapter 6. As we will see, disputes over land tenure are often centered not on the physical ownership of a plot of land, but over wildly differing and poorly apprehended cultural beliefs about the "appropriate" use of land.

Local Perceptions of Land in Iruya

In the *departamento* of Iruya, land is by far the most important productive resource. Subsistence farming is the basis of the economy. Even those few households with a member who has full-time employment or who have small commercial enterprises still keep animals and have large gardens to supplement their cash income. Every household has access to land—there are no truly landless families. In such a land-dependent economy, the significance of land and the value attached to it go well beyond the merely productive.

Most of the land in the *departamento* is still owned by absentee landowners, as it has been since the early colonial period. The entire *departamento* is divided between three major fincas, or farms.[2] Only a few households are located on land that does not pertain to one of these fincas. For generations, the finca owners—all absentee—have taken little or no interest in how land is distributed or used locally, beyond the collection of rent for cultivated land and a fee levied per head on grazing animals.

The notion of *intensive* farming is tremendously apt in Iruyan agriculture. While new land may occasionally be brought into cultivation, most of the land that is not used for planting is extremely marginal, because of its slope, distance from irrigation canals, or altitude. Because there is no new land available, cultivated land is carefully tended to maintain its productivity. Small plots, often just a few meters on a side, are passed from one generation to the next. Regular fallow periods are integrated into a cycle that extends over as many as seven years as crops are rotated. Each small plot that a family cultivates each year is integrated into its overall subsistence strategy with great care and planning. Each plot of land is laboriously planted, fertilized, irrigated, weeded, harvested. Almost all work is done with hand tools—hoes, shovels, spades, and pitchforks. Even if a local farmer had capital to invest in machinery, this is not land where one could farm with a tractor. The ground is too rocky and uneven, the plots too small and irregularly shaped, the slopes, even of cultivated fields, too dramatic.[3]

The practice of farming in Iruya is intense. Equally intense is the relationship that the people have, as farmers, with the land that they cultivate. People spend long hours throughout the year working on these very small plots. They know the qualities and quirks of each field—where it is too cold for corn, which can bear two crops in a season, where there is not enough sunlight for green vegetables, where there are too many rocks, which field is best for which of the many varieties of potatoes that are the staple of the local diet. Like smallholders throughout the world, Iruyan farmers practice "production based on skill as opposed to scale" (Netting 1993, 49). Part of this skill is an intimate knowledge of the land.

Because so much land is not suited for cultivation, most of the land that any household has under cultivation has belonged to the family for generations. One young Kolla woman explained: "My mother's land is her inheritance. It belonged to her parents, and before that her grandparents. Like that. It is all hereditary." The tiny plots that most people farm today are the result of fields being carved up over generations to pass on to children. Children grow up helping their parents in the fields, so that the knowledge of the land is passed down directly, as an equally important heritage.

The resultant patchwork of fields means that a typical family's holdings may be spread over several miles. A shepherd, standing on top of a high ridge with me, pointed out his fields. He began with his house, nestled in a narrow canyon, where he had a small garden. About a half mile away, on the other side of a smaller ridge, he indicated the field where he grew potatoes. When asked if he grew corn, he strode to the other side of the peak, and pointed to three little parcels separated from each other by gullies. Across the river from those fields, he grew peas and beans in several more neat plots of land. From our bird's-eye view, he could also point to his corral and the grazing lands used by his animals, high above the cultivated terraces. From this lofty perspective, the tour took only a matter of minutes. On the ground, however, the distance between holdings was considerable. As in much of the Andes, a system of vertical field diversification means that most households control rights to land at several altitudes, enabling them to spread their risk and produce a greater variety of staple crops (Sallnow 1987).

The land that lies above the cultivated zone, as well as the steep hillsides above and below it, is not as empty as it appears to an outsider. To local eyes, this land too has a great deal of value. Animals are set loose to graze, and wander freely along the slopes. Firewood is collected from scrubby bushes and woody plants. Herbs and wild plants are occasionally gathered for remedies and for use as seasonings. There are few wild animals, but vicuñas, a wild camelid, still roam the upper heights of the mountains and are occasionally hunted for their wool, which fetches a good price.[4] Trails over the mountains link communities.

But the most valuable land lies along the river valleys, high enough above the flood level of the river to keep it safe during the wet season, but low enough to permit irrigation canals to provide water. One of the worst calamities that can fall upon a household is to watch a field close to the river be swallowed up during one of the summer floods, as the course of a river changes and destroys a low-lying terrace beyond repair. The rivers regularly shift their banks, carrying all of the soil away and leaving only boulders and stones.[5] Despite this risk, in the narrow fertile zones above the rivers, there is little land that goes uncultivated.

Stone walls, scrupulously maintained, divide one neighbor's plot from the next, marking partitions that may have been in place for a century or more. In other places, the boundaries are not physically marked, but they are agreed upon and recognized. Until the recent legal battle for formal land titles (see chapter 6), access to land has been based on usufruct rights. Usufruct rights can be sold, although this occurs only very occasionally. Since most land has been legally owned by a finca owner, such sales are rare since the buyer has little security that his/her purchase will be respected by the absentee landowner. In practice, landowners evince little concern for cultivated land beyond levying fees for its use. Usufruct rights to cultivated plots belong to their owner on an individual rather than a household basis. Both women and men inherit and control land. Inheritance is flexible, with no preference given to children according to birth order or gender. In practice, although individuals own land separately, household landholdings are managed together, taking into consideration all of the household's claims on land.

An Iruyan Cosmology

Much of the work on indigenous ecological management has focused particularly on cultures that traditionally relied on hunting and gathering (as, for example, Anderson 1996 and Reichel-Dolmatoff 1976). Such subsistence systems rely on the use of naturally occurring wild plants and animals, a practice that requires social controls in order to remain sustainable. These controls may be expressed in myths or cosmological belief systems which link the natural world with human behavior. In the agricultural society of Iruya, similar controls also exist. The "root metaphors," to borrow Colin Scott's term, are centered on a personified earth and the spirits which protect it.

In the daily farming of this marginal territory, land is highly personified, like someone that you work with rather than a mere medium of production. Plots are small, tiny, and must be closely and carefully tended by hand. The land that is useful for cultivation is scarce and treasured. Relationships with the land are intimate and emotional. This feeling may be reinforced by the dramatic landscape and geography of the valleys. Cultivated land is nestled in the river valleys or on low terraces. Verdant cultivated fields contrast sharply with scant brown grasses and cacti of the higher altitudes.

Space and landscape are important components of spiritual belief throughout the Andes, pre-dating the Conquest and even the consolidation of the Incan Empire. The lofty mountaintops have long been regarded as sacred places. In the high Andes of Argentina, pre-Incan peoples made sacrifices, including even human sacrifices, on the highest peaks on special occasions or in times of crisis, in order to appease, cajole, or placate gods (Schoebinger, 1997, personal communication). The Andean belief in the sacred qualities of the natural landscape was only reinforced by the Spanish practice of building churches and shrines on existing religious sites (Sallnow 1987, 52).

In Iruya, the tallest and most distinctive peaks continue to have spiritual significance. Often, they are considered to be guarded or protected by spirits, and there are shrines built on both peaks and at high passes. In some cases, these shrines are attributed to patron saints, and people say that their offerings are to ensure a safe journey. The road into Iruya is marked by a large shrine at its highest pass that casual visitors might mistake for a trash dump due to the volume of offerings left there. Expensive consumables, such as cigarettes, alcohol, and soda, are left as offerings, and the empty containers litter the enclosed space of the shrine. The stumps of candles line the top of the low stone wall. There is no statue of a saint or other Christian symbols at the site, although there is a makeshift stone altar marked by the dark residue of candles.

Some sites have been sanctioned by the Catholic Church. The highest point in the village of Iruya is marked by a small cross atop a shrine filled with artificial flowers, maintained by a group of churchwomen. Well outside the village, on one of the highest peaks ringing the valley, a large cross marks a remote pass accessible only by foot. The parish priest, a young Claretian missionary, pointed it out to me, distantly visible from the road if one knew where to look. He cheerfully described the arduous pilgrimage he had made with local church members, at their request, to dedicate the site and place the cross. In other cases, such a syncretic transference has not occurred, and non-Christian practices are frequently denied or hidden from observers. Non-Christian practices, where they have not been legitimized through linking them to Catholic beliefs, are furtive and private.

Despite the pervasive influence of the Catholic Church in the valleys of northern Salta, pre-Christian religious practices and beliefs persist, although much transformed from earlier versions. In this, Iruya is not dissimilar from other parts of the Andes. For example, in a study of a Runa village in Peru, Sarah Skar (1993) found that extensive rituals to local gods persist. In this village, the Christian god is seen as one among many; while people lack close ties with Catholicism, they turn to it to gain benefit from prayer and ritual blessing. Despite 400 years of Catholic presence in the area, Catholic missionaries in the Runa village have failed to eradicate a fundamental difference of belief about the nature of the universe and the place of people in it, a difference which Skar argues is not resolvable by a "syncretic compromise" (1993, 230). In a study of Bolivian miners, June Nash finds that their religious system represents a "compartmentalization in time and space" of different belief systems, with no sense of dissonance, so that, for example, Christianity is positioned on Sunday and above ground, while traditional deities are associated with Tuesdays and Fridays and below ground (1979, 7). In both cases, Christian and non-Christian religious systems coexist, albeit with differing degrees of ease and comfort. In Iruya, Christian and non-Christian beliefs also coexist in an uneasy compromise of silence and syncretism.

The natural landscape is tripartite in Iruya. The highest peaks are too cold and barren to provide grazing for domestic herd animals and are one of the few "wild" spaces in the local landscape. In this wild space, the spirits themselves manage the resources. There is little of use or interest to the local people on a practical level on the mountaintops—it is an undomesticated realm. In the intermediate herding zone, communities have long managed the grazing lands as common property. In this zone, microclimates created by hills and rivers determine what areas provide the best fodder for animals during each season. While land is abundant, useful plants and accessible water sources are not. The distances over which herds are moved, although not impressive in kilometers, are considerable in terms of travel time. To bring herds from the summer to winter grazing areas, for example, may take up to two weeks. During the rainy season, when animals are kept closer to the villages, they may still stay as much as a day's walk from the farmer's house. The grazing zone, familiar to herders and farmers, is part of "civilized space," even though to an outsider this part of the landscape may appear somewhat barren. The third space, the thoroughly domesticated realm of house and field, is where the relationship with the *pachamama* is the strongest.

The most prominent non-Christian belief is *pachamama* worship (see chapter 3). Pachamama beliefs frame an understanding of the relationship between people and the environment that is distinct from the "rational maximization" of capitalist farmers. The land itself, the earth worked by farmers, is not conceptualized as an inanimate resource but as a personalized force. Moreover, the *pachamama* is not a benevolent mother-goddess, a New Age incarnation of Nature. The *pacha* is a powerful, capricious god that needs to be placated, sacrificed to, and cajoled into yielding the harvest that allows families to survive. The idea of sacrifice, in particular, is intimately tied to farming and subsistence agriculture. For ritual occasions, and for each planting and harvest, small sacrifices are made, offerings that are buried in the earth (as described in chapter 3). Beyond those symbolic sacrifices, the idea of "sacrificing oneself" to the land is a common expression in Iruya. Maintaining a farm is seen as a labor of love and sacrifice, a lifestyle that is chosen because of the continuity it allows with one's family and the land. Asked about rural life, a middle-aged woman replied, "Here we don't have money. But with the sacrifice of oneself, the earth yields its harvest."

Pachamama worship remains a hidden and secretive practice in Iruya. In part, this secrecy is because the Catholic Church itself represents one of the few stable outside institutions that conveys resources into the area. Although the Church has recently begun to welcome rituals such as those associated with the *pachamama* as representative of local cultural traditions, this has come after many years of suppression. Many villagers remain reluctant to alienate this source of potential material gain by admitting to practices that the church has historically condemned. It is also due in part to a deep suspicion of outsiders.

Not only the church and its clergy, but anthropologists and tourists, are viewed skeptically as strangers ready to take advantage of local people and traditions. My questions about non-Christian beliefs were generally met with closure and curt denial. My closest informants sometimes acknowledged that such practices exist, but denied their own involvement, and hastened to reassure me that people were "really" worshipping saints.[6] One of my experiences illustrates the common reluctance to trust strangers with knowledge of local spiritual practices. On a holiday picnic with some neighbors, one of the children, a bright girl about ten years old who frequently visited me, began to describe how her two-year-old cousin had been brought to a local *curandero,* a healer, for a recent illness. Her mother, overhearing her gleeful description of candles, herbs, and prayers, quickly cut her off, and curtly told me that they had, of course, taken the baby to the doctor.

Distrust of strangers and their motivations is probably a rational and justified attitude from a people who have been exploited by generations of landowners and tax collectors as well as others who have entered the community for their own purposes. Despite the booming tourist trade in Iruya, and the potential boon for the local economy that this influx of outsiders represents, there is a lingering suspicion of tourists, and they meet with only a lukewarm reception. Inhabitants of nearby towns such as Humahuaca have discovered that there is money to be had in "ethnotourism"; many inhabitants there cheerfully parade through town in exaggerated local costumes during festivals and hawk woolen goods and pottery that are usually purchased cheaply across the Bolivian border. In Humahuaca, as in other large towns across the puna, there is a renewed pride in indigenous identity. There, *pachamama* rituals are a routine part of festivals. In more isolated areas such as Iruya, however, such sanitized rituals, devoid of much of their original spiritual content and removed from the realm of genuine belief, represent a loss of a tradition that is still vibrant and immediate elsewhere (cf. Nash 1979; Sallnow 1987) and a betrayal of a relationship with the earth that is too close to the practices of daily life to be shared casually with busloads of outsiders.

Ecological Management

While authors such as Anderson (1996) and Scott (1996) emphasize the role of mythology in hunter-gatherer cultures, some of the concepts about the relationship between myths and environmental management can also be applied to agricultural societies like Iruya. In Iruya, one myth that regulates the extraction of a natural resource is the story of the *duende* that protects the vicuña herds.[7] Vicuña live in the upper altitudes of the mountains around Iruya. Always rare, but increasingly so in the last twenty years, their wool is prized for its softness and warmth. According to a local myth, wild vicuña and llama herds belong to the *duende* who lives in the mountain. Elsewhere in the region, the *duende* is called *el coquena,* "an ecological god living and acting in the territory of the

Collas. At the present time, there are many older people who continue to believe in the *coquena,* defending the hunters' animals" (Olmedo Rivera 1990, 174).

The *duende* has one arm that is made of soft wool, and the other arm is an iron pike. Like the *pachamama*, he must be given a proper sacrifice if a hunter wishes to take animals from the "*duende's* herd." Hunters who abide by this requirement are gently stroked by the spirit's woolen hand, and he continues to care for the herd. But hunters who ignore the *duende*, or who try to take too many animals without need from the herd, are smitten by the iron arm. This myth was invoked in Rodeo Colanzuli to explain why one local man suddenly found himself unable to walk: apparently, he had been hunting vicuña frequently on the mountain in order to sell the wool and had failed to make the proper supplication to the *duende*. The myth also provided an explanation for the dwindling numbers of vicuña to be found in the mountains. Because hunters were taking too many animals for profit rather than out of need, the *duende* had moved his herd elsewhere, to a safer location.

The *duende* is just one of innumerable spirits that populate local mountaintops. The priest Jesús Olmedo Rivera describes many of the gods and spirits common in the region (1990, 172-176). Interestingly, in his description of traditional gods and contemporary spiritual beliefs, Olmedo associates spirits that are benign and positive with saints and Christian beliefs. There are a number of saints, for example, that protect domestic herd animals. Others are patron saints for fiestas, towns, and homes. Negative spirits, however, retain their indigenous names and qualities, and are not subsumed into the Christian "devil." Most of these negative spirits are not in fact "evil" in the Christian sense, but are instead demanding and at times capricious, and many are associated with undomesticated nature. Along with the *duende* or *coquena*, there is the *tío*, god of mines (see also Nash 1979), who may protect miners or deliver misfortunes on them. The *momo*, god of the carnival, is symbolically buried in the earth at the end of each season and dug up the next year.

To be sure, to a certain extent these are fables told to children and curious anthropologists. Spirits such as the *duende* do serve as a cautionary reminder, however. While the *duende* might not literally have struck the hunter that lost the use of his legs, there was a genuine belief that the man in question had been overexploiting a resource. His current ailment was attributed to his failure to act according to accepted precepts governing the hunt of the vicuña herd. In order to find an explanation for why misfortune fell upon this particular individual, and not his neighbor, local people saw that it was due to his lack of respect for the spirits governing the use of resources. By overexploiting the resource, by neglecting the rituals that create bonds between the earth and its inhabitants, this man had left himself open to supernatural influence. The consequences of negligence, in this case, were high.

There are other traditions of shared management, cultural practices, and expected behavior that do not have such a neat myth to explain the rules and their consequences. While these practices and beliefs do not quite fit into the idea of "cosmology," they certainly work to regulate the use of resources according to practices that are based on careful observation and an intimate knowledge of the landscape. Such practices include the obligations of each household to contribute to community labor projects, such as building and maintaining roads and clearing irrigation canals. These "public works" projects are undertaken for the benefit of the community as a whole, and while there is no overarching force that demands the labor contribution, social pressure and sanctions applied informally by the community—practices such as social ostracism, for example—ensure that every household complies with little protest. Collective labor reinforces community solidarity and the interdependence of households, while at the same time allowing the community to accomplish major projects that could not be done by any single household. Of course, in practice, the regulation of common resources such as irrigation water may be fraught with conflict and tension. As Robert Netting (1993) has indicated, rules governing the use of such common resources have been enacted specifically to head off potential problems and disagreements. Still, tensions exist, both where informal or explicit norms and rules have been violated and in cases where one party feels disadvantaged by the rules that are in place.

In the case of irrigation canals, as an example, the collective nature of the project helps to ensure that the resource is managed carefully. In Colanzuli, for example, the community met to plan a new canal that would provide water for both drinking and irrigation. One afternoon, representatives from a number of families met atop a hill to survey their options and plan where the canal could go. Once the canal was completed, it would be governed by the same unwritten but scrupulously followed norms as other irrigation canals. Irrigation "turns," or periods of opened irrigation gates, are meted out to each family by consensus of the households served by a particular canal. Households generally comply with opening and closing their gates for the prescribed intervals. The group deciding where to lay the canal rejected one plan because, although it would be easier to build, it began too close to several corrals, and the water would not be safe to drink. Another route was rejected because it was too circuitous and would lose too much water. Yet a third option was dismissed because it would allow a household who refused to contribute labor—unfairly, they felt, since although the household head was a widow, she had three grown sons living at home with her—to benefit from the canal. Finally, an acceptable route was found, and as dusk was drawing near, the villagers quickly descended. Because the project benefits the community, rather than a single household, it was difficult, if not impossible, for any one family to monopolize the resource; others would not agree, and would not aid in a construction project that they did not feel was fair. The needs of those further downstream were considered, as they were kin and neighbors to those planning this new upstream project. The common management of this vital resource, like the management of common property in land, follows community norms and rules and regulates the use of the resource itself.

Ownership, Rights, and Land Titles

Rights to land are closely held and tightly guarded in the community. Usufruct rights are defended, respected, and upheld. A young agronomist working in the region marveled at local respect for usufruct rights:

> Even if a piece of land has been unused for ten years, a good piece of land, the neighbors will say, "No, that belongs to José," and they will not use it. Even if he has moved away, with his whole family. And José may not even *own* the land, with a legal title. It might just have been used by his family for many years. Until he gives it to someone else, no one will even move a stone.

In this way, usufruct rights are a relatively stable and secure local institution. Certainly, boundaries may be disputed or violated by neighbors. With no recourse to outside court systems, because of a lack of legal titles, local people have been forced to devise ways to mediate their own disputes. When such mediation fails, violence or long-standing feuds may be the result. The depth of such conflicts attests to the strong institutions that govern access to land.

Most of the land in the Iruyan valley is formally owned by outside landlords who collect rents from local residents. Farmers realize that their rights to land vis-à-vis outsiders and the state are precarious. The conversion of vast tracts of land and pasture into fincas during the colonial period and subsequent centuries of having to pay tributes and rents for the land that they use have relegated the local economy to a level of minimal subsistence. More recently, the sale of one finca to a foreign timber company, and its subsequent resale to another logging interest, has emphasized the perilous nature of usufruct rights that have been in place for so many years. People realize that the legal owners of the land that they use have the right to evict them, to use their land for other purposes. The need for local farmers to control legal titles has thus been brought forward as a pressing and immediate issue of concern, which I will discuss at greater length in chapter 6.

Land titles are not sought after merely because farmers do not want to pay rent, however. The relationship that Iruyan villagers have with their land is intimate and spiritual. Land is valued it not only for its productive capacity, but for the power that is embodied within it. The land of the Iruyan farmer is nurturing and life-giving, but it is also demanding and harsh. The "root metaphors" of the Iruyan cosmology entail suffering and silence, as well as growth and renewal. In rituals, the earth is given sacrifices, so that it in turn will yield its bounty.

The Wichí and Their Land

> There is nothing here, but we are native to this place. We aren't going anywhere.
>
> Enrique, Cacique, Kayip

For the Wichí of Los Blancos, just as for the Kolla of Iruya, land is the basic means of production. The landscape of the Chaco stands in stark contrast to that of the mountains and valleys of Iruya. So it should come as little surprise that the beliefs and values that the Wichí hold of their landscape offer a similar contrast to those of the Kolla. Where the Kolla measure land in small increments of fractions of hectares, in Los Blancos land is measured by kilometers, by hundreds of hectares. But for the Wichí, the hectares themselves are of little consequence. What is important is that *here*, there is a grove of algarrobo trees, and *there*, there is a year-round source of water. For the Kolla, the land itself—the physical earth—is significant, personalized, and useful. The soil is rich and carefully tended. For the Wichí, in contrast, land itself has little material value. The soil is dry, almost sandy, and easily exhausted. Instead, the usefulness of land is as a container of resources.

While the Wichí do very little farming, they rely on access to land in order to hunt and gather, to cut wood for use or for sale, and to graze their animals. Every household employs a diversified strategy that utilizes nearly all of the natural resources available in the area—water for drinking, an amazing variety of plants and animals for consumption, shade for shelter. The resources of the *monte*—the undomesticated space that surrounds the small villages—are essential to daily subsistence.

Natural Resources

Alfonso, a middle-aged community leader from Los Blancos, noted, "The land is very important. Without land, we cannot live." But it is not the land itself, as it is in Iruya, that is significant to the Wichí, in their daily lives or in their cosmology. Instead, it is the wild resources that the land contains. At a meeting of representatives from a number of communities, Alfonso addressed this issue:

> We have to think about our natural resources, the resources that we have in this zone. What you see in the countryside, what is used. We use wood, for example. And this is our life. We have to look together to see what our problems are. We have to ask, what is there, what is no longer there. The elders have a lot to tell us about nature. Our race, our Wichí people, is always growing in number. And we always use all the resources, the wood, the rivers. This is the life of indigenous people.

Researchers working in Wichí communities agree that the use of natural resources is central to Wichí subsistence. Carrasco and Briones (1996, 199) cite an unpublished study that documents the use of numerous and varied resources: at least twenty-eight kinds of mammals, ten reptiles, seventeen birds, twenty-one species of fish, twenty types of honey, more than seventy wild plants, and twelve cultivated plants indigenous to the region.[8] The great variety of plants and animals used has provided a varied and rich diet, and it also protects the Wichí from risk when any one resource is scarce. While some species are clearly preferred over others, and form a more basic part of the Wichí diet, the great variety of species that *could* be used ensures a source of food and materials when preferred species are unavailable.

The use of an incredible range of species is dependent on a vast store of knowledge about the properties of plants and animals and the uses to which they can be put. While much knowledge may have been lost as a result of a decline in hunting and gathering practices, the Wichí retain an impressive knowledge of native species. For example, Joaquím, a man who prides himself on his knowledge of hunting and gathering, took me for a short walk around the village of Kayip, a tour which took no more than an hour and covered less than 3 kilometers. He pointed out at least twenty different kinds of plants that comprise basic elements of daily subsistence. Most are used for food, while others are used for the raw materials for housing and crafts. Many plant varieties have more than one use; one type of *chaguar*, a spiny succulent, is valued both for the fruit it produces every year and for its spiky leaves, which are made into string that is used in a number of items such as carrying sacks and previously, clothing. Over a larger area, as well, there is a detailed knowledge of resources that are available in terms of plants and water, as well as the range and migration routes of many animals. This knowledge may extend over many kilometers.

For all that the Wichí, unlike the Kolla, utilize large expanses of land, their knowledge of their territory is no less intimate. This knowledge extends to both a local area where resources are used more intensively, and a larger area where resources may be used more infrequently, but are nonetheless important. This landscape is mapped in the collective imaginary, with locations having cultural and material significance.

> All of the places, with their names in our language . . . are important to us. They are important because they are places where we live or where we have lived; they are places where we travel to take advantage of the things that we find there; they are also places that speak to us of our history. The names have significance—they tell us of the plants, of the animals, of the soils, of the waters or of something that happened in that place. (Letter from Wichí community of Lote 55 to government officials, cited in full in Carrasco and Briones 1996, 215)

Locations are marked with names that both evoke and reflect knowledge of how resources are distributed over space, as well as marking cultural history. For the Wichí, the practice of hunting and gathering is

> something more than a form of subsistence that is adapted to environmental conditions. The[ir] territory is the sociocultural space where they produce and reproduce the resources that are vital for their material and symbolic existence. [It is] a complex space where they create techno-environmental notions that yield information about the locations where resources and memories of historical accounts are found, of a time which, even though it has past, continues to be in use today (Carrasco and Briones 1996, 199)

The Spiritual Landscape

Keith Basso, in a study of place names among the Western Apache of North America, notes that place names serve as linguistic symbols which are highly evocative (1988, 103). Basso (1988) considers the relationship between mythological space, the place names that refer to myths, and the ways in which people make sense of the natural or physical environment. He notes that it is difficult to understand a "foreign" environment, one which one is not used to, especially without a cultural filter (1988, 100). In such a situation, one lacks the ability to makes sense of the environment and its significance, as one would be unable to make sense of a foreign language. "Features of the local landscape, no less than utterances exchanged in forms of daily discourse, acquire value and significance by virtue of the ideational systems with which they are apprehended and construed" (1988, 100). Landscape is thus highly symbolic, an instrument of thought and behavior. For the Wichí, place names also powerfully evoke historical and mythological events. Wichí place names refer to tragic or comic incidents, often generations previously; they refer to the physical characteristics of a place, serving as a mnemonic; they mark the passing of individuals and villages.[9]

In traditional Wichí mythology, described by Niels Fock,

> the Chaco perception of the landscape [is as] an eternity, a canvas wiped clean each time the rivers overflow across the plain. (1982, 28)

According to Fock, this plain represents cultural space, the dimension of daily life and mythology. In the "cultural plain," time and space are marked by "ecological periodicity": times of shortages and plenty and the corresponding movement of the people between rivers and inland spaces (1982, 28). In marked contrast to this cultural space is the wilderness, a dimension that corresponds to the underworld. "Should one stray from known routes out into the wilderness, one might come face to face with Lawo [the god of the woods and rivers, considered extremely dangerous]" (Fock 1982, 28). The wilderness "clearly belongs to nature and is therefore uncontrollable and dangerous. From it pestilence comes whispering; under it live the dead, returned to nature" (1982, 28). The mythic landscape is divided into above ground, corresponding to the material world, and below ground, the world of the dead. The dead do not live on as spirits, but are consigned to the underworld. "Survivors deeply mourn a death for a short period; wailing, they walk up and down the paths used by the deceased and destroy his property until, a mere week later, he is never mentioned again by name" (Fock 1982, 28).

For the Wichí in the communities around Los Blancos, the spiritual landscape described by Fock has been eroded by Christian missionization. Gods that formerly held a place in the Wichí pantheon, both benign and destructive, are generally considered to be evil, demonic spirits that formerly held the Wichí within their power. The conversion of the people to Christianity released them from the power that the evil spirits formerly had over them. Questions that I posed about the traditional gods were generally met with a blanket condemnation, and few in the communities had more than a passing familiarity with traditional myths. The bipartite landscape described by Fock has been replaced with a Christian cosmovision of earth as an intermediary space between Heaven and Hell.

Abundance and Scarcity

The Wichís' traditional system of ecological management tended to preserve a equilibrium in the natural environment. The director of Fundapaz describes this pattern of resource use:

> I have argued with people, some whom had a lot of knowledge about the culture, that the Wichí aren't conservationists. These people say that they are, that they used to live in harmony with nature. But I see them more as predators. It is true, that there used to be more of a balance, but it was because they were nomadic. They could move to a new area, and the old area could recover. But within an area, they use everything. They don't leave anything at all. When they get honey, for example, they will take all of it, the whole panel. They sometimes cut down the tree [to get the honey]. If they find a nest, they take all the eggs, they don't leave any. It's just that before, the territory was big, and they were nomadic. Now that they are settled, it is different, but they still have the same customs.

Historically, low population density and the nomadism of bands contributed to preserving an equilibrium of reproduction of useful species—and, as noted in the study cited above, there are very few species that are not put to some use. When a useful resource was encountered, it was maximally exploited. However, the localized maximization of resource use may be consistent with an ethic of resource management, as long as social and cultural mechanisms prevent the long-term overexploitation of resources. In some hunting societies, switching hunting from one species to another, as species are perceived to decline in numbers, is a strategy used to maximize resources over the long term (see Feit 1973, 1978). Under precontact conditions, such strategies may have enabled the Wichí to "use up" a resource in one location, maximizing their short-term harvest, while also optimizing long-term resource use. With competition from *criollos* and territorial dispossession, however, such strategies have been rendered ineffective.

Maximizing resource use over the short term was not a careless strategy, but a practice founded in the beliefs and values of the Wichí. Hunting and gathering is not based on an ethic of the production and stockpiling of resources. Basic necessities do not have to be produced, but found—things exist, and the work of people is to look for them (Von Bremen 1987, 12). One component of this worldview is the idea that resources are plentiful. Because the Wichí are able to use so many of the species that live in the monte, there is nearly always something available. And when there is not, a nomadic people simply move to where there are more resources.[10] The year itself is divided into several parts based on the availability of important resources: "the forest's blooming" (*tawoy hatlay*) in August, "the ripening of fruit" (*lecheniyo*) in November, "the end of the algarrobo harvest" (*nohhuaikyuk*) in December, "the blossoming of the quebracho tree" (*kyethl kyukthlaw*) in February, and the season when there is "nothing to eat" (*lopetl*) from April until September (Fock 1982, 9).[11] While there may be shortages and crises, they are viewed by the Wichí, for the most part, as phenomena that are natural, periodic, and episodic. The redistribution of goods is geared to the short-term satisfaction of needs, with little long-term planning or storage. When short-term needs can no longer be met in a particular area, the group moves on.

The objective of the traditional Wichí economy is not to transform nature, but to take advantage of plentiful resources. In the Wichí worldview, people do not dominate nature. Instead, what is needed is knowledge of the techniques to access resources. In the past, magical practices were also considered important to success. The power, character, and/or force of the individual constituted an important element of their magical power (Von Bremen 1987, 13). Individuals learn through the example of elders and through the accumulation of experience, and the knowledge that a person possesses is one of his or her most valued qualities. When describing someone, the Wichí frequently begin by listing his or her skills and knowledge: "My mother knew how to make a skirt from *chaguar*, she knew how to make water jugs, and where to find the clay." Through increasing one's power, knowledge, and skills, one does not need to dominate or transform the natural world, but instead is better able to take advantage of the resources that are available.

Ecological Degradation

Until the introduction of herd animals and the settlement of the Wichí into permanent villages, the indigenous use of resources was eminently sustainable, in part because they utilized such a wide variety of species. Traditional practices of hunting and gathering ensured the reproduction of resources and the maintenance of an equilibrium in the environment. Now, however, permanent settlements and the presence in the region of herd animals have created grave ecological difficulties for the sustainability of Wichí ecological management.

Permanent settlements have created a situation in which the most valued species have been overutilized within a small radius, often to the point of their elimination. The same phenomena may also have occurred with species which are naturally uncommon, but are valued for a specific use. Formerly, the resources of one area were allowed to regenerate as bands moved through a zone. Because the population density remained low, an equilibrium was established that preserved useful species. As these plants or animals were subjected to a more intensive pattern of use, they lost their resilience and ability to reproduce. At the same time, herd animals have contributed to the degradation of resources through their consumption of young delicate plants. Moreover, cattle, in particular, trample and compact the soil, making it less hospitable to plant life and contributing significantly to erosion. Traveling through the monte, it is easy to identify areas of higher concentrations of cattle, as well as the zones surrounding settlements, by the desertification that has occurred. In such areas, there is no plant life at all over much of the ground, while in other areas there are pockets of undesirable plants, especially cacti, which have little consumption value for either humans or animals.

Over the long term, habitat degradation has decreased the number of animal species available locally. Most of the largest animals have been much reduced in numbers over the last twenty or thirty years. Increased population, the use of rifles and shotguns, and the addition of *criollo* hunters have all contributed to this reduction.[12] Some species, such as the grey fox, have been hunted virtually to extinction. In a case of the global market and fashion industry having a local impact, the fox was hunted not for food, but to sell its fur, which for a short time was a valuable international commodity.[13] Wichí hunters must travel increasingly long distances in order to encounter their prey—requiring them to cross more property boundaries.

Older Wichí, as well as older *criollo* settlers, describe a landscape that bears little resemblance to the monte around Los Blancos today. In the past, they say, there were large open expanses of grasses. Such grasslands provided a habitat for numerous animals and birds. The grasslands were one of the earliest casualties of cattle, and persist only in a few isolated pockets. With the loss of habitat, many birds and mammals are much more rare in the region, if not completely gone. The elders also note that there were more, and larger, trees. Many of these were cut down to provide materials for the construction of the railroad, and later to be sold for timber. Of particular concern to the Wichí is the decreasing number of algarrobo trees. Algarrobo provide carob beans, the staple of the Wichí diet and one of the few resources that is stockpiled at the time of harvest to last nearly the entire year. The trees are nearly sacred and the Wichí never willingly cut them down. Algarrobo "gives life, as much to animals as to people." The location of algarrobo groves is said to mark areas that are fertile, areas where water rises close to the ground. On the mental maps that the Wichí create of their territory, the location of algarrobo groves, and even individual trees, is one of the most important geographical markers.

Despite the lamentations of some that the natural environment is not as plentiful as it used to be, ecological conservation is not a pressing concern in Wichí communities near Los Blancos.[14] Most community leaders are interested in finding new ways to use the resources available to them. In some of the communities, the prospect of gaining legal title to their lands presents new opportunities for the utilization of the natural environment. For example, the Wichí presently are not permitted to conduct logging on the lands that they are claiming, which are now owned by the state. Instead, the right to harvest lumber is sold to commercial loggers, who contract the Wichí as laborers at a much lower price. The wood is still being cut on the land, but the Wichí receive only a small fraction of its value. At least three factors are at work in such a case against ecological conservation and a more sustainable use of resources. First, the current practices of the Wichí tend towards short-term maximization of resource use. Strategies that may once have encouraged long-term sustainability of hunting and gathering have been rendered unworkable by sedentarization and population growth. Second, the perilous economic situation of the Wichí communities means that the pressure to meet immediate subsistence needs mitigates against any conservation concerns. Conditions of poverty encourage the overuse of resources to enable short-term survival. And third, the Wichí consider that the resources are already being exploited, with others gaining the benefit. In such circumstances, they consider themselves better able to manage the extraction of a given resource than their *criollo* neighbors or outsiders granted a permit by the government. Outsiders have little or no regard for indigenous systems of resource management. The Wichí find themselves facing a very real "tragedy of the commons," where the land that they claim is being exploited by others with no long-term stake in the region. Pragmatically, they realize that if they aren't the ones to cut down the trees, others will do it for them, and they will see none of the slim benefits that this exploitation offers.

"Using" Land

Since *criollo* settlers first arrived in the western Chaco, there have been conflicts over land. A former teacher in Los Blancos, an educated woman of about fifty, described her impression of this historical conflict:

> When I was studying to be a teacher, we had to read a lot of history. There was one book that I read that really made an impression on me, about the history of the region and the colonization of this area. There were a lot of problems between the *criollos* who came to settle here and the indigenous people. They didn't live like they do now, in villages. They moved all over, and *they thought all this land was theirs*. They were even cannibals. So when the *criollos* came, there were a lot of problems, conflicts. [Emphasis added]

Her lurid tale of cannibalism notwithstanding, her attitude towards the indigenous claim for land typifies the point of view of the *criollos*: the Wichí have the belief that the land is theirs, a belief that, to the majority of the *criollos*, is nearly incomprehensible. The ongoing conflict between the Wichí and the *criollo* settlers over land rights remains one of the most serious obstacles to creating secure land rights in the region. It is based in essentially different ideas about what land is for and what constitutes legitimate "use" of land.

The *criollos* living near Los Blancos now are second or third generation settlers. Their parents and grandparents arrived with the advent of the railroad. For the most part, these were poor families, recruited from other parts of Argentina by a government eager to establish its claim to a contested border region. A few others, families which continue to comprise the local elite, arrived as merchants and labor contractors. In exchange for their presence, as Argentine citizens, in the unwelcoming Chaco, the settlers were promised free land on which they could build their homes and farms. In fact, legal titles never emerged, and most of the settlers, like the Wichí, established their homesteads on land that technically belonged to the government.[15]

When the settlers arrived, they eagerly went about reproducing the kinds of farms and ranches that existed in the southern areas that they were from. Cattle, goats, and sheep were introduced. Small farmsteads were laboriously carved out of the unforgiving natural environment. Most of the farmers, with little capital and unproductive land, were able to create small marginally self-sufficient households. Today, wealth among *criollo* farmers can be measured only in relative terms. The most prosperous households may own a herd of one or two hundred cattle. No other crop or animal produces any significant surplus, and even the cattle have a fairly low market value compared to those raised in more lush environs. Given such marginal conditions, the *criollo* culture places a high value on creating and maintaining small, independent ranches modeled after the kinds of farm enterprises that exist in more productive regions.

Criollo homesteads mark a use of space that is entirely different from the ways in which the Wichí use the environment. A *criollo* home exists in a domesticated space, one where the boundaries between farm and monte are carefully established and maintained. A typical rural household occupies two or three small adobe buildings in the center of a completely denuded patio. The center of this patio is covered by a thatch awning, creating an outdoor living space that is protected from the hot sun in the dry season and from the worst of the rains in the wet season. The patio is the center of domestic life. Families cook, eat, and sleep on the patio, using the house itself more as storage space than as living space. The buildings and patio are surrounded by a sturdy fence, usually constructed of intertwined thorny branches that keep animals out. A large area around the outside of the fence is usually also bare of the plants of the monte, stripped by domestic animals that are brought in at night. Outside of the fence, there is a paddock for goats and sheep, also ringed by a fence. Another pen, where cattle are kept during the dry season, is surrounded by a post and beam fence. If the family is fortunate to have an artificial pond, it is usually located within sight of the house compound and ringed by a thick fence with a small gate. At a distance of several hundred meters, the monte resumes. The area of the monte immediately surrounding the farmstead is used to graze goats and sheep. Small garden plots, surrounded by thorny fences, are located just within the edge of the monte, where shade protects the plants.

Criollo households are visibly and tangibly domesticated space. The boundary between the monte and the house is clear. It is evident to the *criollos* that the household is "using" space even in the monte. Cattle and goats, turned loose to graze in the monte, are understood to need a certain area in order to forage successfully.

Wichí households and villages, in contrast, do not create such clearly delineated boundaries between monte and house. Small houses are usually made of thatch, rather than adobe, which blends visually into the monte that approaches close to the house. Small areas around the house may be bare of ground cover, but only incidentally as a result of increased foot traffic. There is no deliberate effort to keep a patio area clear of plants. Fences are built around gardens and animal pens, but there are only rarely fences around the houses themselves. Most houses are built close to or under trees which provide shelter. Most notably, the Wichí houses are not dispersed on separate ranches, like the *criollos*, but cluster in small villages.

Despite the absence of clear land titles, the *criollo* settlers have established boundaries of usufruct, and families are considered to have *de facto* ownership of large areas, usually two hundred or more hectares, around their homestead. When asked to map their landholdings, *criollo* men could clearly delineate their property boundaries and those of their neighbors. However, these boundaries, while recognized and accepted by settlers and their neighbors, are permeable. Many settlers, perhaps even most *criollo* households, use land in one way or another that either belongs to someone else or is considered to be public land. Most obviously, animals are allowed to roam freely and cross unfenced boundaries. But some households have their house on land that is considered to belong to someone else, while others have their well or pond outside of their own boundaries. At present, such arrangements are private agreements between neighbors, and only rarely present problems. However, when private land rights are established by the government (see chapter 6), such informal arrangements may be an increasing source of conflict.

A permeability of property boundaries also exists between the settlers and neighboring Wichí villages. *Criollos* and their animals frequently use land claimed by the Wichí to obtain one of their most important resources—good grazing. The Wichí, in turn, enter *criollo* ranches to gather algarroba and to hunt. This arrangement has led to a tacit compromise: the Wichí do not bother the cattle that enter land they view as theirs, and the *criollos* allow the Wichí to use and cross their land. Most of the time, this somewhat tenuous relationship allows the Wichí and the *criollos* to both get what they need from the monte. Occasionally, however, there are conflicts, particularly over water, which is a scarce and important resource for both communities.

Uneasy Neighbors

The primary source of tension between the *criollo* settlers and the Wichí is their differing concepts and practices of land use. The Wichí recognize that their ways of using land are not valued or understood by the *criollos* or even by the larger society. In a petition to the government, a group of Wichí communities near the Pilcomayo state:

> The *criollos* do not understand [us] and they criticize us, saying that we are lazy and we do not know how to work. But they do not understand that we work in a different way. So they ask, "Why do the indigenous people want land if they do not have cows? Maybe they want to eat it." The truth is that we are part of the land. We have always lived here, since the beginning. When God made the world he put us on this land. . . . Like the trees, we are born of this land. The land belongs to us because we belong to the land. (Letter from caciques and representatives of the communities of Lot 55 to the provincial government of Salta, cited in Carrasco and Briones 1996, pp. 214-229)

In this statement, the Wichí are clearly basing their claim to land not on the productive use that they make of it, but on their relationship to the land itself, which they view as unique. They claim a spiritual relationship to their territory, which they recognize is not viewed as valid by *criollos* who have opposing claims and interests.

From the point of view of the *criollos*, the Wichí do not make productive use of land. While they understand that the Wichí hunt, for the *criollos* hunting is a form of sport or recreation rather than an important subsistence strategy; it does not comprise work that requires land. Because the Wichí have few animals, and do not make large farm or garden plots, there is a persistent belief among the *criollos* that the Wichí do not "use" land at all.

The differences in ideas about land use are rooted in conceptions of property. The Wichí do not have a belief in private property, and view the elements of the natural world as inalienable. In the same letter, the caciques go on to argue that the *criollos*

> are not owners of the monte and of the river. They did not plant the trees; they do not raise the bees; the animals of the monte are not theirs. The things that we take from the monte are not owned by any man. God is their owner. (Letter from caciques and representatives of the communities of Lot 55 to the provincial government of Salta, Carrasco and Briones 1996, p. 226)

From the perspective of the Wichí, the encroachment of the *criollos'* herd animals is seen as an increasing problem. The same document cited above notes that there have been considerable ecological changes, most notably the loss of open grasslands. This destruction is blamed on cattle and has forced the community to change its subsistence practices. "We have to travel far to where we can gather, to where there are no *criollos*" (Letter from caciques and representatives of the communities of Lot 55 to the provincial government of Salta, Carrasco and Briones 1996, p. 223). There is also concern expressed about the increased presence of fences and increased enforcement of private property boundaries, both practices which inhibit the ability of Wichí hunters to move freely through the monte. This restriction of movement presents a concrete barrier to pursuing subsistence practices such as hunting and gathering. For communities near Los Blancos, their access to the river is blocked in many areas by *criollo* farms bordering the Bermejo River, where fences are commonly erected to limit access. Although the communities do not make frequent use of riverine resources, because of the distance between them and the river, it does act as an important resource in the leanest time of the year. Perhaps more importantly, fences represent a symbolic loss of territory. The threat of exclusion is a perceived danger to the communities and is something that they fear will occur as land is increasingly privatized. In their letter to the government, the caciques express this fear: "The fences of the *criollos* do not serve to close in their cattle, but to close in us" (Letter from caciques and representatives of the communities of Lot 55 to the provincial government of Salta, Carrasco and Briones 1996, p. 225).

Historically, the relationship between the *criollos* and the Wichí has been marked by violence and bloodshed. The single most important cause of this conflict has been the battle over land. A Wichí leader in Kayip recounted:

> At first, the whites came. They said that they had to kill everyone, for the land. . . . The whites thought that they would come and take all of this land. That they would kill all of the Wichí. I tell you that the Wichí were desperate because of this. . . . Our ancestors shed their blood for this land. The blood ran like water.

Suspicion and fear persists on both sides. In the Pilcomayo region, violence continues to be a problem: "In the past, if someone disappeared in the monte our ancestors blamed a tiger. Now, if one of us disappears, we think that it is the *criollos*. If we go out [into the monte], we must go in groups of two or three" (Letter from caciques and representatives of the communities of Lot 55 to the provincial government of Salta, Carrasco and Briones 1996, p. 226). Near Los Blancos, overt violence is not as common, although not eliminated.[16]

In many ways, the relationship between the Wichí and the *criollos* is analogous to a study of aboriginal communities in northern Australia by Howard Morphy (1993). In the region of Morphy's study, landscape is an area of conflict between the aboriginal people and European settlers. The European settlers, like the *criollos* in the Chaco, denied the previous history of the land, as settlers moved into what they perceived and depicted as an "unused" environment (1993, 206). Morphy argues that the concept of landscape provides a discursive frame for metaphors employed in the struggle over land titles (1993, 205). The contested region is symbolic to the Europeans as representing the region's "potential" value, future value as grazing land (1993, 210-215). The early European outposts took the form of cattle stations, which Morphy describes as "a mode of colonization and expropriation, rather than viable business enterprises" (1993, 215). In fact, the early European settlers, again like the *criollos*, were marginal members of their own society, as were the outposts themselves, which received few government services and were ultimately unprofitable (1993, 215-216).

The creation of a cattle range in the region involved both physical and conceptual transformations of the land. The settlers brought with them their own experience of other landscapes that conditioned their implicit ideas of landscape. In northern Australia, argues Morphy, the European and aboriginal people "have coexisted and interacted in the region over a long period of time, yet in some respects it can almost seem as though they occupied different conceptual space/times" (1993, 207). Morphy briefly outlines how the aboriginal cosmology holds that features of the landscape have been shaped by ancestral beings who also left spiritual forces which are embodied in the land forms (1993, 232). Links between the present and the past, both mythical and historical, are continually reforged, with the landscape serving as a mnemonic device (1993, 234).

For the Aborigines, "the colonial process ended up structuring the Aboriginal population to fit into the landscape as it had been transformed by European settlement and gave the people no option but to articulate with the life of the cattle stations" (1993, 237). The local group, which had formerly occupied a large area, became centered on a much smaller area. In this process, they lost some of the intensity of knowledge associated with a larger area, while at the same time intensifying their connections with the smaller area adjacent to the cattle station (1993, 237), in a process of transformation of indigenous knowledge. This process was amplified by the fact that the stations were located in areas that were already ecologically and geographically apt for use, where there was already a concentrated aboriginal population. Thus, as land claims issues arose in the early 1980s, the Aborigines and Europeans had attachments to the same places (1993, 239). The European settlers assigned value to land based on its historical significance, as a site of early colonization, and economic potential, while for the Aborigines, the landscape has been mythically transformed, and places have spiritual significance, as well as holding resources of economic value.

Similarly, white settlers in the Chaco, encouraged by the government, saw the landscape of Los Blancos as an empty space awaiting colonization. Its potentiality lies in its ability to be divided into farms and ranches. Their homesteads and farms are carved out of the monte, representing a domesticated space in the midst a rather barren wild landscape which is scrupulously held back. For the Wichí, the same monte represents a fertile, territory. It is not barren or inhospitable; its plants and animals are useful to those who possess the knowledge and luck to find them. It is not empty, but mapped and familiar. However, the Wichís' occupation of the monte has come to be structured by the colonial process and contemporary institutions of landownership.

Conclusion

Both the Wichí and the Kolla have elaborate cosmological systems that sustain a relationship between the land and the spiritual and physical well-being of the people who occupy it. Situated within their cosmologies are systems of ecological management that represent a systematic understanding of the ways that the natural world functions and the role of humans in this functioning. The arrival of outsiders and the introduction of European systems of land tenure disrupted these indigenous systems, rendering them if not ineffective, then impotent in the face of legal and actual changes in the environment. In contrast to these indigenous understandings of landscape, which were created and re-created *in situ*, the cosmology of later settlers, the *criollos* in Los Blancos and capitalist land owners in Iruya, was derived from another set of ecological systems, and like the cattle ranchers of Australia, they imposed it on the local landscape in a process of dramatic transformation. In both cases, the cosmology that explained the role of humans in the world and provided a framework for the understanding of the local environment was unavoidably and irreversibly altered.

Colin Scott argues that indigenous ecological knowledge is gaining a more powerful voice in response to international environmental concerns and to aboriginal demands to directly manage environmental resources within or affecting their lands (1996, 69). In the Cree case offered by Scott, the jurisdiction over such resources is contested, and both "science" and indigenous knowledge are used to attack and defend Cree opposition to development projects. In Argentina, indigenous ecological knowledge has not yet come into its own as a motivating political force. However, this line of argument has begun to appear as another justification for indigenous land claims. In a political meeting in Colanzulí, one of the small villages near Iruya, a community leader seized upon a statement made by Menem:

> Finca Santiago is a reflection of the world. We have defended the earth, the air, the water. President Menem said, "The whites came as destroyers. Now we realize that the Indians were better caretakers than we were."

In a case study of Australian aborigines, Kenneth Maddock (1991) examines the emergence of a discourse of sacred space in Australian land claims. Maddock argues that while there has been a decline of the importance of religion in the West, there has at the same time been increased interest in "re-evaluating" Australian aboriginal culture as spiritual, especially in the relationship between society and the land (1991, 213-214). This is an argument that could also be made for North and South America, where a fascination with indigenous spirituality has popular currency.

Since the late 1960s, Maddock notes an increased use of the idea of sacred sites in Australia, beyond the anthropological literature, which he argues is a reflection of concern for aboriginal rights and their cultural survival (1991, 220). As the aboriginal rights movement gained momentum, anthropologists began to act as mediators between the aborigines and the legal system, during the 1970s (1991, 223). Maddock traces the entry of the idea of sacred sites in the legal system as it was adopted from the anthropological literature (1991, 223-226). Once the idea of sacred sites passed into the legal system, however, anthropologists lost control of the discourse that defined the concept of sacred site (1991, 226). Similarly, as the idea passed into popular usage in the 1980s, lawyers also lost control (1991, 227). The consequence of the idea of sacred sites, and their recognition, "both spiritualizes and domesticates the environment, including the cultural as well as the physical environment" (Maddock 1991, 231).

Unfortunately, Maddock (1991, 231) does not address the most interesting question that he says this analysis raises: why did the "sacred" come to be associated so closely with land, rather than other aspects of social organization which were as closely related to aboriginal cosmology? While he claims not to address this, one implicit answer may be in the very advocacy of native rights that he discusses. As land is understood as the basis for cultural and economic survival, the ability to define that land as sacred provides a key discursive and moral tool. If the land is inherently linked to cosmology, in an explicit way, the appropriation of that land becomes a form of cultural violence that the post-colonial era finds hard to defend. Ultimately, this identification of land rights with identity confers some moral power, but it also may leave indigenous peoples in constricted spaces.

Now, as both the Kolla and the Wichí mobilize to claim legal title to land that they consider theirs, their cosmology and its relationship to the natural world is beginning to come to the forefront. In the case of the Kolla, as the process of land reclamation begins, the people of Iruya have been motivated by two factors. The first is their material ties to the land, as the basic resource of subsistence production. Secondly, the Kolla people do have strong emotional ties to the local landscape. However, in making a claim that the government finds itself unable to deny, it is the second factor, based in indigenous cosmology, which gives the Kolla priority over poor white Argentines, who also rely on land for their subsistence.

In the letter to government officials by the caciques of Lot 55 quoted earlier, Wichí leaders have a vested interest in convincing government officials that they do have a unique and irrefutable claim to land, and as such, they are employing a language and metaphors that they have found reason to believe may be successful. Basing land claims on spiritual ties to the land is a tactic that has been used with great success in other cases of indigenous rights worldwide, and the Wichí are aware of this. This is not to say that the strong cosmological and emotional ties of the Wichí to the land are not true or are less valid, nor would I suggest that to be true in other cases. However, indigenous groups in Argentina, as elsewhere, have learned to base their claims on arguments that have some currency and efficacy in a national and international context of indigenous rights that recognizes such claims as having priority over simple arguments of economic necessity, which may be no less true or important for people in their daily lives.

Another base for land claims that both groups have found resonates with both their own experience and the sympathy of outsiders is the invocation of ancestors and their struggle to maintain their land and culture. In a political meeting in Los Blancos attended by the province's governor, one of the most articulate and thoughtful of the Wichí leaders reminded the crowd of the historical ties of his people with the land that they were claiming: "This is the land of our ancestors. Our ancestors lie below this earth. Now we are standing here with our foot atop this land." The claim to ancestral land was used by the Wichí as one factor to prioritize their needs over those of the *criollos*. Another leader argued: "The *criollos* want titles too. But the law says that the Wichí are more entitled to land titles. Because they were from this land. And we have to remember that our ancestors lost their blood like water for this land." In fact, the battles referred to by this speaker were not for land rights as they are now understood by the Wichí. But the fact of conflict between the indigenous people and early settlers is invoked and re-created as a representation of the struggle over land.

Because the idea of an indigenous right to land based on cosmology and the spiritual relationship of an indigenous people with its territory finds sympathy in an international discourse of human rights, it has been used to bolster indigenous claims to land in the province of Salta. Arguing that the Kolla and Wichí employ cosmological concerns as a strategy in their land claim struggle is not to argue in any way that individuals in these communities do not have ideas about the relationship between humans and the natural environment that are very different from those of individuals in the dominant culture, nor is it intended to diminish the important role that ideas of nature and its spiritual qualities play in indigenous cultures. The very fact that these arguments are able to be marshaled as an effective strategy points to their salience in local culture.

The understandings of the natural world that were an intrinsic part of indigenous, pre-Conquest cosmologies have been irrevocably altered as a result of changes introduced by colonialism. Transformations in systems of land tenure have alienated indigenous peoples from their land; new technologies have altered the ways in which people interact with nature; Christianity, along with other colonizing agents, has introduced and inculcated an entirely different framework for understanding the role of humans in the world. Clearly, indigenous cosmologies have undergone radical change as well. In many ways, systems of native ecological beliefs and knowledge have lost their salience, and in some regions they are vanishing altogether as unique forms of being and knowing. As this body of knowledge and belief has been seized upon as tool for political change, however, it may be reinvented and reenergized as a focal point of indigenous culture. Indigenous ecological knowledge, embedded in and intimately part of spiritual beliefs about the natural world, is being re-created and invested with new meaning. It is emerging as a focal point for indigenous identity, identities that set the Kolla and the Wichí apart from other poor rural Argentines in their efforts to claim land.

Notes:

1. Scott borrows the term "root metaphor" from the work of Pepper (1942) and Ortner (1973) to describe a metaphor that is "pervasive in a knowledge discourse."
2. One of these fincas, where San Isidro and a few smaller villages are located, has already been successfully reclaimed by local farmers.
3. Crops were often grown even on fairly steep hillsides. The largest, flattest tract of land in each tiny interior village was generally reserved for the soccer field, a social space seen as vital.
4. Vicuñas are a protected species, and hunting them is illegal and at the present time uncommon, as they are scarce.
5. The Iruya river is part of the Bermejo basin that eventually drains into the River Plate, which empties into the Atlantic at Buenos Aires. Small mountain farmers are regularly, if unfairly, blamed for silt problems further down river (see Reboratti 1996).
6. Because of my work with OCLADE, I may have been seen as somehow connected to the Catholic Church, heightening people's reluctance to discuss other spiritual practices with me.
7. *Duende* is best translated as "dwarf" or "gnome." Here, the word is used to refer to a similar earth-dwelling spirit, but without the cheerful or diminutive aspects of that those terms may convey in English.
8. This study, which is unpublished and for which Carrasco and Briones do not provide a full citation, was conducted by Dr. Cristobal Wallis and other researchers in a number of communities along the Pilcomayo River. I believe that a similar study in the region where I worked would yield comparable results, although there may be some differences in the exact species utilized due to ecological variation between the two regions.
9. An extensive mapping project was carried out in the Pilcomayo region in 1990-1991 that documented thousands of place names in that area.
10. Whether hunters and gatherers live in conditions of chronic scarcity or have a relatively easy time meeting their subsistence needs is a question of much debate in the anthropological literature (see, for example, Lee 1993 and Wilmsen 1989).

11. The identification of seasons may vary according to region or dialect. A report of Lhaka Honhat, a Wichí organization in the Pilcomayo region, identifies the seasons as: *chelchup* ("flowering of the *quebracho colorado*"), *fwiyettilh* ("time of cold"), *yaychup* ("when there is fruit"), and *inawop* ("when the trees flower") (Lhaka Honhat 1995, 21).
12. The *criollo* settlers of the region use many fewer species than do the Wichí. While hunting is not a part of their normal subsistence strategy, it is enjoyed as a sport by many men. They prefer the largest mammals, such as the small deer that are common in the region, and *souri*, a large flightless bird, as well as armadillos, which are considered a delicacy by both Wichí and *criollos*.
13. Now that fox fur has passed from fashion demand, there is some indication that the fox population is starting to make a comeback.
14. There is some indication that conservation is an issue in other Wichí communities, especially those near the Pilcomayo (Lhaka Honhat 1995, 17-23; Wallis, personal communication). The reasons for the difference in ecological attitudes present a compelling issue for future research.
15. Until the recent land reform described in the next chapter, only five *criollo* families owned land, out of perhaps five hundred families in the region. Most of those who purchased land legally were members of the merchant elite.
16. There is a fear of entering the *criollo* community at night. I was not allowed by my Wichí hosts in Kayip to go to the *criollo* village alone at night, and was told that it wasn't safe. In another incident my husband and I were run off a homestead that we accidentally passed too closely at night by a farmer who clearly thought we were Wichí.

Chapter 6: Claiming Property in Two Communities

> If an indigenous person does not have land, his culture dies. We want our territory in order to live our communal lifestyle that they have been trying to destroy for the last five hundred years, in order to impose an individualistic lifestyle on us. . . . This is our situation with regard to land: we want the land to continue living with our customs and economic organization. We have an alternative economy that permits us, a little, a certain freedom from the system and from the market. We want the land to live, and not to accumulate.
>
> José Maurín, Kolla, Jujuy[1]

In 1996-1997, a process of "repatriation" of land to indigenous communities was taking place in the province of Salta. The Argentine constitution, revised in 1994, contained a provision (Article 75, Clause 17) that specifically granted indigenous communities rights to lands which they "traditionally occupied." The constitutional clause was just one step in an ongoing struggle by native communities to retain some rights over territories that they claimed (see Nahuel 2001). Land claims were an active issue in both Iruya and Los Blancos, and both OCLADE and Fundapaz played a key role in the land claims of the communities where they were working. The contentious issue of land repatriation brings to the forefront some of the most interesting issues in the relationships between the communities and the NGOs.

This chapter considers recent land claims made in both Kolla and Wichí communities. It addresses the ways in which the rights of indigenous peoples have been regarded in law and in fact as distinct from those of other poor rural populations. In many ways, the political and ethnic situation in Argentina is more comparable to cases in North America and Australia than it is to the rest of Latin America, in that the national population is predominantly of European descent, and indigenous groups are clearly differentiated as such (see, for example, Asch 1989; Scott 1988; Morphy 1993; McIntosh 2000). In both of the case studies presented here, land was successfully claimed after many years of political struggle by the communities. Also in both cases, the NGO in the community was highly involved in this process, in both the initiation of claims and the long legal and political negotiations involved.

In order to situate the current land claims in their historical context, I begin this chapter with a history of patterns of land tenure in Argentina. Then, because the land claims are based on the communities' status as indigenous, I consider how Argentina has dealt with its indigenous population, in law and in fact, and look at how the government was involved in the process of land repatriation. In the second part of the chapter, I turn to the case of the Finca Santiago in Iruya. Patterns of land tenure in the Andean highland of the finca have been based on the extraction of rent from the local population since the early colonial period. The efforts of local residents to reclaim the finca were initiated and supported by the Catholic Church, and by OCLADE, as part of its mission to liberate the oppressed. Yet, as I move on to look at Fundapaz and the Wichí, we see that Fundapaz took an even more active role in the actual process of claiming land. After a long and tiresome legal battle, the Wichí communities were granted titles in 1997, a process I consider in detail. In both communities, I briefly consider the kinds of changes implied by legal landownership, in the form of the communal titles that they received.

Argentina: Land and Peoples

Land Tenure in Argentina

A history of patterns of land tenure in Argentina is a tale of ongoing conflict. Unlike other parts of Latin America, the lands of what was to become Argentina were, at the time of the Conquest, sparsely settled. The native population was predominantly nomadic, the most important exception to this being the Kolla and other peoples of the northwest. As Argentina developed as a nation, control over national boundaries by the state entailed the elimination and marginalization of the indigenous tribes, rather than their incorporation as a laboring class as was common elsewhere such as Mesoamerica and the northern Andes.

The Tucumán region, extending through the northern and northeastern parts of modern Argentina, including what is now the province of Salta, was colonized in the second half of the sixteenth century. By 1681, seven hundred estates were established in Tucumán, most lying to the south of the city of Córdoba (Cushner 1983, 10). These settlements were important as a buffer zone between Spanish and Portuguese holdings. Spanish control was erratic and unstable, and in this early period, towns and *encomiendas* were founded but then were often deserted under pressure from hostile indigenous groups, in what Nicolas Cushner terms a "piecemeal approach to conquest" (Cushner 1983, 9). The region was sparsely settled, and land was so plentiful that neither a decrease in population nor resettlement was necessary to make land available for Spanish settlers.

As elsewhere in the New World, a tremendous decline in the native population occurred between the 1640s and 1700 (Cushner 1983, 83). By 1729, there were only twenty-eight native villages in the region; unlike the more densely populated areas in Peru, there was no systematic "reduction," or resettlement, of native communities. Rather, there was a tendency for the native population to intermix with Spanish settlements instead of forming separate communities

(Wood 1986, 56), particularly since Spanish settlements were placed to take advantage of existing indigenous population centers (Scobie 1971, 36).

In the central region of Argentina, the great pampas surrounding Buenos Aires, the lack of labor and great distance from trade centers in Peru made ranching more profitable than agriculture (Cushner 1983, 162). The dominance of the pastoral economy quickly came to shape patterns of landholding and class structure. The value of cattle, raised primarily for their hides, was so low that large estates were needed, since small holdings could not support enough cattle to make the operation sustainable. In the seventeenth century, the Crown began to sell large *estancias* (estates) in the countryside around the Rio de Plata. This created an ultra-wealthy landowning class whose members presided over their holdings as absentee farmers, living in Buenos Aires and visiting their rural properties only occasionally (Scobie 1971, 56-57). Gradually, the frontier of Spanish control expanded in towards the interior of the pampas, southward and westward of Buenos Aires, pushing nomadic indigenous groups into increasingly marginal areas and increasing armed conflicts. Over the course of the seventeenth and eighteenth centuries, pressure on land increased, and landownership became more important. Land prices gradually rose (Gibson 1966, 152-154), and "very little land ever reverted to Indian control" (Gibson 1966, 157).

The elite governments of the early nineteenth century implemented a number of policies that shaped the future of the Argentine economic and geographic landscape. Some of the leaders most central to the development of the Argentine state saw the nation's vast landscape as a threatening, barbarous emptiness (Shumway 1991, 133). Steps were taken to fill this "empty" landscape, to civilize the wilderness and (re)populate it with white colonists. One of the most prominent figures of this period, Domingo Faustino Sarmiento, believed that settlement was

> a necessary step in eradicating the nomadic life of the gauchos and Indians. . . . For Sarmiento and his generation, capitalist development would not only bring prosperity to the pampas; it would also end the 'barbarism' of the pampa's natural inhabitants. (Shumway 1991, 136)

Subjugating the Argentine "wilderness," including its "wild" native inhabitants, was seen as essential to national progress (Shumway 1991, 136). Accordingly, in 1824, a "land reform" program allowed individuals to lease public lands for twenty years for minimal rent. The benefits of this program went mainly to the wealthy: by 1830, just 538 individuals and corporations had received 20 million acres. The best land was distributed to families in the ruling oligopoly. Eventually nearly all of this land became private property, concentrating ownership and leaving little land available (Shumway 1991, 101). Legally, in this period, indigenous populations were considered to be equal to whites. This status may actually have contributed to their dispossession by removing barriers to the expropriation and sale of lands occupied by indigenous communities (Levaggi 1990).

Juan Manuel de Rosas, a military dictator who ruled Argentina from 1829 to 1852, proceeded to "liberate" more land from indigenous peoples, creating an economic boom in the centers of power (Shumway 1991, 121). The Spanish *porteños* viewed the pampas as a land to be tamed and settled, and the natives were the only obstacle (Shumway 1991, 133). In the late 1870s, the government intensified wars against the remaining indigenous population, displacing them and making new lands available for white settlement. "These lands were intended for immigrants who would fill [former president] Alberdi's dictum *gobernar es poblar*, 'to rule is to populate'" (Shumway 1991, 279). However, homesteading generally failed, as a result of a banking system which refused to extend credit to small landowners and the limited agricultural potential of much of the new land (Shumway 1991, 279-280). Most of the countryside remained in the hands of the landowning elite.

In the late nineteenth century, a wave of European immigration and campaigns of military conquest in the pampas resulted in a proportional increase of people of mostly European descent. Political leaders at the time encouraged increased European immigration, in the belief that groups from northern Europe would make a superior contribution to increasing the nation's productivity (Shumway 1991, 146-147). Racist ideologies legitimized the subjugation of native peoples and the appropriation of their "unproductive" land, forcing most of the nomadic hunter-gatherer groups into wage labor (Shumway 1991, 144). Subsequent waves of immigrants from Europe, especially from Italy and Spain, followed, with major influxes of population from 1904-1914 and in the 1930s. Net immigration from 1880-1910 alone was more than two million (Davis 1995, 72), although many of these were seasonal migrants who came to Argentina for high wages during the agricultural season, then returned to Europe (Taylor 1948, 102). Those who decided to stay most often became tenant farmers, and most settled in the coastal regions and on the pampas. These immigrant populations changed the face of the Argentine nation and left an ethnic legacy that is distinct from elsewhere in Latin America. Argentina developed a racialized class system where nearly all of the wealthy landowners were *criollo* (white, or creole), tenant farmers were newer European immigrants, and most hired laborers were either *mestizos* or poor *criollos*.[2] The native population was relegated to the lowest rung of the class ladder. From the 1910s until the 1940s, wars against native populations were abandoned in favor of assimilationist policies that encouraged the development of settled agricultural communities (Carrasco and Briones 1996, 19).

The pattern of an elite landowning class persisted into the twentieth century. By 1937, there was a rural population of 1.5 million, while 20,000 urban-based landlords owned seventy percent of the agricultural land. Only one third of farm occupants were owners (Ivereigh 1995, 109). The population was characterized by an urban elite, a small group of rural landowning farmers, and a larger class of rural semiproletarian workers. The landholding pattern, of large cattle estates requiring little labor and monopolizing much of the arable land, precluded homesteading. Instead, a system of tenant farming developed, generally based on short-term contracts of one to five years. Carl Taylor's (1948) description of rural life in the 1940s shows that the tenant farming system was generally detrimental to both the quality of life in rural areas and the long-term agricultural development in the region. Short-term contracts meant that there was a great deal of instability of farm occupancy, and a lack of commitment by both tenants and absentee owners to the long-term productivity of the land (Taylor 1948, 195, 202). Farm capital was held by the owner of the land, and the contract usually specified how much land was to be planted in a given crop. The tenant's commercial opportunities were thus limited, and Taylor says that upward mobility, from laborer to tenant to owner, was rare (1948, 203).

The global effects of the Great Depression prompted efforts to industrialize. Import-substitution policies reduced the share of imports in consumption from forty percent in 1928 to twenty-six percent in 1938 (de Janvry 1981, 66). However, the industrial sector continued to suffer from a lack of foreign exchange and numerous regulations and tariffs (Scobie 1971, 182). Because Argentina had no peasantry except in the far north, the industrial sector did not have access to surplus labor from an unemployed or marginal population; the ongoing scarcity of labor increased the political power of organized labor (Lehmann 1990, 46). A new industrial elite emerged, separate from the traditional landowning class. In rural areas, the Depression created further land concentration and agricultural mechanization, which forced out many seasonal laborers and tenant farmers. Small farmers faced the problems of scarce credit, debt bondage, and low prices due to poor storage facilities and the purchasing power of cartels (Ivereigh 1995, 109). Migration to urban areas continued to be high; by the late 1930s there were over 70,000 migrants to Buenos Aires each year (Ivereigh 1995, 109). While the economy was industrialized to an extent, it still depended heavily on agricultural production. By the early 1940s, almost ninety-six percent of exports were agricultural products; moreover, about seventy-five percent of industrial products were processed crops, such as food, beverages, tobacco, textiles, and leather (Taylor 1948, 420).

State Policies and Indigenous Peoples

In 1943, another military coup brought the most controversial figure in Argentine history, Juan Perón, into power. Perón was a populist figure, and he and his second wife, Eva, were widely loved. Under Perón, the state's system of social support was greatly extended, generous social benefits introduced, and the government's bureaucratic structure expanded. Perón was strongly nationalistic, and the state supported rapid industrialization and investment in infrastructure. By the end of the Second World War, there had been a large increase in industrial development, mostly in coastal cities, and an increase in the relative power of the industrial elite (Scobie 1971, 185-187).

Nationally, Perón did little to advance the cause of land reform. Perón's most important base of power was in the urban working class, and there was little impetus to significantly change the structure of landownership, with the alienation of the landowning class that such a move would entail. While Perón failed to make significant land reforms, there was some liberalization of state policy towards Argentina's indigenous peoples. In 1945, a large group of Kolla from Iruya and the Humahuaca valley staged the "*Malón de Paz*," a march on the Peronist government in Buenos Aires to demand land rights and increased educational opportunities. They met with Perón himself, but ultimately returned to the north unsuccessful. In denying their land claims, Perón reportedly declared that the marchers did not represent the "true indigenous inhabitants of our north" (cited in Zapiola 2002, 2). However, the publicity surrounding this event prompted a series of decrees guaranteeing native rights and granting some land to resettled groups. The rights granted under these provisions took a circumscribed form, prohibiting the sale of land and dictating the structure of native settlements (Carrasco and Briones 1996, 20), and were unevenly implemented. In the province of Jujuy, where most of the Kolla were located, large tracts of land were turned over to native inhabitants, but there was little change in Salta, where the landowning elite was more entrenched. In the period that followed, the state's attention to indigenous land rights trailed off, and there was little change in rural areas. In 1958, usufruct rights were established, as well as recognition of some common property rights (Carrasco and Briones 1996, 21). However, there were still many limits on how such land could be used, and it was inalienable.

Beginning in the 1960s, official policy began to encourage the active participation of indigenous people in their own development. In the 1970s, for the first time, "the idea of 'historic reparation' towards native populations that had been stripped of, and marginalized from, their territories appeared in the official vocabulary" (Carrasco and Briones 1996, 22). An indigenous political leadership emerged, as several regional and national advocacy groups were formed.

In 1985, national law 23.302 created a new agency of indigenous affairs, INAI, which was given the responsibility of adjudicating land claims as well as overseeing other efforts to improve conditions in native communities. Law 23.302 included strong language calling for the transference of land to indigenous communities. Communities were to be given "lands apt and sufficient" for their economic development. Titles were to be adjudicated by INAI, and the normal fees for transferring land titles were to be waived. The lands turned over to native communities would be free from federal taxes and any other fees, but they would also be inalienable. Additionally, communities would be prohibited from renting or leasing land, and community members were required to occupy and use the land that belonged to them. Land could be granted under individual or communal title, depending on the desires of each community.

Despite the measure's convincing language, little immediate progress was made in most of the nation. The federal government failed to appropriate funds to purchase land where necessary and lacked the will to expropriate significant landholdings. Provincial laws lagged behind federal laws, slowing the process in many cases. This was particularly the case in areas such as Salta where many communities occupy land held by the province. In some cases, the failure of indigenous communities to meet federal guidelines and regulations, often criticized as unduly complex and culturally inappropriate by advocates, further slowed the process.

The national constitution, revised in 1994, now for the first time includes a provision that guarantees indigenous rights, including the right to land. With regard to the question of land, it essentially reiterates the basic provisions of law 23.302, that each community has a right to the land that they have "traditionally occupied." The inclusion of this language in the constitution brought considerable power to bear on the subject. It meant that provinces that remained reluctant to comply with 23.302 would have little choice but to change their own laws to bring them into accordance with constitutionally mandated rights. Indigenous groups and NGO advocates were active in promoting the inclusion of this language, after a long process of negotiation and compromise. The final ratification and acceptance of the ILO Convention 169 in 2000 on indigenous rights has continued to add momentum to the discursive and legal support for indigenous land rights (Nahuel 2001). However, while constitutional changes have spurred some movement toward the titling of indigenous lands and the promotion of other rights for the indigenous peoples of Argentina, they have not acted as a panacea for the many issues and challenges faced by native communities, nor has the process of bringing provincial law into conformity with the national law been completed smoothly or quickly. Even where laws have been enacted, their implementation is sometimes slow or nonexistent.

Expropriation and the Neoliberal State

Both the federal and provincial governments have been significant players in the process of land reform in both of the case studies under consideration. The relationships between local communities, the NGOs that have served in this instance as their advocates, and the state have been conflictual more often than not. The strategies that indigenous groups and their advocates have developed in their dealings with the state have been an important aspect of their land rights struggle.

The Argentine government has been open to land claims made by indigenous peoples. There has been no significant movement towards a more generalized process of land reform that would include large rural white or non-indigenous populations. Where white or *criollo* farmers have received land, as in the Chaco, this has been incidental to the process of titling lands to indigenous communities. Apart from this very small and limited white population, there has not been any dialogue on rural land reform for nonindigenous communities. The Argentine government's openness towards land reform targeted towards indigenous populations, and indeed the inclusion of rights specific to its indigenous population in its constitution, has largely been in response to pressure brought by indigenous rights organizations both internally and internationally. At various times, indigenous groups have enlisted the assistance and support of international rights organizations such as Cultural Survival, ICCO, and Oxfam. The government, highly conscious of its international image, has made considerable efforts to reform its laws and policies regarding indigenous peoples to bring them into conformity with a global discourse on human and indigenous rights.

However, "there is a great distance between the recognition and the effective implementation of indigenous rights" (Carrasco and Briones 1996, 35). The factors contributing to the state's willingness to implement land reform have been complex and interrelated. As land claims have developed throughout the nation, there have been different motivations on the part of the state in each case, depending on the timing, the policies and platforms of key individuals, and local and provincial political contexts. In Salta, the successful land claims cases of both Finca Santiago and the communities around Los Blancos have been due at least in part to the isolation of each region, the lack of significant resources, and the relatively low cost to the state of land reform.

In other regions, particularly where indigenous peoples have been located on and laying claim to land that does contain valuable resources, the provincial government has systematically created delays, contested indigenous claims, and at times just completely ignored native claims. An exceptionally contentious case exists in the zone to the north of Los Blancos where a group of Wichí communities located along the Argentine side of the Pilcomayo have made a collective claim to a very large area. The government had been planning an international roadway through the contested region, and delayed negotiations with the native communities until after construction had begun. The communities strongly opposed the proposed route of the road, which would divide their lands through the middle. Although the government argued that the bridge is crucial to international trade and in the interests of Mercosur, the roads on either side of the bridge are not paved for hundreds of kilometers. The Wichí argued that the road not only represented an unwanted government intrusion into their territory, but would bring considerable traffic, increased white settlement, and environmental destruction to an area that had previously been relatively inaccessible. After repeated incidents of bad faith bargaining on the part of the province, during which agreements were made and then violated, the Wichí communities staged an occupation of a bridge connecting the Wichí community of Misión La Paz and the Paraguayan border. The occupation, which lasted from August 25 until September 16, 1996, was highly publicized. Again the government met with the Wichí communities, persuading them to abandon their protest without making any lasting concessions. The land claim of the Pilcomayo communities remained unresolved until 2001, more than five years after the occupation.

In regions where mineral resources are the chief concern, the government has been working to ensure access to those resources despite the process of granting titles to native communities. In some areas of the highlands, there has been considerable pressure for people to agree to take individual, rather than communal, titles. With individual titles, the government retains subsoil rights, and possesses the power to buy out owners in order to resell mineral rights to private companies. With communal titles, by contrast, the government is restrained from such expropriation. Sister Rosa, who works for ENDEPA, is on the advisory board for OCLADE, and is active in indigenous land struggles, described the situation in Susques, a town in the high Andes to the west of Iruya:

> The government is pushing very hard to get the people to accept individual land titles. And this is an area very rich with minerals. We know, for example, that there is some gold, there is silver, there are other minerals. . . . Because of the minerals there, we are afraid that if people take individual titles they will lose their land. A number of companies have already entered [the region]. They are there to see what land they want. They think that because they are indigenous lands, they will be cheap and easy to take. Many of them are from other countries, and the government is ready to sell them the land.

According to Rosa, the government's strategy to promote individual titles is deliberately deceptive and misleading:

> They are trying to confuse the people. They say that the Church can't give people the land, that we are encouraging the people to take communal titles but that the only ones who can give the titles is the government. They try to make the people afraid, like they had better take individual titles or they won't get anything. They are telling people that the church is wrong. They are confusing the people. So we protested. . . . We are fighting so that they will give the land titles in the form that the communities ask for.

With the strong support of the Catholic Church, administered in Susques as in Iruya by the Claretians, the consensus in the community is for communal, and inalienable, titles.

In cases where the formal arrangements for granting titles to indigenous communities has been agreed upon, the actual transaction typically is excruciatingly slow. Reboratti (1996, 94-95) notes that there are considerable technical problems with expropriation. The government must determine the amount of compensation due to the owners, where the land is in private hands. Furthermore, the agency responsible for the administration of titles, INAI, is described by Reboratti as lacking the organizational capacity for the process. And in any case where there is an agreement, but titles have not yet been produced, there remains the risk that the government will not comply within the specified time frame and the expropriation law will lapse.

Claiming Land in Iruya

Constitutional changes provided a new impetus and momentum to struggles by indigenous groups to gain titles to land which they viewed as rightfully theirs. One of these reinvigorated land claim efforts was being enacted in Iruya in 1996-1997, the period of field research. In the community of Rodeo Colanzulí, one of the small villages in the *departamento* of Iruya, community members were mobilizing to gain title to the Finca Santiago, a private landholding that has encompassed their community since the colonial period.

Andean Land Tenure

It would be misleading to discuss "traditional" patterns of land use in Iruya and Rodeo Colanzulí. Local institutions of land tenure have changed as legal, political, and social contexts have shifted. However, there are long-standing patterns of land use which form the backdrop for the current land tenure dispute. These patterns are similar to those found elsewhere in the Andean region.

Michael Sallnow (1987) discusses pan-Andean corporate village organization in upland and lowland peasant communities based on his research near Cusco. In the highlands, community members usually hold heritable rights to particular plots in the lower cultivable zone and usufruct rights to cultivate yearly plots in the upper seasonal zone. Grazing rights to pasture in the highest usable zones and to fallow are held in common. The community has reversionary rights to all land, and sale or lease to outsiders is often forbidden. To retain their rights, community members have certain formal and informal obligations, including attendance at community meetings, supporting communal work projects, following irrigation and fallow rules, participating in sponsoring fiestas, and holding civil offices. In lowland communities, land is usually privately owned and the community retains little, if any, land in common.

Closer to Iruya, Ricardo Abduca (1995) examines the rural property system in a region that straddles the border between northern Argentina, in the province of Jujuy, and Bolivia. In Abduca's case study, the community has defined how local space is used depending on microgeography. Land falls into three categories: cultivated land, cultivated pastures (*potreros*), and communal pastures. Both cultivated land and cultivated pastures may be bought, sold, and rented, but the community retains rights over irrigation. While cultivated plots are alienable, "they are sold first to people who are 'from here,' an affiliation which is demonstrated by 'having family': by marriage or by descent" (1995, 89), to prevent land being sold to anyone outside of the community. Abduca strongly argues that pastures and other lands are not open access, as they have been portrayed by some authors, but commons, with access regulated by the community. While pastures are communally owned and regulated, most households maintain a small dwelling in the pastures for use there; the land immediately surrounding this is considered to be private, and care is taken by others to avoid herding animals too close.

The community also sets levels of required labor contributions, mainly to maintain and repair irrigation channels. These rights and obligations are defined in terms of household or family, rather than individual, possession. Every household has to contribute male labor to maintain the irrigation canals. One recent problem created by a seasonal exodus of migrant labor is a lack of available labor for maintaining irrigation canals at the proper time of year; fewer families are able to send labor, choosing instead to pay a fine. Sometimes problems arise when families are only able to send women or children to meet their labor obligations, or if they only offer to send labor at the wrong time of year. This crisis, Abduca argues, is not only a problem of production, but one of community morale: there are no rituals associated with this community labor, and it is difficult to reinforce a sense of "the basis of [the community's] integration as a group" (1995, 91).

The Community of Rodeo Colanzulí

Rodeo Colanzulí, located in the *departamento* of Iruya, includes three small villages: Colanzulí, Río Grande, and Campo Carreras. The communities are located on the top of a bluff overlooking the river valley, between the river and the higher hills to the northeast. The cultivated fields extend the length and width of this bluff. They are connected by a road that links the area with Iruya and bigger population centers on the other side of a high mountain pass. The three communities are separated from one another geographically by deep arroyos, but the people of the three villages share one *Centro Vecinal* (Neighborhood Association) and are connected through multiple kinship ties. In all, the three villages encompass ninety-nine households.[3]

The area is relatively isolated, with limited access to basic services. The nearest hospital is located in Iruya, although there is a health post staffed by a nurse in Río Grande. There are two primary schools, located in Colanzulí and Campo Carreras; the school in Colanzulí has a small dormitory for children whose families live too far from the village to be able to walk every day. Only Campo Carreras has potable water, although there are currently plans to build cisterns in the other two centers. Electricity is only available in the schools and a few private dwellings that have installed solar panels. While many families have radios, the only television is in the school in Colanzulí.[4] Communication is limited to a two-way radio in the health post.

Rodeo Colanzulí has a total of approximately 100-120 cultivated hectares. Of this amount, about half is left fallow in any given year. This land is distributed relatively evenly between households. The household with the most land has about 5 hectares, while other households, generally those of young families, might only have a quarter hectare. The majority of households have less than one hectare, divided between several small plots. The limiting factor in agricultural productivity is not land, but water. While most families have at least some of their land under irrigation, there is generally a lack of water to bring more land under cultivation or expand production.

The History of the Finca Santiago

Northwest Argentina is one of the few parts of the country in which fincas have remained an important form of land tenure, despite "their present social and economic dysfunction" (Reboratti 1996, 6). Finca Santiago, which encompasses Rodeo Colanzulí as well as three other communities, was created just after Argentine independence when changes in provincial and international borders caused older, larger fincas to be broken up.[5] The present Finca Santiago extends just over 125,000 hectares, spanning a variety of microclimates from east to west. Rodeo Colanzulí is located on the western extreme of the Finca, at approximately 3,600 meters above sea level. This zone is cold and dry. To the east of the community is a small chain of mountains, and as one crosses this natural barrier, the landscape drops sharply, giving way to thick *yungas*, semitropical forests. Until the 1970s, when the community of Isla de Cañas was founded by a number of families from another part of the finca, the semitropical zone was virtually uninhabited and used only for winter pasture.

Reboratti describes significant ecological changes that occurred during the colonial period (1996, 54-55). Llamas were pushed to higher altitudes, as the European herd animals, which did not do as well up high, took over the lower grazing lands. Transhumancy was introduced, and there was a degradation of pasture, combined with increased erosion, especially at higher altitudes, since the European animals were more destructive of native plants which held the soil. There was also a shift from irrigated agriculture to seasonal agriculture, as land use became more extensive and less intensive, and overall productivity decreased. The plow was introduced, and soil quality lessened. Nicolas Cushner notes that land had symbolic value as well as material value for Spanish, as much as for the people who were already located in the highlands (1982, 26). For the Spanish, the transformation of land tenure represented the replacement of one ruler by another and the establishment of "civilization" as new systems of production allowed them to grow European foods.

Historically, Finca Santiago has been owned by absentee landowners who have never lived in the community. In 1906, the finca was purchased by the Patrón Costas family from the family who had owned it since the 1830s (Reboratti 1996, 61, 88).[6] Patrón Costas, along with several associates, was also the owner of a large sugar plantation, Ingenio San Martín. By the early 1900s, sugar was becoming an important crop in the lowland region east of the finca. The sugar harvest is marked by seasonality and requires intensive labor for only a few months of the year.[7] From 1880 to 1920, most of the labor for sugar plantations was recruited from the Chaco, especially among the Wichí. This involved considerable problems with transportation, and while the Wichí were cheap labor, they were not seen as reliable. The intense seasonal labor needs of the sugar harvest at Ingenio San Martín meant that Finca Santiago itself was much more valuable to the owners as a source of inexpensive, seasonal labor than for the small amount of rents that could be extracted.

The people of Rodeo Colanzulí perceived the system of rents and seasonal labor in the sugar harvest as a tremendous burden. Residents were required to pay two types of rent, one for cultivated land and another fee for the right to graze animals, which was charged per head. Grazing fees allowed animals to be grazed in the open pastures in the hills surrounding the community and in the lowlands to the east. Rents had to be paid in cash, which generally had the effect of forcing people to work on the plantation.

Elena, a middle-aged woman in Colanzulí who has been a leader in efforts to claim land, described the life of the tenant farmers:

> If you couldn't pay, pay in cash, you had to go to work. They used to take people to the sugar fields to work, to get enough money to pay the rent. They used to come and take people away to work.

At times, this was accomplished through force or the threat of force. Elena continued:

> My grandfather told me, that back then, if you didn't have the money [for the rent], they would come and take you, and make you go work, however they wanted. . . . If you wouldn't go work, they would come and take your animals, for the rent. Whatever little you had, they would take.

There was also the threat of eviction:

> When I was a little girl, they said that if we didn't pay the rent, the owner would bring other people to live here, to work here, and we would all have to leave. I remember that.

These complaints echo those expressed in 1945 during the *Malón de Paz*, when tenant farmers complained that the labor demands of Patrón Costa were "impossible to refuse, because [if you did] the police of the plantation would appear with Winchesters, pistols . . . and force us to work" (quoted in Zapiola 2002, 2).

The incorporation of the villages of the finca into the plantation labor system began a process of semiproletarianization. An almost feudal system of labor control developed, as farmers from Finca Santiago were required to work at San Martín, without benefiting from market forces or the choice of conditions on another plantation. In a self-perpetuating cycle, subsistence production was reduced as labor was siphoned off. The decreased harvests increased people's need to work on the plantation in order to continue to pay their rent. Labor on the plantation was further coerced through a system of debt peonage. The landowners provided merchandise on credit, and then deducted the amount from a worker's earnings. Lodging and food for the time that the worker spent at the plantation was also deducted from earnings. An older man remembered, "They would take you to the sugar fields, give you a bag of maize, and then make you work to pay for it." A worker very often found that at the end of the sugar harvest, the cash left to him from his earnings was, at best, just enough to cover his expenses for the harvest season and what the household owed in rent, or at worst, that the family was left in debt. A middle-aged woman, now a prosperous farmer, described her family's experience:

> My parents, my grandparents, they all always had to pay. They had to pay for the land, and for the animals. The money all went to pay the rent. There was nothing left for clothes, for food, nothing. Everything went to pay the rent.

The finca itself seems to have been of little productive importance to its owners, beyond acting as the principal source of labor for the plantation. As Carlos Reboratti describes, "In more than a half century they made no investment whatsoever in the Finca" (1996, 88). Because the villages within the finca were located on private property, the government also failed to make significant investments in the area, such as roads, schools, or other public services such as systems for potable water. Families within the community did not generally have a sufficient surplus to enable them to make productive investments such as installing irrigation. Even if it had been possible, the insecurity of their claim to the land made it unwise to do so. Beyond the threat of eviction, "if you improved your land, by putting irrigation or a well, the landowner would look at it and charge you more rent," as one resident explained.

In the early 1950s, the Patrón Costas sold the finca to another owner, a Spanish corporation.[8] The sugar industry was introducing more mechanized processes, and the labor that the finca provided was no longer crucial.[9] By the 1960s, the mechanization of production was so thorough-going that the need for labor was considerably reduced, resulting in more labor market instability for the finca's highland occupants, who had by then come to depend on seasonal work (Reboratti 1996, 79-80). The finca's new owners were interested in the prospect of commercial development in the eastern part of the property. They did continue to collect rent on the agricultural land and herds of the local population, but with less vigor than the Patrón Costas. One can imagine that the rent itself was of little monetary value to an international firm, and they were not interested in using it, as the Patrón Costas had been, to coerce labor. In the mid-1980s, the highland tenants of the finca began to refuse to pay rents on the land.

Perceived pressure on grazing land due to the increased level of logging in areas which had been used as winter pastures was one of the most immediate incentives to protest. One member of the OCLADE board of directors described the changes:

> What happened was that companies started coming in and taking out all of the wood, in the area where the people pasture their animals. The pastoralists were pushed further and further up in to the hills. Then they finally got so there was nowhere for them to go any more. And taking out all of the wood like that, it is very bad for the environment. So the people started looking to see what they could do, looking to the situation of ownership. That all started in 1985 or 1987.

The process of organizing the community to stop paying rents was by no means easy. Elena, who had been active in organizing local protests, explained, "Some people were afraid to stop paying. They thought that they might get evicted, or even arrested." However, with some support from the Catholic Church, which was active in the area, the community began to mobilize. In 1989, the community formed a Centro Vecinal in order to organize themselves in the battle to gain title to the finca. The centro became important as a locus for opposition and local organization. One of its founders said, "We have used the center to allow the people of the community to meet together. . . . We believe that this is our land, and we want to have our own secure place, our land that no one will be able to take away from us."

While the owners of the finca were less interested in the payment of rents than in the profit from lumber, they initiated some efforts to collect the rents that were due to them. Elena described this: "In 1989, 1990, around then, many of us stopped paying. They stopped coming to try to get it, because we wouldn't pay anymore. Then politicians came. They said that we had to pay, that he was the owner and it was his land." However, the community continued to refuse to pay.

Faced with increasingly recalcitrant tenants, the finca owners approached the provincial government and offered to give the government the highland grazing zone, in exchange for which they wanted the government to pay for clearing two hundred hectares in the jungle to allow the expansion of commercial agriculture (Reboratti 1996, 89). The government failed to formally respond to the repeated requests of the owners, and no action was taken.

In 1993, the finca was leased to a different Spanish timber company. Like the finca's previous owners, the Spanish company had little interest in most of the land of the finca. Rather, they were primarily interested in the extraction of wood from the jungles in the eastern part of the finca. The mature forests of the eastern jungle of the finca contained a number of commercially valuable species. This forest had not been subject to heavy use previously, due to its distance from villages, the scarce numbers of the herd animals which the highland villages grazed there, its inherent impenetrability, and the difficulties of commercial logging in the region (Reboratti 1996, 31-32). The timber company immediately began extensive logging operations, opening up much of the previously untouched region with logging roads and rapidly extracting the most valuable lumber. This logging has continued until the present time. This extractive industry does not represent a source of employment for the community of Rodeo Colanzulí, as it brings in its own workers from elsewhere.

Finally, in May 1994, faced by continued protests and lobbying by the population of the area and various NGOs, a constitutional article requiring that land be turned over to indigenous communities, and continued requests from the finca owners, the federal government took action. A law (24.334) was passed according to which the government would purchase all of the lands of Finca Santiago, and then pass the titles to the indigenous communities of the finca. Finca Santiago was one of several fincas to be retitled around the same time in the region. At the beginning of 1995, over 164,000 hectares in the area were under some process to transfer legal title, and another 100,000 hectares were being considered (Reboratti 1996, 95).

The reclamation of the finca has been seen as a major victory by members of the community. One community leader proudly declaimed, "The question of the land is the question of independence. With this, I think that people will start to see that they can do things, that they can organize and accomplish things." However, the actual process is long and complicated, and its outcome is far from ensured. The law passed by the government in May 1994 (federal law 24.334 mentioned above) is an agreement to purchase the land from the current owners. This purchase will take place in three payments, made over three years. The amount that the government is paying for the land has not been disclosed.

The first payment was made on March 19, 1997. With this payment, the control of the finca was passed to the Department of Social Development of the federal government. In the meantime, the community has gained legal recognition, in the form of *persona jurídica*, which enables it to act as a corporate group. The Centro Vecinal of Rodeo Colanzulí, with the other three communities of the finca, has established a General Council, the *Consejo Kolla de Finca Santiago*, to coordinate the question of the reclamation of the finca and the management of the land. This council consists of several elected representatives from each community.

After the purchase is complete, the finca will be the property of the federal government, which will then turn it over to the provincial government. The provincial government has agreed that it will survey the land and turn over the title to the residents, a process which observers generally agree is complicated and expensive. The survey and distribution of titles will be conducted under the auspices of several new government agencies, some federal and some provincial, and some of which have yet to be formed.

Under the current provisions of federal law, land that is being returned to indigenous communities may be titled either privately or communally, with the decision being left to the community. In Rodeo Colanzulí, the question of whether titles will be communal or private, or whether some land will be reserved as common property and some titled individually, is still not settled. The legal agreement, as it now stands, is that the title to all of the land will initially be granted to the Centro Vecinal once all three payments have been made and the survey is complete. The Centro Vecinal will then oversee the process of distributing land to its members. The current plan suggested by the Centro Vecinal, as explained by one of the leaders of the community, is that

> the Centro Vecinal will give out individual titles to each owner [for the land that is currently cultivated]. They won't be able to sell the land for five years after that. The pasture will all stay communal property. There will be an internal agreement, here in the community, about selling land. For example, people would first sell their land to their own children, then to others here. This would be so that land will not be lost to outsiders.

As in the case described by Abduca (1995; see above), there is a strong feeling that the land should stay in the hands of people "from here," a sentiment which is no less powerful for being informal.

Communal Property in Colanzulí

Colanzulí does have a long tradition of managing grazing lands as common property. Although rents have been paid for many years for cultivated land and for grazing rights, the actual management of the land has largely been left to the community. At the present time, the community is facing the considerable challenge of formalizing the rules by which it will govern itself and its property. The Centro Vecinal of Rodeo Colanzulí is in the process of writing a set of by-laws that define the rights and responsibilities of members of the community. When describing this process, one community leader said, "We decided there were three important areas: water, land, and animals. So we formed three groups, which met to look at what we should do in each of these areas." Sister Rosa, a nun working with the centro on these issues, described her advice:

> We say, look, how did your grandparents manage the pasture land? They know this. They already know how to manage their lands, so that everyone has their own land to farm, so that everyone can have animals in the pasture.

Many of the resulting by-laws are straightforward, simply formalizing practices which are already in place through custom. For example, people are required to maintain the irrigation channels that run through their land and to help maintain those that bring water down from the river; this is a long-standing practice to which people are already accustomed. When looking at the number of animals that can be grazed, the centro has suggested that the only animals that need to be limited are burros. This is based on local knowledge that burros are more destructive than other grazing animals and tend to be kept in the village.

The rules that the community has formulated represent a distillation of such beliefs and practices and are focused on the space within the villages.

Rules regarding access to communal grazing land have not been as thoroughly laid out, which may also conform to a kind of commonsense approach to commons management. Researchers working in natural resource management in the area have noted that overgrazing does not appear to be a problem in the common pastures (Reboratti 1996).[10] Local farmers raise only enough animals for their own consumption and perhaps a few for the local market. The market value of animals raised on this rugged terrain is low, and transportation costs are high. As with other local products, the potential for commercialized husbandry is nearly nonexistent. Herd animals do represent a kind of capital, and farmers may have more than they strictly need. However, the members of the centro do not feel that there is any immanent danger of an individual or single household overusing the common grazing area, or of a dramatic increase in the total number of animals. In fact, local perception tends to be that there are fewer animals than formerly. Burros, in particular, are kept less frequently and in fewer numbers, since motorized transportation is fairly readily available and much faster and more convenient. As the practice of weaving has declined and the market value of wool and woolen goods has dropped, it is likely that there are also fewer sheep, which are less favored for their meat than cattle or goats. The number of cattle and goats may be increasing to compensate, but the capital invested in these animals is collected only slowly. Moreover, herding is only one element of the subsistence strategy of most households. There is a great deal of labor involved, as animals must be moved from distant pastures and fed during the dry season with alfalfa and other fodder crops. Herding involves some risk to capital; it is not uncommon for animals, particularly cattle, to suffer a fatal fall or become lost when turned loose to graze. Rather than invest in a larger herd, which represents security but little potential gain, many families choose to invest instead in education for children, in improved irrigation, or in migrant labor.

While the threat of amassing large herds is seen as remote, the ability to graze some animals on common grazing land continues to be an invaluable resource for local households, who depend on a diversified subsistence strategy. Despite the important role of common pastures, there is some local opposition to accepting a communal title for any part of the finca. Sister Rosa explained,

> Sometimes the people don't understand what it means to have communal title. They think that it means that they have to share everything. They are afraid that this means people will fight more. We try to explain to them, that no, they will still have the same property that their ancestors had.

She went on to describe some of the most obdurate divisions within the community:

> The people fight with each other for different reasons—because some are from one political party and some are from another, because some are evangelicals. This is a big problem in some communities. The evangelicals generally encourage the people to take individual titles. They tend to stay separate from the rest of the community, and they don't want to have to work together.

In Rodeo Colanzulí, a religious divide follows geographic divisions. Most of the evangelical families live in the uppermost community center, Colanzulí, while the residents of Río Grande and Campo Carreras are Catholic. Sister Rosa's assessment that the evangelical families tend to argue more strongly in favor of individual titles appears to conform to the perceptions of local residents.

The Role of the Catholic Church and OCLADE

As the struggle to gain title to land commenced throughout the highlands in the late 1980s, the Claretian order and the prelature of Humahuaca played a key role. The church acted to mobilize popular support for land claims, placing itself at the forefront of the political struggle. Through sermons from the pulpit and the personal networks of its clergy, local activism was developed and encouraged. Links within and between local parishes provided key organizational frameworks.

The organizational capacity of the church was one of its strongest assets in this region where towns are remote and poorly integrated, travel difficult, and phones scarce. Over the years since the Claretian order had arrived in northern Argentina, the church had been building community organization through networks of lay personnel. It had created newsletters and systems for distributing pamphlets. The Claretians had instituted series of workshops, retreats, and seminars for lay leaders. All of these means of communication and organization were turned to the cause of land reform. The church enlisted legal support both locally and in the national capital, primarily through the medium of ENDEPA, a Catholic organization whose mission was specifically to minister to the needs of indigenous communities. While the Catholic Church has been a key player in land claims issues, OCLADE itself has played a less prominent role because of its structural position in the church organization, and because of its views of development in the region.

Defending the Dispossessed

The role of the Catholic Church, and by extension, OCLADE, in the land reclamation efforts of the people of Finca Santiago had less to do with the material resources of the church than it did with the moral authority and the ideological legitimization that church support provided to the struggle. The church also possessed crucial the human capital, in its network of educated, concerned people. Having the support and encouragement of religious leaders motivated local residents to take on a battle which some had believed was impossible. A middle-aged woman active in the Colanzulí parish described the galvanizing influence of the bishop:

> People didn't believe, before, that the expropriation of the land was possible, when they started to fight. When Padre Pedro [Olmedo, the bishop of the prelature of Humahuaca] came, he said to fight. But it had been years this way. People were afraid. People from outside have always lied, have said things would happen that never happened. The people here were scared.

The residents of Rodeo Colanzulí knew and trusted the bishop, who had been the resident priest in Iruya for some ten years. When he promised that it was possible to claim land titles, it was not discounted as an empty hope offered by a well-meaning outsider, but as a voice coming from a trusted and authoritative leader.

Given the church's strong attention to the issue of landownership, it is perhaps surprising that OCLADE itself has not taken a leading role in promoting land claims. In part, this is due to the structural position of OCLADE in the church organization. Land claims issues were delegated to ENDEPA, which took on the functions of enlisting and acting as a medium for legal advocacy, organizing local meetings, and publicizing information on indigenous rights. Because the legal aspects of land reform had been assigned to ENDEPA, OCLADE tended to take a back-seat approach and did not identify land reclamation as one of its central missions. Despite the structural limitations of OCLADE's position in the Catholic organization, however, its leadership could have chosen to take a more proactive approach to supporting local land claims.

In fact, the leadership of OCLADE failed to take a prominent role in the land reclamation effort because of its leadership's larger view of regional development. A narrow definition of "development" caused the organization to limit itself to narrowly defined, "achievable" goals that addressed issues such as female literacy and child malnutrition. This enabled the organization to continue to gain outside funding and government support and demonstrate "progress" to both its external audience and its immediate clientele. Projects that addressed changing relations of production or the conditions of production in any substantive way were neither proposed nor embraced.

Moreover, OCLADE's vision of "appropriate" development for the region, as I have laid out in previous chapters, hinged on the ennoblement of subsistence production. Landownership, by contrast, is seen by the residents of Finca Santiago as a critical element to allow them to invest in commercial production. OCLADE's deep ambivalence about increasing market involvement of local farmers translates into a lack of involvement in the land claim issue.

The leadership and field staff of OCLADE did not take a proactive role in the Finca Santiago land claim, despite the active involvement of the leadership of the prelature on land claims issues more generally. However, some of OCLADE's work in the region provided local residents with the tools that they needed to pursue their claim independently of the NGO's assistance. In all of its work, OCLADE defined its mission as one of "support" for local initiatives. OCLADE's self-designated role was that of conscientization, of training, and of empowering local leaders to take action on behalf of their communities. In the objectives that the prelature laid out for the NGO, the first is "the conscientization of the Colla people," the promotion of human rights and human dignity, and the defense of indigenous rights (Olmedo Rivera 1990, 278).

Obviously, the work of community organization does not lend itself to "achievable," measurable goals. It is at this juncture, however, where the religiously motivated, idealistic elements of OCLADE's philosophy come into play. Community organizing and consciousness-raising do not require specific projects or funding. They are, instead, seen as part of the underlying objectives that frame the NGO's work as a whole. Through providing training, promoting political awareness, and sponsoring concrete projects that require members of the community to collaborate, it is felt that the communities will be more capable as a whole, possessing a trained leadership that will be equipped to advocate on behalf of its neighbors.

In fact, the NGO and the church seem to have been largely successful in this mission. Most of the community's leaders in Rodeo Colanzulí, from those who were most active in encouraging their neighbors to refuse to pay rent to those who have taken on administrative posts in the Centro Vecinal, are those who have been most active in the church and with OCLADE. They include the leaders of Rodeo Colanzulí's women's groups, the lay leader for the local parish, and the animal health outreach worker, as well as others. These are the members of the community that have received training in concrete skills and in social organizing, who become more aware of the problems and issues in their communities, and who developed skills that allow them to act as leaders and mediators within the community. At least one of these people expressed the feeling that she had, in fact, "outgrown" OCLADE, that they are no longer as progressive and proactive an organization as she feels is needed in her community. But, she added, she is grateful to them for the "start" that they gave her.

A constant subtext in OCLADE's agenda of training and community organizing has been the promotion of local indigenous identity. Indigenous identity has been explicitly linked to the right to make land claims, as the national constitution contains no provisions for the restoration of land to nonindigenous communities. As discussed in chapter one, a sense of local identity that is specifically identified as "indigenous" is problematic in Iruya. Some researchers in the area have gone so far as to claim that the recent embrace of Kolla identity has been a thinly disguised pretext for a land grab with no basis in fact.

> In other places in Argentina, indigenous groups clearly exist, given that they recognize themselves as such . . . and are also recognized as such (for better or worse) by the rest of society. But in [Iruya] . . . any *campesino* . . . speaks of himself as a *criollo* and never as an "*indio*," an identity which they concede

> with a certain disdain to the indigenous people from the Chaco that they know from the plantations. Furthermore, they have not maintained, not even as simple *campesinos*, a sense of social cohesion or a strong communal spirit (Reboratti 1996, 95-96).

Reboratti (1996, 95-97) goes on to argue that there is no archaeological basis for a continuous occupation of the land by ancestors of the people who live there now. The Kolla are a tribe more commonly placed in the region near Lake Titicaca, far to the north in Bolivia, and Reboratti argues that there is no evidence of any link between those Kolla and people claiming Kolla identity in northern Argentina. Given what he characterizes as the "weakness" of local community organization, he cautions against the danger that those individuals and small groups claiming a Kolla identity may be setting themselves up as a local elite who will wrest control of the land from both its current owners and their own neighbors who are less determined to portray themselves as "indigenous" (1996, 97).

Such arguments are based on poor ethnographic evidence and a limited definition of what constitutes ethnic identity. I would argue against Reboratti's characterization of community organizations as weak or nonexistent. In fact, local communal institutions, although perhaps weakened by migrant labor and the consequent absence of many men from the community—artifacts of the Finca system itself—are vibrant. Further, Reboratti's understanding of ethnic identity is highly circumscribed, and also quite contrary to what I found in my research. While there is an ambivalence about indigenous identity in the community, there are certainly no "ethnic" divisions, as Reboratti suggests, between *criollos* and *indios*.[11] Despite the weakness of Reboratti's claims in this area, they have been seized upon at various times by the government, which has attempted to argue that the inhabitants of the region do not meet the criteria of an "indigenous" group. These arguments have successfully been defeated in the Finca Santiago case, as in most of the other contested land claims cases in the northwest highlands.

The valorization of indigenous culture has been a major agenda of OCLADE and the church. All of those active in the organization deny that land claims issues constitute a primary, or even an explicit, motivation in affirming a local identity that is specifically indigenous. The prelature and its institutions believe that they have a leading role in promoting educational efforts that teach the inherent value of local culture and traditions, as well as a responsibility to respect the culture and allow space for local traditions and rituals (prelature of Humahuaca 1997, 10). Such an "indigenization" of religion is a common agenda of the liberationist church. This role is seen and defined as an intrinsic element of promoting social justice and human dignity. Given the high stakes involved, however, a politicization of ethnic identity was perhaps inevitable.

In a study conducted by the prelature in 1996, a sense of cultural inferiority and isolation was defined as "a constant question . . . [that makes people feel] that they are not listened to or recognized by governments and public institutions, as well as the feeling that they are worthless, and for this reason they are not motivated to express themselves, participate, and complain" (prelature of Humahuaca 1997, 9). According to this line of thinking, a sense of cultural inferiority led to a reluctance to make demands on the government, even for things which the community is rightfully entitled to (prelature of Humahuaca 1997, 10). Thus, while promoting a sense of indigenous identity is not understood as a political end in itself, or as a direct tool to establish the validity of land claims, it is seen as an underlying factor in the ability of local people to effectively advocate for their own rights.

OCLADE's part in promoting indigenous identity and local ethnic awareness begins with the children that attend the preschool program and the mothers who work there. Celebrations of local tradition are encouraged: everything from encouraging little girls to carry their dolls in ponchos tied to their backs to the title of OCLADE's new periodical, *Yareta*, named for a medicinal highland plant. The embrace of cultural traditions is selective and paradoxical, as certain elements of local culture, such as a timidity about public speaking on the part of women, are rejected as oppressive. In accordance with their own beliefs based on liberation theology and Western liberalism, OCLADE and the church take an active role in a re-creation of a Kolla culture that is sanitized and made more palatable. Certain elements of "traditional" culture are emphasized and reified, while others are neglected and abandoned.

One of the elements of local culture that has been made into a defining mark of indigenous identity is a relationship with the land. Subsistence production is strongly associated with indigenous identity; it is part and parcel of what it means to be Kolla. Subsistence farming is associated with a contemporary way of life, a glorious ethnic past, and an enduring local tradition. On the part of the nonlocal leaders of the church and OCLADE, this way of life is implicitly counterpoised with an idealized opposite of the qualities of Western and Argentine culture that are most inimical to a vision of social justice—individualism, commercialism, consumerism, corruption.

In its writings and teachings, the prelature has stressed a sense of innate connectivity between the Kolla people and their land. A revealing passage describing the relationship between the Kolla and the land by Jesús Olmedo, a leading figure in the prelature, is worth citing at length:

> The Colla man [sic] carries [a sense of loyalty to the land] so deeply within his being that he not only remains loyal to the land, but fully identifies with it. The land of the *puna* and the Colla are two realities that complement one another, and they cannot be understood separately.
>
> The Colla is born attached to his land, as one aspect more of all that is earthly, and assimilates by osmosis all that the earth offers. He is a part of the landscape. And he meditates and he lives; maybe because of this the Colla is sad, as the landscape of his mountains is sad. The immensity of the *puna* has

> given its shape to his suffering heart, but with strength that withstands the test of sun, of cold, and of suffering. All this he has learned and assimilated from his land, so that he cannot forget it because far from [his land] he loses his identity and he feels profoundly foreign. And when, because of necessity or circumstance, the Colla leaves his land and travels to the city, or to the plantation, deep within he feels like a stranger in Paradise, anxious to return to the land that gave birth to him. To be more specific, we would say that the Colla never feels his life is fully realized far from his land, because life is not only bread and work, but also the landscape and the mountains, the songs and the fiestas. Only in this way, assimilating and loving the *Pachamama*, the Colla feels that he lives, that he works, and that he suffers. (Olmedo Rivera 1990, 177)

This passage conveys a belief in a deep supernatural connection between the Kolla and the land. The Kolla is so connected to his natal land that he feels "foreign" elsewhere, unfulfilled and bereft. This bond is implicitly unlike that of the European or Argentine to a landscape. The landscape of the puna mystically imprints itself on the mind and personality of the Kolla, according to Olmedo's interpretation. It is impossible, in this vision, for a Kolla to happily and willingly leave this homeland, to migrate elsewhere for economic opportunity or mere wanderlust. Yet the relationship between the Kolla and the landscape of the puna, as imagined by Olmedo, is not an entirely felicitous one, marked as it is by sadness and suffering. Again, this suffering is ennobled, as an intrinsic part of the Kolla identity, bestowed upon them by the very land to which they are so connected.

At the same time that a relationship with the land is construed as a foundation for Kolla identity, there is recognition that the Kolla themselves are, for the most part, disenfranchised from that land. The church aligns itself with the dispossessed, in keeping with its discursive base of liberation theology. The fact that the Kolla are alienated from their land is compounded by the idea that a relationship with the land is an intrinsic element of Kolla identity. The political cause thus becomes clear: to join the Kolla in a struggle to reclaim their land. As in the case of Finca Santiago, this may entail a steady program of consciousness-raising (*concientización*) in the beginning.

In its daily programming, there is a recognition on the part of OCLADE and the church that the land is the primary means of production in the rural highlands. The political cause to reclaim land does not ignore its value as the basis of subsistence on a material level. Put simply, people need their land to farm because it is the only way that they have to make a living. This instrumental interest in land possession, however, pales in importance to the symbolic relationship between the Kolla as a people and their ties to the land that are rooted in an ethnic imagining.

Los Blancos Case Study

Access to land is a frequent topic of conversation in the Wichí villages near Los Blancos, at informal gatherings, at community meetings, and when discussing local concerns with outsiders. The Wichí agree: they need land, and they need firm rights to that land. Throughout the province, Wichí communities have been trying to gain legal land titles for the past fifteen years, with varying degrees of success. Most of the communities around Los Blancos finally received legal communal land titles late in 1997, after many years of raised expectations and collective struggle.

A Long Road

Alfonso, a middle-aged community leader in Los Blancos, recounted his involvement in the community's efforts to gain legal land titles: "Ten years ago, I was a hunter. Then, I didn't know anything about all these papers." With a smile, he added, "Now I am still a hunter—a hunter of papers." He explained that he has come to understand that it is the papers that will allow the Wichí to continue to hunt. Alfonso tried to explain how the awareness of the need for land rights developed in the community:

> Years ago now, Fundapaz said that it wanted the indigenous people to have their own land. There were many people who questioned that, asking, "Why do we need the land? When I die, what difference will it make?" Then we started to fight for the land. Then later, other people said, why do the indigenous people need so much land? And the [Wichí] people got annoyed!

As Alfonso relates, Fundapaz played a critical role in fomenting the process of land reclamation.

In the mid-1980s, Fundapaz, along with the Bishopric of Oran, began to initiate efforts to have legal land titles ceded to Wichí communities. From the point of view of Fundapaz, work on issues of economic development in the Wichí communities hinged on their ability to create permanent investments in infrastructure and the preservation of their access to the monte and its resources. Acquiring secure land rights was seen as the fundamental basis for economic development, for community organization, and for the work of the organization in improving local living conditions. The NGO began to lobby the government to turn over large blocs of land to the communities located on them. At the same time, the local development team began the crucial work of raising awareness in the Wichí communities of the importance of landownership and the tenuous nature of the usufruct rights that they had, until that time, taken for granted.

The interest in land rights was immediately spurred by the redemocratization of the Argentine government. According to an annual report of Fundapaz from the late 1980s,

> It is evident that the nation is going through the difficult process of the rebirth of democracy and the participation of its citizens. As the [democratic] system is consolidated and assured, participation is encouraged in all spheres of life. (Fundapaz 1988/89, 5)

During the same period, the provincial governor was also more open to issues of indigenous rights in the province.

The initial years of democratic government were filled with optimism. The Wichí communities of the region were located on land that belonged to the provincial government.[12] This implied that the process would be less complicated than if they had been located on private lands. Governmental ownership of the land was a relic of the late colonial expansion into the western Chaco. No large estates, as existed in the highlands, had ever been created in this barren corner of the country. The land was ill suited for any kind of commercial exploitation, and the region had continued to be poorly regulated and marginally developed. For the Wichí, however, land titles were an increasingly important issue. Permanent mission settlements established in the 1930s and 1940s had contributed to a loss of control by the Wichí over resources. As settlements concentrated the population, and nomadism as it had formerly been practiced was virtually eliminated over a very short period, *criollo* settlement increased. The new Wichí villages consolidated control over a much smaller range, while losing access to much larger areas.

Despite the minimal value of the land itself, the bureaucratic wheels of the provincial government ground on with inexorable slowness. Before the government was willing to give up any land, it first set about confirming that there was indeed little of value. The national petroleum company conducted a series of surveys searching for oil or gas reserves. The new roads that this survey required crisscrossed the monte. According to Fundapaz,

> The search for petroleum, the construction of roads and the installation of large [numbers of] white workers and laborers, has contributed in recent years to accelerate the process of collapse of the Wichí world, increasingly affecting their contact with nature and inner peace. (Fundapaz 1988/89, p. 8)

The roads opened up previously inaccessible sections of the monte to white use and *criollo* settlement. Their unerringly straight paths cut through game trails and fragile microenvironments. After months of searching, no commercially viable fuel reserves were found, and the process of land repatriation continued.

A second obstacle was the presence of *criollo* settlers in the region. *Criollo* farmers had carved out their settlements dotting the area claimed by the Wichí. Wichí claims were careful to avoid large *criollo* towns and villages, but individual ranches were so widespread that avoiding all of them was virtually impossible. Tensions between the two communities increased, escalating periodically into violent incidents and the destruction of property. The Wichí were encouraged by Fundapaz and others to see the land as theirs, and became increasingly ready to assert their rights of ownership. A view developed that the *criollos* were infringing upon the resources that the Wichí considered vital to maintaining their cultural integrity. The following passage, a statement by a Wichí man from Salta, eloquently conveys this sentiment:

> The cows eat during the night, and when we come to gather [fruit] we find them. The cows and the goats eat the algarroba [carob] and after midnight they gather together in some place and then they eat and they leave only the seeds. When it rains, they grow, but what happens then is that the animals come and they eat them and then that's it. We are jealous of the animals that come here and eat our food. But I believe that these animals have an owner. . . . The *criollos* come and they put up fences. And when one wants to enter they say, "No, this is mine." But on the other side [of the fence] there is no [algarroba]. Then finally we do not know where to go, unless we say, "This is mine, this belongs to us." Many times one runs up against the white people, and this is why we are submitting papers to the government to make our request. We do not want money, or anything, only that we want the land. We try not to get annoyed, or to kill the other person but to talk. We are asking for what is fair. What we are asking for is the title, [because] if we do not have the title no one gives us credit, no one respects us. I cannot speak more of this because it is a very long story. If I talk for a whole day I would not finish the story. This is the half of what my grandfather told me happened. The region was very beautiful before, when the people planted, made gardens, and the only thing they ate were the wild animals. They didn't eat beef. There were no pigs, there was nothing, and you did not worry because you could go out and there was food, there was a harvest. This and no more will I say. (Quoted in Carrasco and Briones, 1996, 33-34)

The increasing tension between *criollos* and Wichí led Fundapaz to begin to work with the *criollo* communities around Los Blancos. Creating a consensus between the two populations about property boundaries became one of the NGO's central projects. In a series of meetings, the two groups were brought together to discuss boundaries. This was not always a smooth process, as I will discuss below, but gradually, a consensus emerged and the process was able to go forward. Fundapaz played the role of mediator and, at times, arbiter. Once Fundapaz established a certain credibility with the local *criollos*, they began to request that the NGO sponsor development projects in their communities. Fundapaz gradually increased its work in the *criollo* communities, creating projects for the *criollo* farmers.

The process of yielding land titles proceeded over many years. Periodically, there would be some sign of progress, as agreements were signed by the government to turn over specified regions to the Wichí. Land was set aside for each community and boundaries for *criollo* ranches were established. In the town of Los Blancos, because of the need to accommodate *criollo* ranchers and towns, the Wichí were promised land that was located over 15 kilometers from the actual location of the village. Despite periodic bursts of progress, the actual land titles remained elusive, as the government repeatedly failed to complete the process.

Fundapaz encouraged the Wichí communities to strengthen their claims by resettling on the land that had been promised to the communities in the preliminary agreements. Marisol, a Fundapaz worker, encouraged such a move at a meeting in the Wichí community of Los Blancos, exclaiming,

> What happens if a government agent goes by and sees that the land which has been given to the communities is just monte? They will say, the Wichí do not need that land! They need to see houses, buildings. They need to see that people are living there. Living there full-time, with their goats and their children.

Another Fundapaz worker went on to note that the agreement under which the community was to receive the land stated clearly that it had to be occupied and used by the Wichí. Once again, the concept of land "use" comes into play, this time with ominous importance. The Wichí, like other nonagricultural societies, use land without the same markers of settlement that white settlers create, such as buildings and deforestation. In their own territorial divisions, they employ other, more subtle signs of possession such as hunting zones and burial grounds (Carrasco and Briones 1996, 65). The hypothetical government agent in Marisol's diatribe would be looking for visible signs of "use"—houses, fences, domestic animals, etc. As Marisol remarked afterwards, without a hint of cynicism, it would be preferable if the new Wichí villages could be seen from the road, since the government agents would not be inclined to hike far through the monte to see the new communities. The "use" value of undeveloped monte to the Wichí, for whom it provides a vital reservoir of resources, is not apparent to the government, whose agenda is to visibly develop and transform the countryside.

In each village, a number of families moved to land that the government had agreed was "theirs," despite the hardship and expense that this entailed. These families could generally not avail themselves of day labor opportunities, as the new settlements were too far from *criollo* settlements. The infrastructure that did exist in the more well-established communities—schools, communal buildings, reliable sources of water, a church—was absent in the new villages, and the process of developing such amenities was begun again. In one of the new communities, or colonies, Fundapaz acquired funding to build a community center. The building itself was of little use to the six families who lived in this new village. Even after its completion, it was rarely used even as a storage space. The families did welcome the paid work that the project provided, however. More significantly, the building was a visual marker of "use," a sign that the community existed, an accomplishment that could be pointed to in an effort to further consolidate a claim to the land.

Once colonies began to be established in the new lands, Fundapaz concentrated its efforts in other development programs on helping the colonies, at times in preference to the stem communities. Ostensibly, such concentrated efforts were to remedy the lack of infrastructure in the colonies that had already been developed in the older communities. Since many building projects included allowances for labor, it also helped to encourage families to stay in the colonies when no other paid work was available. In part, as in the above example of the community center, this effort had the dual motive of establishing a presence in the newly claimed territory. The projects also served to reward those who had moved. Fundapaz's team was fully cognizant of the sacrifices made by the families who moved onto the land. In the case of the colony of Cacique Abregu, Vicente said, "Most families don't want to move to the monte. They are from town, and they are more comfortable there. But they have to use this land, or they could lose it."

Fatigue and Resistance

Although the Wichí have come to espouse attaining land titles as one of their most pressing common goals, there is a continued feeling in the community that the land issue originated not within the community, but with Fundapaz. As Alfonso expressed above, "Years ago now, Fundapaz said that it wanted the indigenous people to have their own land." As the process dragged out over years, this sentiment sometimes turned to resentment, that Fundapaz introduced a cause that at times appeared nearly impossible, a chimera. A sense of fatigue with the issue set in.

In June of 1997, rumors were circulating that the titles would be distributed that year. In a meeting with the Fundapaz team, Don Sebastián, the pastor of Misión San Patricio, complained,

> We have been fighting for this land for 16 years. We are tired of talking about land. Sixteen years, we have been waiting for the titles to this land. The government lies. Fundapaz lies. We just want the titles.

Vicente, the Fundapaz worker conducting the meeting, tried to explain the complexities of the final stages of the land title process. Don Sebastián dismissed him out of hand, saying, "Look, Vicente, you're new. We have been fighting for sixteen years already. You were born the day before yesterday." A younger man added that before Fundapaz came and started talking about the land, they didn't worry about land titles, that the Wichí "just lived peacefully." Don Sebastián continued to explain to Vicente, with exaggerated patience, that there are other problems of the community that need more urgent attention, and dismissed the topic of land titles for the remainder of the day.

One of the most intractable issues in adjudicating land titles, from the point of view of the government, is the conflict between Wichí communities and *criollo* settlers. The government has been unwilling to intercede between the two groups, insisting that boundaries be established and agreed upon by mutual consent of those concerned before it will consider petitions for titles. Given the level of hostility that has prevailed on this issue between Wichí and *criollos*, and the profoundly interwoven patterns of access to land, the government's insistence on an independent agreement has been an enduring obstacle.[13] With the government's approval, Fundapaz undertook the role of intermediary and mediator to hammer out agreements locally. At times, when the conflict was particularly persistent or deep-rooted, this role segued into that of arbiter.

Conflicts between Wichí communities and Fundapaz over land titles went beyond a sense of weariness and futility, at times escalating to a more serious rift in the relationship between the NGO and the community. The most serious rupture occurred in the communities of Kayip and Capitán Page, where a serious disagreement arose about the ownership of land close to the Wichí community. Guillermo, one of the young Wichí leaders of Kayip, explained it this way:

> There were some people who wanted more land. They wanted this land here, and for us to move far back into the monte. There were two or three [*criollo*] families who were asking for more land. And they were new—they had only been here 8 or 10 years at the time.

Faced with recalcitrance on both sides, Fundapaz brought in an independent engineer to consult with both sides and draw up boundaries. According to Guillermo,

> You know, this is when we had problems with Fundapaz. They brought in an engineer, and he agreed with those new families. The *criollos* who were always here, they weren't disagreeing with us. But the engineer wouldn't listen to us.

Fundapaz supported the work of their consultant, and submitted a plan with the boundaries placed as the *criollo* settlers had lobbied. Kayip refused to accept this plan, asserting, as Guillermo continued, that "they weren't listening to us. Their engineer only listened to the *criollos*, the families who were new." This created a break between the community and Fundapaz, which withdrew from its work in the village in an atmosphere of hostility and mistrust on both sides.

The leaders of Kayip mounted a bid to get the government to conduct a new land survey with one of its engineers. Their efforts were vindicated when the government engineer agreed with the boundaries requested by the community. The *criollo* families that were requesting land within these boundaries were given other land elsewhere.

Fundapaz stopped working in Kayip for nearly a year. Again, according to Guillermo,

> For a long time Fundapaz didn't come here at all. You know, when they started, they didn't work at all with the *criollos*, only with the [Wichí] communities. Then they started working with the *criollos*, later. To make an agreement

> about the land. . . . Then after a year, more than a year, we wrote a letter. To fix things with them. After that, they came and started working with us again.

I asked if the letter had asked Fundapaz to return to the community. "No," he replied. "We just said that we wanted to have a good relationship with them, a friendship. Like before."

To a certain degree, what the Wichí community saw as the failure of Fundapaz's advocacy has been attributed by some of its members to one particular worker on the Los Blancos team.[14] As it was explained to me, they felt his ties of kinship to local *criollo* families compromised his advocacy of Wichí interests, as he repeatedly, according to them, sided with *criollos* in various disputes. In the view of many in Kayip, Fundapaz failed to represent the interests of the Wichí community, and they rejected not just the individual whom they saw as responsible, but the entire organization.

From the point of view of Fundapaz, the conflict was due to unrealistic expectation of the role of the NGO by the community. As time went on, the director of Fundapaz came to view the NGO's withdrawal as ultimately having positive consequences for its relationship with the community. "We needed to create a relationship that was more mature. . . . We had to realize that we can't and don't have to respond to any demand that they make of us." Some of the misconceptions and miscommunications, he said, "are historical in the relationship—[the idea held by some of the Wichí] that Fundapaz keeps money that the community is entitled to, that the delay in the titles of the land is due to some action or lack of action by Fundapaz." He felt that this pattern was broken by the realization on both sides that Fundapaz could leave the community.

Given the highly charged nature of the issue of landownership, and the absence of any other effective institution in the area of Los Blancos, there is little doubt that without Fundapaz as the key actor in negotiating agreements between Wichí and *criollo* communities, no such agreements would have been reached. This role, although necessary, caused tension and mistrust in the relationship between the Wichí and the NGO. The Wichí had come to see Fundapaz as "their" organization, a patron of sorts. Much as the missionaries of a previous generation, Fundapaz had acted for a number of years as an intermediary between the Wichí communities and the larger societies. It was a conduit of resources, and, perhaps more importantly over the long term, an advocate that the Wichí viewed as both powerful and effective. Fundapaz's strategic decision to begin working with *criollo* communities on the land claim issue, and to continue to work with them as a development organization, created a wedge of unease in its relationship with the Wichí.

In the interests of negotiating a settlement that would move the process forward, Fundapaz alienated some of the Wichí communities. In particular, certain of the Wichí leaders felt that Fundapaz could no longer act as an effective advocate for their interests. They viewed the attempt at creating closer ties with the *criollos* as a betrayal of a relationship characterized, at that time, by paternalism and patronism. As Fundapaz positioned itself to advocate the big picture, so to speak, of gaining land titles in a way that would be *possible*, given the social and political context, some of the Wichí perceived this move as a threat to the interests of their communities.

The Final Stages

By 1996, agreements had been signed and were in place. Still, the actual titles had not arrived. Many Wichí leaders, having little faith in agreements, were dubious about the validity of their claims without the actual physical title to the land in hand.

Over the course of time, Wichí leaders have learned to be wary of politicians and their promises. Before elections were held in 1997, for example, local politicians made a tour of rural communities to raise support. In Capitán Page, representatives of the ruling party promised several construction projects that would provide months of labor for both *criollos* and Wichí. Reviewing these projects, Guillermo, a local young leader, noted in a serious tone, "We have learned not to believe the *politicos* until you see the things actually come." In this, residents of Kayip seemed to possess far more political savvy than their counterparts in the *criollo* village of Page, who enthusiastically embraced the politicians' unlikely plans. Although the *criollo* community stood considerably more to gain through open and visible political support, and was thus more likely to make a show of their political allegiance for local officials and candidates, there was a genuine sense of naivete, a belief that the political payoffs would, in fact, arrive. Members of the Wichí community, in contrast, were more likely to be skeptical of projects and plans, willing to take advantage of those which did materialize but putting little faith in political largesse. Government promises that land titles were forthcoming, and Fundapaz's reassurances in the later stages of delay, were thus met with little credence.

By mid-1997, rumors began to circulate that titles would be awarded in August. Fundapaz and other NGOs heard that the governor would come early in August to personally hand over the titles. At that point, it was not clear if all or only some of the documents would be ready. The Fundapaz team shared this information during their regular meetings in the communities, but with cautious caveats. As Marisol said in one of these meetings, "This is only a rumour. We heard he was coming in February, remember, and again May 1. So this might be like that, and he might not come at all."

As July wore on, it became apparent that not all of the titles would be ready. Rumors continued to fly, as government officials declined to share any definitive information. As far as the Fundapaz team could determine, the government wanted to have all of the titles ready, and some of them were being held up by incomplete paperwork. In meetings in the Wichí communities, Marisol emphasized, "The problem is not with Fundapaz, it is with the government. At this point, it is out of Fundapaz's hands. We have to wait and see what happens."

The title of one of the communities, Cacique Abregu, was in limbo because of a complicated legal arrangement. Cacique Abregu did not have independent legal status as a community, and was considered part of the community of Los Blancos for legal purposes. It thus had no independent land claim. The land that its colony was located on had been given to the community by Kayip. The land title for this tract, some 1,200 hectares, was supposed to be separate from titles of both Kayip and Los Blancos. However, the title could not be issued to the community because of its lack of legal status. The community considered applying for independent status now, but decided to wait because the process was long and quite expensive. There was also the possibility that the process would be changed imminently as a result of constitutional changes to make it easier for indigenous communities to obtain legal status. The indefinite status of the title caused considerable consternation in the community. The cacique of Abregu, a gentle elderly man, went to speak to the leaders of Kayip in order to reassure himself and his community that they would not renege on their gift. Joaquím, one of the leaders of Kayip, recounted this meeting,

> I told him that the land will always belong to you. [The cacique] always asks me if we'll come and say we want that [land] back, and I say no. He asked me again, last week, and I told him again. He is worried.

By the end of July, it had become apparent that the August date that had been circulating was not going to happen. Fundapaz renewed its efforts to spur on the government process in Salta, as team members continued to reassure the communities. In a meeting, Vicente broke the bad news:

> With the titles, we have to continue to hope. It will be delayed more. The titles are not ready. . . . [The director] is going to check on this, to see what exactly the problem is. But don't get discouraged. There is a signed decree, an agreement by the government.

Despite such reassurances, community leaders were becoming increasingly frustrated. After spending time in the provincial capital, the director of Fundapaz became convinced that it was titles north of Route 81 that were holding up the process. This included the land that had been awarded to the Wichí community of Los Blancos and numerous *criollo* holdings. Fundapaz continued to maintain the position that all of the titles should be issued at once, in fear of provoking local conflicts if Wichí titles were distributed before those of the *criollos*.

In the meantime, rumors continued to circulate. At a regional meeting of Wichí leaders in late August, a provincial representative asserted that the Wichí communities would have to pay six hundred pesos for each title. This statement provoked a wave of nervousness in the communities. The director of Fundapaz, learning of this rumor, hastened to assure local leaders that it was not true. The politician, he said, might have misunderstood the process, which waived fees normally assessed for real estate transactions. Or, more cynically, he pointed out that the politician in question may have been trying to raise fears so that he later could take credit for having "taken care of" fees which did not exist in the first place.

By mid-September, rumors once again began to circulate, this time that titles would arrive in late October, days before the provincial elections. This rumor was met with considerably less excitement, as weary community members and leaders had little confidence left. However, in early October, it was officially announced that the governor would arrive the next day with the titles. The communities scrambled to send representatives to Los Blancos to receive the titles. Fundapaz sent its truck out to bring as many people as it could. Others walked or bicycled in.

Predictably, the event itself was dominated by political propaganda, with the governor and members of his party taking personal credit awarding the titles. In the crowded school where the official ceremony was held, *criollo* settlers and Wichí leaders mingled uneasily, as politicians circulated shaking hands. The Wichí pastor of Misión San Patricio, Don Sebastián, began with a prayer, noting that God created men and women from the land itself. Speeches by politicians, each commenting on how hard he personally had worked to process these titles, were followed by brief comments from the president of the *criollo* association and a Wichí leader. Finally, the titles were distributed with great fanfare. The politicians disappeared in short order, and the crowds drifted home, most of them to homes which they now legally owned.

Not all of the titles were distributed in this ceremony. Most notably, the Wichí community of Los Blancos did not receive their title; it arrived some weeks later, along with titles for a few *criollo* homesteads which had been caught in the same bureaucratic morass. When all was finalized, the Wichí community of Los Blancos had received some 2,100 hectares, Misión San Patricio 4,500 hectares, Cacique Abregu 1,200 hectares, and Kayip 9,300 hectares. The amount given to *criollo* households varied; about two hundred families received from several hundred to a thousand hectares each—for a total far larger than what was received by the Wichí population, and with much more land per capita. These titles were individual rather than communal, and usually, but not always, were given in the name of the male head of household.[15]

The differences in the amount of land granted to Wichí communities did not depend on their population or the dependence of the community on natural resources, but on their locations and the presence of *criollo* ranches in their vicinity. It is also not a coincidence that Kayip, the community which was most vocal in its own advocacy, received more than twice the number of hectares as the others. There is still some land in the region which has not been adjudicated, including a large area designated in earlier agreements as an "indigenous reserve" that lies between Misión San Patricio and the Bermejo River. Although it is far from the communities, and not used much by any of them, they see this tract as important to preserving an access route to the river.

The Wichí communities received communal tenure to their land. This entails certain restrictions that are specific to this kind of land grant to indigenous communities. The community is not allowed to collect rent for the land, to subdivide it, or to sell it. They are not required to pay taxes. It must be "used" and occupied by members of the community. *Criollo* settlers, who received individual titles, are not subject to the same restrictions, although they are not permitted to sell the land that they received for a specified number of years.

Unlike in Rodeo Colanzulí, there was no debate in the Wichí communities about whether to accept communal or individual title. In part, this is because the Wichí do not think of land as individually owned, as alienable. "Private property" is a relatively recent concept for these communities. It is also due to the ways in which the Wichí use the monte. Hunting and gathering require access to large areas, in order to guarantee access to important species throughout the year and in times of shortage. This access is best preserved through common property. It would be nearly impossible to divide up the monte, with its wild resources, between Wichí households in a way that they would find equitable. The prospect of individual land titles was never discussed or debated as an option in the Wichí communities.

What was created by the titling of land to Wichí communities and *criollo* households was, then, a dual system of ownership. By titling some land individually, free of constraints and regulations, and other land communally, with numerous restrictions and protections, the state created two classes of owners, and perhaps ultimately, two kinds of citizens. The Wichí strongly support the kinds of communal rights that this system affords them. As this generation has watched their access to land steadily decline, eroded through white settlement, the guarantee that some land will always remain for the Wichí is reassuring and comforting. It is seen as a way to guarantee that the Wichí culture, with its ties to the land, to hunting and gathering, will persist. Leaders of the Wichí communities see it as a way to better exploit the resources of the monte, without having to ask permission or worry that access could be blocked. For advocates, such as Fundapaz, collective land titles are seen as a tool for ecological conservation, enabling the development of a management system of common resources that will ensure their long-term protection. In the future, however, the Wichí may find that the restrictions on their ownership of land place them, as individuals, in a different category than their *criollo* neighbors. It may limit their possibilities in the market economy, which plays an increasingly important role in Wichí economic strategies. However, at the present moment in time, the benefits of communal land tenure are welcomed, without a sense of inequality.

Owning Land

The receipt of the titles, for both *criollo* and Wichí, set off a flurry of projects and proposals that had been awaiting just such a development. Fundapaz had been planning several projects, especially in the *criollo* villages, that had been put on hold because the funding source required legal landownership. These were immediately set into motion. In the Wichí communities, an important project would provide funds for each community to enclose a significant area of its land, up to 1,000 hectares. This fencing could be used to protect vulnerable parts of the monte, or areas which contained particularly useful resources, such as water and algarrobo groves, from grazing animals.[16]

Despite the initial promise of such projects and the renewed optimism that the long-awaited land titles spurred in the communities, Fundapaz and other observers advised caution in thinking about regional development. Secure land titles do encourage certain kinds of infrastructural investment and are an improvement over the insecure usufruct rights that formerly prevailed in the region. However, they are not the panacea to all of the region's issues. Land titles could even introduce new conflicts in a region where land is by far the most important resource. First, *criollo* homesteads nearly always use more land than what they were given titles to. As fences go up, conflict between neighbors could increase. Secondly, the Wichí have never built fences, lacking the kind of permanent claim to land that enclosure implies. As the Wichí begin to enclose parts of their land, ethnic tensions could also increase.

Within the Wichí communities themselves, other issues may arise that have not yet been foreseen locally. In a study of the involvement of the Wichí and other recently nomadic peoples in plantation labor in northern Argentina, Héctor Trinchero and Juan Leguizamón (1995) point out that indigenous "communities" are best understood as artificial constructs rather than a truly indigenous form of social organization. Like early *reducciones*[17] and later mission villages, contemporary indigenous "communities" in the Chaco are best considered to express the organization of a surplus rural labor force rather than a distinctly *indigenous* form of organization (1995, 19-20).[18] Here, the idea of communities as an artificial construct is useful, although removed from the context of labor force organization discussed by the authors. There are considerable implications for land titles as community property, in a context where the community itself—the mission village—has been created recently, and from the outside. Titles are not awarded to an indigenous grouping, such as the clan or extended family, but to a mission village, a community which has been in existence for at best some sixty years. Granting land titles, and legal status, to mission villages transforms them into a permanent, legal social arrangement which does not reflect the historic nature of Wichí social organization.

For example, one issue that has not been addressed locally is the continuing mobility of individuals between settlements.[19] Defining which individuals have rights to land within a given community's landholdings may become problematic as individuals move between communities. Although ties of kinship and affiliation permit such mobility, there is as of yet no indication of whether community membership may become more rigidly defined as a result of claims that members may make on communal resources. The question of how an individual can make a claim on land as a resource, in a culture where land has not been seen as an individually ownable thing, remains open. It may be that family ties which currently entitle an individual to settle in a given community may be extended to define rights to land. It is also possible that access to land in any Wichí community may be open to any individual, regardless of kinship ties, who is recognized as Wichí. In marked contrast to the highlands of Iruya, where residents are accustomed to having a set of rules defining use and access, the Wichí continue to have a strong sense that all Wichí have a right to the resources of the monte. In the absence of undue pressure on local resources, this open access to communal property may continue to serve as the framework for Wichí subsistence.

Fundapaz: Conservation and Stewardship

In the Chaco Salteño, the questions of land tenure are set against a backdrop of environmental and economic concerns. On a daily level, this is a more technocratic and bureaucratic process, one in which the productivity of the land is measured against the economic needs and possibilities of its inhabitants, both Wichí and *criollo*. But underlying a dry accounting of carrying capacity are questions and assumptions about the Wichí and their relationship with the land, and how that relationship is to be played out in an increasingly taxed environment.

The policy of the state, in recent years, has been to "develop" the indigenous groups of the Chaco. The provincial constitution emphasizes that land is for "rational" production (Carrasco and Briones 1996, 208).[20] Hunting and gathering is portrayed as "cultural backwardness" (Carrasco and Briones 1996, 209). The rights of indigenous peoples to have land is not entirely negated, but their use of their territory for traditional subsistence practices is relegated to the realm of the cultural, clearly less valued and of lower priority than "productive" use of the same land. The dominant cultural norms clearly favor herding, which is an economic activity of high prestige throughout Argentina. Land policies are shaped by a bias towards using land as open rangelands, despite low productivity and ecological destructiveness in the fragile lands of the Chaco. The indigenous people themselves have been treated as minors, conceptually if not legally, "culturally backward" people who need to be civilized. Integrationist policies encourage land uses and economic activities that promote "production": settled agriculture, herding, and participation in wage labor and the cash economy.

Fundapaz has acted as a mediator, albeit an uneasy one at times, between such state policies and the indigenous communities. There is a strong recognition of the cultural importance of hunting and gathering and the nature of the relationship between Wichí culture and the landscape they occupy. This is tempered by a sense that given the actual ecological and political context of the region, the Wichí need other alternatives for their subsistence, and that this inevitably entails changes in lifestyle and even culture.

In its advocacy for native communities, Fundapaz mobilizes the argument that the Wichí need their land in order to maintain their traditional culture. In its daily praxis, the Los Blancos team struggles to maintain a balance between instituting development programs and creating a space for the maintenance of Wichí culture. The director noted ruefully,

> Sometimes the team worries too much about time, about getting things done. They worry about finishing things. When they were building the center in San Patricio, for example, it was the beginning of December and they wanted to get it done so that they could say it was done by the end of the year. But everyone was hunting, going in the monte. I told them, "Wait, why push the project when there are things they can do in the monte? It is better to have the work from projects during this time of year, and the months when they can hunt, let them hunt." We need to reflect on the cultural aspects of working with the Wichí. We need to look at what we need to change [about our work]. We have our discourse, and our practice.

The problem, he continued, is putting the discourse into practice, of keeping an awareness of cultural sensitivity in day-to-day activities.

In its daily work, Fundapaz's focus stayed on the ecological environment of the Chaco. Projects were considered carefully in terms of their potential environmental impact. At times, the team refused to promote projects requested by the Wichí, such as introducing cattle, because it was felt that the ecological consequences outweighed any potential economic benefits. The Los Blancos team included several specialists in ecology and natural resource management, and scientific knowledge of ecosystems and the local environment was scrupulously deployed. There was also a recognition, however, of the tremendous knowledge of the Wichí about their territory and its resources. Such knowledge was respectfully sought after and eagerly accepted by the team, who employed this source of information along with other, "scientific" sources, in their work in the region.

Conclusion

As communities of Iruya and Los Blancos have labored to win titles to the land that they consider theirs, their rights to that land have been explicitly linked to their status as indigenous peoples. This status has given them specific rights, but also specific constraints, which are not shared by other poor rural groups. The discourse employed by the state in granting such rights tends to focus on righting historical wrongs. The other principal actors involved in this process, the

Catholic NGOs and the indigenous peoples themselves, tend to focus more on the particular nature of these peoples' relationships with their land.

As Akhil Gupta and James Ferguson note, "Even people remaining in familiar and ancestral places find the nature of their relation to place ineluctably changed, and the illusion of a natural and essential connection between the place and the culture broken" (1992, 10). Ironically, as actual place becomes less important in the transient and shifting global economy, the idea of culturally and ethnically distinct places has become more important (Gupta and Ferguson 1992). For both the Kolla and Wichí, the process of land reclamation acted to sharpen and define ethnic identity. An identity as *indigenous* marked the land claim issue from its inception, defining individuals as entitled to specific rights and subject to certain restrictions. At the same time, indigenous identity has been reshaped and redefined by a bureaucratic legal process that defines what it means to be indigenous and what the costs and benefits of that definition are (Briones 2000).

Both the indigenous communities and their NGO advocates have emphasized an emotional and cultural tie to land in the quest to win land titles. At times, this relationship is idealized and romanticized. In other instances, it is employed deliberately as a political tool. Throughout the process of land repatriation, in both communities, the unique relationship of an indigenous community with its land has been invoked as an irrefutable moral argument. Indigenous identity, in turn, has been linked to a "natural" connection to land, which in turn provides the basis for political legitimacy (cf. Clifford 1994).

Indigenous communities are portrayed as having been

> pushed by white men to lands which are dry and inhospitable, or in some few cases, fertile but small in area, insufficient to allow them to maintain their cultural norms and to live in dignity. . . . Without land . . . one lives as a slave to the white man. (Fundapaz 1988/89, 3-4)

In the discourse of Catholic NGOs, land acts as the means for these indigenous communities to live "in human dignity." It does not merely provide a means of subsistence—in fact, the land-based traditional subsistence strategy of these communities is usually inadequate to their present needs. Rather, its greatest importance lies in acting to provide a cultural space.

Notes:

1. Quoted in Carrasco and Briones 1996, 32.
2. Poor *criollo* laborers have been romanticized in the form of the *gaucho*, one of Argentina's national symbols and the subject of a substantial literary tradition (see Shumway 1991).

3. This figure comes from data collected by health care workers (*agentes sanitarios*), who take a household census every three months, going door-to-door to all of the dwellings in the community. The data used here come from the census dated March 14, 1997. I am grateful to Armando Tacacho and the hospital in Iruya for sharing the data from this census with me.
4. The only channel that it receives is the Bolivian national network.
5. These other communities are Volcán Higueras, Río Cortaderas, and Isla de Cañas. They are all located at a considerable distance, in terms of travel time, from Rodeo Colanzulí, across the mountains to the east. There are few ties between the communities. The research for this paper was conducted in Rodeo Colanzulí, thus I am not going to discuss the other communities or the relations between them to any significant extent here.
6. A report produced by the Centro Vecinal of Rodeo Colanzulí gives this date as 1909.
7. May through October.
8. Again, the dates given by Reboratti and the report do not coincide: Reboratti gives the exact year as 1951, while the community report states that it was in 1950.
9. At the present time, the sugar produced in Salta is of poor quality and high price, and not competitive, but is maintained with state support (Reboratti 1996, 70).
10. Unfortunately, most local residents have had little access to the results of this kind of research.
11. In fact, I never heard anyone in the community refer to him/herself by either term.
12. Some of the mission communities around Embarcación were located on private land that belonged to the Anglican church. Most of this land has been given to the communities by the church. Other communities are located on land held by private owners, and their status continues to be unresolved.
13. This continues to be a vexing issue in the communities near the Pilcomayo, where Wichí and *criollo* factions have been unable to reach any compromise. In an appearance in Los Blancos in 1997, the provincial governor complained that the tensions between the two groups were so high that it was impossible to hold a meeting that both groups would agree to attend. One of my Wichí informants noted that from what he understood of the Pilcomayo situation, there were a few *criollos* who refused to sign on to any agreement, thus blocking a consensus and derailing the entire process.
14. This person was no longer working for Fundapaz when I was in Los Blancos.
15. Most of the exceptions were in the case of female-headed households, often widows with children.
16. In terms of ecological management, it is unclear whether this is a large enough area to provide significant protection of habitats for the wild animal species used by the Wichí. Ecological specialists at Fundapaz feel that the protection of important resources, such as water, is crucial to long-term ecological conservation. I am unaware of any scientific studies on the ranges needed for the wild animal species of the region, and the amount of land that would need to be protected in order to sustain healthy populations.
17. This is sometimes translated as reductions. It refers to villages in which nomadic peoples were forced to settle in the early colonial period, often also organized as missions.
18. The concentration of the indigenous population also served to make land available for white settlement in the region, which I argue was more important than the concentration of the labor force described by Trinchero and Leguizamón.

19. The issue of mobility has been inadequately addressed in some development projects as well, and at times the presence or absence of particular individuals during ongoing projects has been an issue of contention, especially between the NGO and project participants.

20. The provincial constitution is currently in the process of being rewritten, and there may be some significant changes to sections dealing with the state's relationship with its indigenous peoples.

Conclusion

Carlos Reboratti noted that northern Salta has been widely ignored by the rest of the Argentine nation, except "as a rare or curious object, something which is missed or alienated by a public which converts it into a different space, almost foreign" (1996, 7). The inhabitants of this foreign space are equally mysterious to the national gaze.

In the imagination of the NGOs that work in northwest Argentina's remote spaces, the indigenous communities are an alternative societal model. Their lifestyles and values are seen as preferable to the consumerism, corruption, and capitalism of urban Argentina. OCLADE imagines the people of Iruya as sharing their lives, their land, and their work almost as did the early Christians, living collectively and communally. Their very poverty is deemed noble, based as it is on subsistence production and local self-sufficiency. Fundapaz, in turn, sees the Wichí as living more in harmony with their natural environment than others in the mainstream society. A sense of impending ecological crisis colors Fundapaz's work; if the fragile natural environment deteriorates beyond repair, the Wichís' existence, like that of the plants and animals who share their wild landscape, is in peril.

In envisioning indigenous cultures in this way, ties to the land symbolize and enshrine indigenous identity. Their cultural ties to the land are invoked as a key symbolic element of the difference between them and the larger society. It is in this light that OCLADE and Fundapaz take on the contentious issue of indigenous land claims as part of their work towards social justice. Cultural ties to the land are invoked as a key and presumably inarguable rallying point. Landownership is portrayed as the lynchpin upon which hangs the ability of indigenous cultures to preserve themselves and their (implicitly superior) way of life. In Iruya, land claims issues acted as a catalyst to invigorate a sense of indigenous identity. In both cases, the salience of a connection between indigenous culture and the land was seized upon, by both the NGOs and the local communities, as an effective political argument.

These views of the indigenous community, as an *alternative* model, emerge from the religious background of both the NGOs in question. OCLADE and Fundapaz are quite distinct in the ways in which they conceptualize and realize their missions, in the degree to which they emphasize their religious values and origins. Still, they both originated as religiously motivated organizations. In both cases, persons associated with the Catholic Church, living in an indigenous community, felt compelled by the depth of the needs that they perceived around them, to create an organization dedicated to improving conditions in those communities.

Moreover, the impetus to change economic conditions was itself rooted in a deeper conviction that poverty is just one aspect of unjust social conditions. As religious organizations, they take a holistic interest in the human condition. Their motivation is not based on an idea of economic maximization, or improved living conditions, or growth, to the extent that a secular development organization's *raison d'etre* is economic, or educational, or any single issue or set of issues. Instead, their driving force is social justice, interpreted broadly and inclusively. They are interested in improving material conditions as one necessary aspect of improving the whole human condition. In short, improving the material conditions of the communities is a necessary step towards social justice.

The religious background and motivation of each NGO also contributed to its willingness to become involved with land claims issues. Land expropriation is not a popular idea in the contemporary development discourse, but something that was left behind in the detritus of the socialist era. Land claims do not fall into the domain of project funding. OCLADE and Fundapaz, motivated by the quest for social justice, were able to envision a role in the struggle for landownership as part of their overall mission, which was holistic and encompassing. Their ideal of independent indigenous communities, in each case, made landownership an obvious, if difficult, target.

As we have seen, Fundapaz, as an independent organization, took a much more active role in the process of land reclamation, serving as a *de facto,* and at certain times even as an official, mediator between the Wichí communities and the state. OCLADE's involvement, on the other hand, was limited by its structural position as part of a larger religious organization, where others were appointed as the mediator. It was also encumbered by its own reluctance to become involved in changing the structure of productive relations in the region—a reluctance which emanated from its idealization of subsistence production and its misgivings about commercial farming. On a broader level, however, both Fundapaz and the Claretian church saw their own role as that of mediators. They perceived a need on the part of the communities where they were located for someone to "help." Initially, this help consisted of making the indigenous communities aware of their own oppressed, landless condition: a process of conscientization. For Fundapaz, the second step was its own active intervention in constructing feasible agreements between the *criollos* and the Wichí, and intervening with the state to persuade it to ratify those agreements. For OCLADE and the Claretians, the role continued to be one of political advocacy and communication.

Initially, the advocacy of the NGO was accepted and welcomed by leaders in the communities. In these remote and isolated areas, sources of material and political resources are scarce. Religious NGOs represented a stable and committed institution, one which was able to garner a degree of trust, if at times colored by relations of dependence. The Kolla and Wichí accepted the vision of landownership offered by the NGOs and ultimately espoused land reclamation as their own goal. Landownership became intimately linked to a vision of "development" based on a conception of their own position as indigenous peoples within an ethnically homogenous state.

Ironically, in both communities, individuals active in the land cases came to feel that the NGO was not adequately meeting their needs. The NGOs' efforts at conscientization, in fact, led to a degree of local empowerment. To a certain extent, both NGOs felt this tension as a betrayal, even though their own goals were to empower the community and allow it to go beyond the NGO to self-advocacy. To different degrees this tension has engendered some confusion in the roles and positions of each NGO as an agent of development.

The land claim cases serve to illustrate an ambivalence in the NGOs' definitions of development that in turn colors the work that they do in the indigenous communities. Both organizations have a profound respect for the indigenous cultures where they work. They cast them as an alternative model to modern society. They are sensitive to a threat of acculturation and the "loss" of indigenous culture to the encroaching fingers of the national society. The communities are increasingly integrating through the mass media, through improved transportation, and through the need for migrant labor and the continued outmigration of young people fostered by the ever-increasing difficulty of maintaining an acceptable standard of living in the villages.

OCLADE and Fundapaz wage an unconscious battle against their own inclination to "preserve" the indigenous cultures, to create conditions that allow local people to sustain their "traditional" way of life. At their best, they acknowledge that this is impossible. Fundapaz, in particular, has an acute awareness that the Wichí cannot, and do not choose to, continue to live as they did in the era before white settlement. The NGOs illustrate an implicit tension that underlies the work of development: mediating between sustaining an indigenous culture, often idealized and conceived of in the timeless past, and creating projects that promote material and social change.

The views that the NGOs hold about the indigenous communities, and their ambivalence about the desirability of change, shape and inform the development projects that each NGO creates in the community. Particularly for OCLADE, which has been less self-critical in its approach, this underlying tension limits the organization's approach to, and definition of, development. Idealized images of cooperation and communalism emerge from a projection of Christian values onto the local community. As in the case of the failed agricultural cooperative, the failure to live up to these expectations is then cast back onto the community itself.

For OCLADE, subsistence agriculture was an essential part of what it meant to be "indigenous" in Iruya. Subsistence farming was ennobled and glorified, even as it proved unable to provide a standard of living that either the farmers or the NGO found acceptable. But the association, in the discourse of the NGO, between subsistence farming and indigenous identity was so strong that other means of earning a living were depicted as alien and as alienating. Even expanding commercial farming was off-putting to OCLADE, because the entrée of values associated with the marketplace and capitalism were at odds with its image of the noble indigenous farmer. Poverty and suffering, the life of the oppressed, themes which recur in its Catholic discourse, resonate locally. The impoverished subsistence farmer is glorified, even as the NGO introduces projects which attempt to ameliorate that poverty. Because subsistence farming is defined as central to indigenous identity, OCLADE is nearly incapable of undertaking projects that try to change the underlying system of production.

Moreover, the religious nature of the NGO may limit local people's negotiating power in other ways. In the case of Iruya, the direct association of OCLADE with the Catholic Church gives its vision of development and of indigenous life a sense of moral authority. Local people may accept or reject the image that the NGO proffers of their own culture, but its rejection entails a difficult split from a deeply embedded institution, that of the Church. The sharp divide between Catholics and evangelicals in the community is characterized not only by religious differences, but by a division over the nature of local culture and an adhesion to indigenous traditions. The evangelical churches may be acting as a locus of resistance to the model of indigenous culture suggested by the Catholic Church, its satellite organizations, and its members.

Fundapaz, in contrast to OCLADE, has juxtaposed a religious discourse with a more technical and ecological vision. In part, this difference is due to the structural relationship of each organization with the Catholic Church. OCLADE is directly tied to the Church and reliant on it for funding and resources. Religious personnel comprise a large portion of its staff, especially its administration. Fundapaz is an independent NGO that has steadily moved towards secular funding sources and nonreligious personnel, including its administrative staff. In consequence, its model of development is more technically oriented. Although Fundapaz's mission continues to include issues of social justice, its discourse steers away from explicitly religious visions of the existing social order. This is in sharp contrast to OCLADE. While OCLADE creates an emphatic vision of the Kolla culture as apart from, and morally superior to, the dominant Argentine lifestyle, Fundapaz's vision for the Wichí relies on a conception of social justice, derived from its religious origins, as well as on a sense of ecological and cultural sustainability.

Yet a religious idiom of development may permit each organization to be more creative in its approach to projects. The dominant, secular discourse of development emphasizes technical solutions to issues that are defined in highly limited and circumscribed ways. It tends to confine projects to specific ends and means. Religious NGOs such as OCLADE and Fundapaz, however, do not limit their sphere of interest. As their involvement in land claim issues illustrate, a holistic approach allows them to go beyond the narrow confines of specific projects. Arguably, this support translated into concrete material and ideological gains for the communities.

As each organization has recently redefined its mission in the communities, it has focused its own discourse and efforts on empowerment. Both have recognized patterns of dependency and paternalism in their relationships with the communities. On one hand, this new understanding by the NGOs is pragmatic in that it has encouraged a redefinition of some aspects of the local economy as beyond their purview. OCLADE, in particular, has shifted to encouraging local people to pressure local government to meet some of their needs. The consequences of relying more heavily on government resources, however, are dubious in a region where government operations are far from open and impartial, and the capacity of local government, in particular, to impartially distribute resources is in question. Nevertheless, as we have seen in the land claim efforts the NGOs' attempts to increase the ability of local people to act as their own advocates, reducing their reliance on the organizations themselves, have borne fruit.

There are examples of such empowerment and its unpredicted, multi-stranded results in both case studies. As OCLADE distanced itself from the land claim of the people of the Finca Santiago, local residents organized themselves to continue their legal battle. In the process, many of those who had been most involved with and most dedicated to the NGO, as clients, participants, and local organizers, found themselves distanced from the organization. They felt that it no longer was working to meet their needs, and indeed, described themselves as having outgrown it, in a sense. In the Chaco, Kayip made a deliberate split from Fundapaz when community leaders felt the NGO was not acting in their interest. This breach in the relationship had an acrimonious character. Both the community and the organization took some time to reassess their interactions, which had been characterized by a sense of dependency and entitlement. When a *rapprochement* occurred a year or more later, it was with a new sense of empowerment on the part of the community. In both cases, the work of the NGO to increase the community's independence paid off with the community becoming less dependent on the NGO itself. Community leaders, when they felt the NGO was not acting in their best interest or was not sufficiently proactive, set off in search of other resources.

The religious framework of the organization may give local people negotiating power. First, because the goal of the organization is not just to implement one project successfully, or to change specific aspects of local production, but a holistic process of empowerment and a quest for social justice, local people may be able to ask more of these NGOs than they would of other kinds of organizations. They may also be less bound by rules or compliance. The NGO has a commitment to the community that goes beyond one specific project or program. Second, the emphasis on empowerment and conscientization provides tools to allow local people to go outside of the NGO itself for resources. Thus, the goal of reducing dependence may have unintended results, as local people challenge the NGO and its vision of their future.

In the several years since I completed the field research for this study, Argentina has unquestionably passed through challenging times. Economic crisis and political instability have thrown the nation into turmoil. The neoliberalism of the Menem government was resoundingly rejected in widespread protests in 2001-2002. While banking restrictions and currency changes may seem to have little bearing on communities where there are no banks and families do not keep their life savings in American dollars, political instability and a shifting national discourse are felt as keenly there as anywhere in central Buenos Aires. Perhaps one of the key lessons of that can be gleaned is the ongoing importance of NGOs, which remain in place and continue to operate even as government agencies change policies with administrations.

In an era in which the forces of globalization are increasingly contested by local voices, religious organizations that base their work on notions of social justice may indeed offer an alternative model for development. A religious idiom of development may reframe the terms of the debate, shifting the discourse from one which is narrowly focused on projects and outcomes to one which considers the fundamental questions: how do we want to live? How do we work with others in order to allow them to live as they want to live? Although the distance from question to implementation may be considerable, with pitfalls along the way, the first crucial step is this reformulation of the questions of development. The question, really, is not one of development but one of how to live. OCLADE and Fundapaz, like innumerable other organizations working in remote communities, have shown themselves willing to ask this difficult question and to work tirelessly towards difficult answers.

Bibliography

Abduca, Ricardo G. 1995. "Campesinos con ocupación obrera: Relaciones campesinas y dependencia salarial en una cabecera de valle argentino-boliviana." Pp. 81-103 in *Producción doméstica y capital: Estudios desde la antropología económica*, edited by Hugo Trinchero. Buenos Aires: Editorial Biblos.

Aguilar, María Angela. 1993. "Decentralización y gobiernos municipales: Limitaciones y posibilidades." Paper presented at a seminar on "La cuidad y la calidad de vida: El rol del municipio," Consejo de Investigación, Universidad Nacional de Salta.

Aguilar, M. A., and M. E. Sbrocco. 1995. "Tecnologías apropriadas para cocción de alimentos." Working paper, Brace Research Institute of McGill University.

Alvarsson, Jan-Åke. 1999. "Foraging in Town: Survival Strategies among the 'Weenhayek of Bolivia and Argentina." Pp. 23-35 in *Peoples of the Gran Chaco*, edited by Elmer Miller. Westport, Conn.: Bergin and Garvey.

—. 1988. *The Mataco of the Gran Chaco*. Stockholm: Uppsala.

Andersen, Martin Edwin. 1993. *Dossier Secreto: Argentina's Desaparecidos and the Myth of the "Dirty War."* Boulder, Colo.: Westview Press.

Anderson, E. N. 1996. *Ecologies of the Heart: Emotion, Belief, and the Environment*. New York: Oxford University Press.

Asch, Michael. 1989. "Wildlife: Defining the Animals the Dene Hunt and the Settlement of Aboriginal Rights Claims." *Canadian Public Policy* 15, no. 2: 205-219.

Barúa, Guadelupe. 1985. "Principios de organización en la sociedad Mataco." Pp. 1-78 in *Sistemas Socioculturales América*, vol. 1. Buenos Aires: Cefyl Publicaciones.

Basso, Keith H. 1988. "'Speaking with Names': Language and Landscape among the Western Apache." *Cultural Anthropology* 3, no. 2: 99-130.

—. 1996. *Wisdom Sits in Places*. Albuquerque: University of New Mexico Press.

Bateson, Gregory. 1979. *Mind and Nature: A Necessary Unity*. New York: Bantam Books.

Bax, Mart. 1987. "Religious Regimes and State Formation: Towards a Research Perspective." *Anthropological Quarterly* 60, no. 1: 1-11.

Benavides, Gustavo. 1987. "Catholicism and Politics in Latin America." Pp. 107-142 in *Movements and Issues in World Religions*, edited by Charles Wei-hsun Fu and Gerhard E. Spiegler. New York: Greenwood Press.

Berry, Sara. 1988. "Concentration without Privatization? Some Consequences of Changing Patterns of Rural Land Control in Africa." Pp. 53-75 in *Land and Society in Contemporary Africa*, edited by R. E. Downs and S. P. Reyna. Hanover, N.H.: University of New Hampshire.

Berryman, Philip. 1987. *Liberation Theology: Essential Facts about the Revolutionary Movement in Latin America and Beyond.* New York: Pantheon Books.

Bornstein, Erica. 2003. *The Spirit of Development: Protestant NGOs, Morality, and Economics in Zimbabwe.* New York: Routledge.

Boserup, Ester. 1990. *Economic and Demographic Relations in Development.* Baltimore: Johns Hopkins University Press.

Bourque, Susan C., and Kay Barbara Warren. 1981. *Women of the Andes: Patriarchy and Social Change in Two Peruvian Towns.* Ann Arbor: University of Michigan Press.

Braunstein, José A. 1983. *Algunos rasgos de la organización social de los indígenas del Gran Chaco.* Buenos Aires: Universidad de Buenos Aires, Facultad de Filosofía y Letras, Instituto de Ciencias Antropológicas, Trabajos de Etnología, Publicación No. 2.

—. 1974. "Matrimonio y familia entre los matacos." *Cuadernos Franciscanos*, no. 35: 72-79.

Braunstein, José, and Elmer Miller. 1999. "Ethnohistorical Introduction." Pp. 1-22 in *Peoples of the Gran Chaco*, edited by Elmer Miller. Westport, Conn.: Bergin and Garvey.

Briones, Claudia. 2000. "The Politics of Indigenous Representation: Mapuche Views on State Law and Juridical Pluralism." Paper presented at the annual meeting of the American Anthropological Association, San Francisco.

Bunker, Stephen G. 1985. *Underdeveloping the Amazon.* Chicago: University of Illinois Press.

Cardoso, Fernando Henrique, and Enzo Faletto. 1979. *Dependency and Development in Latin America.* Berkeley: University of California Press.

Carrasco, Morita, and Claudia Briones. 1996. *La tierra que nos quitaron: Reclamos indígenas en Argentina.* Buenos Aires: Grupo Internacional de Trabajo sobre Asuntos Indígenas (IWGIA) and Lhaka Honat.

Carroll, Thomas F. 1992. *Intermediary NGOs: The Supporting Link in Grassroots Development.* West Hartford, Conn.: Kumerian Press.

Chambers, Robert. 1983. *Rural Development: Putting the Last First.* New York: Longman.

Clifford, James. 1994. "Diasporas." *Cultural Anthropology* 9, no. 3: 302-338.

—. 1988. *The Predicament of Culture: Twentieth-Century Ethnography, Literature, and Art.* Cambridge, Mass.: Harvard University Press.

Comaroff, John, and Jean Comaroff. 1992. *Ethnography and the Historical Imagination.* Boulder, Colo.: Westview.

Corradi, Juan E. 1985. *The Fitful Republic: Economy, Society, and Politics in Argentina.* Boulder, Colo.: Westview Press.

Crush, Jonathan, ed. 1995. *Power of Development.* New York: Routledge.

Cushner, Nicolas P. 1982. *Farm and Factory: The Jesuits and the Development of Agrarian Capitalism in Colonial Quito, 1600-1767.* Albany: State University of New York Press.

—. 1983. *Jesuit Ranches and the Agrarian Development of Colonial Argentina, 1650-1767.* Albany: State University of New York Press.

Dahl, G., and A. Rabo, eds. 1992. *Kam-Ap or Take-Off: Local Notions of Development.* Stockholm: Stockholm Studies in Social Anthropology, Stockholm University.

Dasso, María Cristina. 1999. "Equilibrio del control y descontrol en la existencia *wichí.*" Pp. 141-166 in *Mito, guerra y venganza entre los wichí*, edited by Mario Califano. Buenos Aires: Ciudad Argentina.

Davis, William Columbus. 1995. *Warnings from the Far South: Democracy versus Dictatorship in Uruguay, Argentina, and Chile.* London: Praeger.

De Janvry, Alain. 1981. *The Agrarian Question and Reformism in Latin America.* Baltimore: Johns Hopkins University Press.

Dorner, Peter. 1992. *Latin American Land Reforms in Theory and Practice: A Retrospective Analysis.* Madison: University of Wisconsin Press.

Elias, Robert. 1989. "Alternative Development in Central America: A Role for Oxfam?" Pp. 1-32 in *Dependence, Development, and State Repression*, edited by George A. Lopez and Michael Stohl. New York: Greenwood Press.

Escobar, Arturo. 1995. *Encountering Development: The Making and Unmaking of the Third World.* Princeton, N.J.: Princeton University Press.

Evans, Peter. 1979. *Dependent Development: The Alliance of Multinational, State, and Local Capital in Brazil.* Princeton, N.J.: Princeton University Press.

Feit, Harvey. 1978. *Waswanipi Realities and Adaptations: Resource Management among Subartic Hunters.* Ph.D. Dissertation, McGill University.

—. 1973. "The Ethno-ecology of the Waswanipi Cree: Or, How Hunters Can Manage Their Resources." Pp. 115-125 in *Cultural Ecology: Readings on Canadian Indians*, edited by Bruce Cox. Toronto: McClelland and Stewart.

Felix, David. 1994. "Industrial Development in East Asia: What are the Lessons for Latin America?" *The UNCTAD Review*: 123-142.

Ferguson, James. 1990. *The Anti-Politics Machine: "Development," Depoliticization, and Bureaucratic Power in Lesotho.* New York: Cambridge University Press.

Fock, Niels. 1982. "History of Mataco Folk Literature and Research." Pp. 1-33 in *Folk Literature of the Mataco Indians*, edited by Johannes Wilbert and Karin Simoneau. Los Angeles: UCLA Latin American Center Publications, University of California.

Fonseca Martel, Cesar, and Enrique Mayer. 1988. *Comunidad y producción en la agricultura andina.* Lima, Peru: Fomciencias.

Frank, Andre Gunder. 1967. *Capitalism and Underdevelopment in Latin America.* New York: Monthly Review Press.

Freire, Paulo. 1970. *Pedagogy of the Oppressed.* New York: The Seabury Press.

Geertz, Clifford. 1988. *Works and Lives: The Anthropologist as Author.* Stanford, Calif.: Stanford University Press.

Gibson, Charles. 1966. *Spain in America.* New York: Harper and Row.

Gill, Lesley. 1987. *Peasants, Entrepreneurs and Social Change: Frontier Development in Lowland Bolivia.* Boulder, Colo.: Westview Press.

Gordillo, Gastón. 1995. "La subordinación y sus mediaciones: Dinámica cazadora recolectora, relaciones de producción, capital comercial y estado entre los Tobas del oeste de Formosa." Pp. 105-138 in *Producción doméstica y capital: Estudios desde la antropología económica*, edited by Hugo Trinchero. Buenos Aires: Editorial Biblos.

—. 2002. "Locations of Hegemony: The Making of Place in the Toba's Struggle for *La Comuna*, 1989-99." *American Anthropologist* 104, no. 1: 262-277.

Gudeman, Stephen, and Alberto Rivera. 1990. *Conversations in Columbia: The domestic economy in life and text*. Cambridge: Cambridge University Press.

Gupta, Akhil, and James Ferguson. 1992. "Beyond 'Culture': Space, Identity, and the Politics of Difference." *Cultural Anthropology* 7, no. 1: 6-23.

Hyden, Goran. 1980. *Beyond Ujamaa in Tanzania: Underdevelopment and an Uncaptured Peasantry*. London: Heinemann Educational Books.

—. 1983. *No Shortcuts to Progress: African Development Management in Perspective*. Berkeley: University of California Press.

Ivereigh, Austen. 1995. *Catholicism and Politics in Argentina, 1810-1960*. New York: St. Martin's Press.

Jelin, Elizabeth. 1994. "The Politics of Memory: The Human Rights Movement and the Construction of Democracy in Argentina." *Latin American Perspectives* 8, no. 21: 38-58.

Kidd, Stephen. 1999. "The Morality of the Enxet People." Pp. 37-60 in *Peoples of the Gran Chaco*, edited by Elmer Miller. Westport, Conn.: Bergin and Garvey.

Koenig, Dolores. 1988. "The Culture and Social Organization of USAID Development Projects in West Africa." Pp. 345-364 in *Production and Autonomy: Anthropological Studies and Critiques of Development*, edited by John W. Bowen and John R. Bennett. Lanham, Md.: University Press of America.

Kulik, Don. 1992. "'Coming Up' in Gapun: Conceptions of Development and Their Effect on Language in a Papua New Guinean Village." Pp. 9-34 in *Kam-Ap or Take-Off: Local Notions of Development*, edited by G. Dahl and A. Rabo. Stockholm: Stockholm Studies in Social Anthropology, Stockholm University.

Lee, Richard. 1993. *The Dobe Ju/'Hoansi*. New York: Harcourt Brace.

Lehmann, David. 1990. *Development and Democracy in Latin America: Economics, Politics and Religion in the Post-War Period*. Philadelphia: Temple University Press.

Leonard, David K., and Dale Rogers Marshall, eds. 1982. *Institutions of Rural Development for the Poor: Decentralization and Organizational Linkages*. Berkeley: Institute of International Studies, University of California.

Levaggi, Abelardo. 1990. "Tratamiento legal y jurisprudencial del aborígen en la Argentina durante el siglo XIX." Pp. 245-284 in *El aborígen y el derecho en el pasado y el presente*, edited by Abelardo Levaggi. Buenos Aires: Universidad del Museo Social Argentino.

Little, Peter D. 1992. *The Elusive Granary: Herder, Farmer, and State in Northern Kenya*. New York: Cambridge University Press.

Maddock, Kenneth. 1991. "Metamorphosing the Sacred in Australia." *The Australian Journal of Anthropology* 2, no. 2: 213-232.

Makower, Katharine. 1989. *Don't Cry for Me: Poor Yet Rich: The Inspiring Story of Indian Christians in Argentina*. London: Hodder and Stoughton.

Marostica, Matthew. 1998. "Religion and Global Affairs: Religious Activation and Democracy in Latin America." *SAIS Review* 18, no. 2: 45-51.

Mayotte, Judith A. 1998. "Religion and Global Affairs: The Role of Religion in Development." *SAIS Review* 18, no. 2: 65-69.

McIntosh, Ian S. 2000. *Aboriginal Reconciliation and the Dreaming*. Boston: Allyn and Bacon.

Merlino, Rodolfo J., and Mario Sanchez Proaño. 1994. "Diversidad e integralidad en las poblaciones Andinas." Pp. 15-34 in *Cultura e identidad en el noroeste argentino*, edited by Gabriela Alejandra Karasik. Buenos Aires: Centro Editor de América Latina.

Métraux, Alfred. 1939. *Myths and Tales of the Matako Indians*. Gothenburg, Sweden: Walter Kaudern.

Miller, Elmer S. 1970. "The Christian Missionary: Agent of Secularization." *Anthropological Quarterly* 43: 14-22.

Mitchell, Timothy. 1995. "The Object of Development: America's Egypt." Pp. 129-157 in *Power of Development*, edited by Jonathan Crush. New York: Routledge.

Morphy, Howard. 1993. "Colonialism, History, and the Construction of Place: The Politics of Landscape in Northern Australia." Pp. 205-243 in *Landscape, Politics and Power*, edited by Barbara Bender. Providence, R.I.: Berg.

Nash, June. 1979. *We Eat the Mines and the Mines Eat Us: Dependency and Exploitation in Bolivian Tin Mines*. New York: Columbia University Press.

Netting, Robert McC. 1993. *Smallholders, Householders: Farm Families and the Ecology of Intensive, Sustainable Agriculture*. Stanford, Calif.: Stanford University Press.

Niezen, Ronald. 1998. *Defending the Land: Sovereignty and Forest Life in James Bay Cree Society*. Boston: Allyn and Bacon.

Norget, Kristin. 1995. "Modernization, Globalization, and the Popular Church in Oaxaca, Mexico." Paper presented at the annual meeting of the American Anthropological Association, Washington, D.C.

Nostro, María Ester. 1992. "Semiótica de un conflicto étnico encubierto: Los indios en la Argentina." Pp. 59-95 in *Propuestas para una antropología Argentina*, edited by Carlos Enrique Berbelia. Buenos Aires: Editorial Biblos.

Nunca Más: The Report of the Argentine National Commission on the Disappeared. 1986. New York: Faber and Faber.

Occhipinti, Laurie. 2002. "Being Kolla: Indigenous Identity in Northwestern Argentina." *Canadian Journal of Latin American and Caribbean Studies* 27, no. 54: 319-345.

Olmedo Rivera, Jesús. 1990. *Puna, Zafra y Socavón: Homenaje al pueblo Colla*. Madrid: Editorial Popular.

Palmer, J. H. 1997. *Wichí Goodwill: Ethnographic Allusions*. PhD Thesis, Oxford University.

Payer, Cheryl. 1991. *Lent and Lost: Foreign Credit and Third World Development*. New York: Monthly Review Press.

Peters, Pauline. 1996. "Who's Local Here? The Politics of Participation in Development." *Cultural Survival Quarterly* 20, no. 3: 22-25.

Picchi, Debra. 2000. *The Bakairí Indians of Brazil: Politics, Ecology and Change*. Prospect Heights, Ill.: Waveland Press.

Pigg, Stacy Leigh. 1992. "Inventing Social Categories through Place: Social Representations and Development in Nepal." *Comparative Studies in Society and History* 34: 491-513.

Porter, Doug J. 1995. "Scenes from Childhood: The Homesickness of Development Discourses." Pp. 63-86 in *Power of Development*, edited by Jonathan Crush. New York: Routledge.

Price, David. 1989. *Before the Bulldozer: Nambiquara Indians and the World Bank.* Washington, D.C.: Seven Locks Press.

Quarles van Ufford, Philip, and Matthew Schoffeleers. 1988. "Towards a Rapprochement of Anthropology and Development Studies." Pp. 1-30 in *Religion and Development: An Integrated Approach*, edited by Philip Quarles van Ufford and Matthew Schoffeleers. Amsterdam: Free University Press.

Reboratti, Carlos. 1996. *Sociedad, ambiente, y desarrollo regional en la alta cuenca del Río Bermejo*. Buenos Aires: Instituto de Geografía, Facultad de Filosofía y Letras, Universidad de Buenos Aires.

Reichel-Dolmatoff, G. 1976. "Cosmology as Ecological Analysis: A View from the Rain Forest." *Man* 1, no. 3: 307-318.

Robertson, Roland. 1986. "Liberation Theology in Latin America: Sociological Problems of Interpretation and Explanation." Pp. 73-102 in *Prophetic Religions and Politics: Religion and the Political Order, Volume I,* edited by Jeffrey K. Hadden and Anson Shupe. New York: Paragon House.

Rosaldo, Renato. 1988. "Ideology, Place and People without Culture." *Cultural Anthropology* 3 no. 1: 77-87.

Rosander, Eva Evers. 1992. "People's Participation as Rhetoric in Swedish Development Aid." Pp. 35-68 in *Kam-Ap or Take-Off: Local Notions of Development,* edited by G. Dahl and A. Rabo. Stockholm: Stockholm Studies in Social Anthropology, Stockholm University.

Rowe, John Howland. 1963. "Inca Culture at the Time of the Conquest." Pp. 183-330 in *Handbook of South American Indians, Volume 2,* edited by Julian H. Steward. New York: Cooper Square.

Ruggiero, Kristin Hoffman. 1988. *And Here the World Ends: The Life of an Argentine Village.* Stanford, Calif.: Stanford University Press.

Sallnow, Michael J. 1987. *Pilgrims of the Andes: Regional Cults in Cusco.* Washington, D.C.: Smithsonian Institution Press.

Scobie, James R. 1971. *Argentina: A City and a Nation.* New York: Oxford University Press.

Scott, Colin. 1996. "Science for the West, Myth for the Rest? The Case of James Bay Cree Knowledge Construction." Pp. 69-86 in *Naked Science: Anthropological Inquiry into Boundaries, Power and Knowledge,* edited by Laura Nader. New York: Routledge.

—. 1988. "Property, Practice and Aboriginal Rights among Quebec Cree Hunters." Pp. 35-51 in *Hunters and Gatherers—Property, Power and Ideology,* vol. 2, edited by James Woodburn, Tim Ingold, and David Riches. London: Berg.

Scott, James C. 1998. *Seeing Like a State: How Certain Schemes to Improve the Human Condition Have Failed.* New Haven, Conn.: Yale University Press.

Sen, Amartya. 1999. *Development as Freedom.* New York: Knopf.

—. 1992. *Inequality Reexamined.* Cambridge, Mass.: Harvard University Press.

Serrano, Antonio. 1947. "Los Matacos." Pp. 97-104 in *Los aborígenes argentinos.* Buenos Aires: Editorial Nova.

Shaw, Carolyn Martin. 1995. *Colonial Inscriptions: Race, Sex, and Class in Kenya*. Minneapolis: University of Minnesota Press.

Shumway, Nicolas. 1991. *The Invention of Argentina*. Berkeley: University of California Press.

Silverblatt, Irene. 1987. *Moon, Sun, and Witches: Gender Ideologies and Class in Inca and Colonial Peru*. Princeton, N.J.: Princeton University Press.

Skar, Sarah Lund. 1993. "Catholic Missionaries and Andean Women: Mismatching Views on Gender and Creation." Pp. 229-250 in *Women and Missions: Past and Present*, edited by Fiona Bowie, Deborah Kirkwood, and Shirley Ardener. Providence, R.I.: Berg.

Snow, Peter G., and Luigi Manzetti. 1993. *Political Forces in Argentina, Third Edition*. Westport, Conn.: Praeger.

Spier, Fred. 1994. *Religious Regimes in Peru: Religion and State Development in a Long-Term Perspective and the Effects in the Andean Village of Zurite*. Amsterdam: Amsterdam University Press.

Starn, Orin. 1992. "'I Dreamed of Foxes and Hawks': Reflections on Peasant Protest, New Social Movements, and the *Rondas Campesinas* of Northern Peru." Pp. 89-111 in *The Making of Social Movements in Latin America: Identity, Strategy, and Democracy*, edited by Arturo Escobar and Sonia E. Alvarez. Boulder, Colo.: Westview Press.

Stewart-Gambino, Hannah. 1992. "Redefining the Changes and Politics in Chile." Pp. 21-44 in *Conflict and Competition: The Latin American Church in a Changing Environment*, edited by Edward L. Cleary and Hannah Stewart-Gambino. Boulder, Colo.: Lynne Rienner.

Stoll, David. 1990. *Is Latin America Turning Protestant? The Politics of Evangelical Growth*. Berkeley: University of California Press.

Taylor, Carl C. 1948. *Rural Life in Argentina*. Baton Rouge: Louisiana State University Press.

Tennekes, Hans. 1988. "Religion and Power: Modernization Processes in Dutch Protestantism." Pp. 31-52 in *Religion and Development: An Integrated Approach*, edited by Philip Quarles van Ufford and Matthew Schoffeleers. Amsterdam: Free University Press.

Trinchero, Héctor Hugo and Juan Martín Leguizamón. 1995. "Fronteras de la modernazación: Reproducción del capital y de la fuerza de trabajo en el umbral al Chaco argentino." Pp. 15-44 in *Producción doméstica y capital: Estudios desde la antropología económica*, edited by Hugo Trinchero. Buenos Aires: Editorial Biblos.

Trujillo, Bishop Alfonso Lopez. 1977. *Liberation or Revolution? An Examination of the Priest's Role in the Socioeconomic Class Struggle in Latin America*. Huntington, Ind.: Our Sunday Visitor.

United Nations Development Programme (UNDP). 1993. *Human Development Report 1993*. New York: Oxford University Press.

—. 2002. *Human Development Report 2002*. New York: Oxford University Press.

Vallier, Ivan. 1970. *Catholicism, Social Control, and Modernization in Latin America*. Englewood Cliffs, N.J.: Prentice-Hall.

Van Kessel, Joop, and Andre Droogers. 1988. "Secular Views and Sacred Vision: Sociology of Development and the Significance of Religion in Latin America." Pp. 53-71 in *Religion and Development: An Integrated Approach*, edited by Philip Quarles van Ufford and Matthew Schoffeleers. Amsterdam: Free University Press.

Whiteford, Scott. 1981. *Workers from the North: Plantations, Bolivian Labor, and the City in Northwest Argentina*. Austin: University of Texas Press.

Wilmsen, Edwin. 1989. *Land Filled with Flies: A Political Economy of the Kalahari*. Chicago: University of Chicago Press.

Wood, Robert D. 1986. *"Teach Them Good Customs": Colonial Indian Education and Acculturation in the Andes*. Culver City, Calif.: Labyrinthos.

NGO Documents and Unpublished Sources:

Animadores. 1997. A publication of the Prelature of Humahuaca. (May).

Equipo de Pastoral Aborigen (ENDEPA). 1992. Report on Meeting with Representatives of Indigenous Communities (Toba, Pilaga, and Mocovi). Parroquia Pampa del Indio, Chaco Province. (June).

Fundapaz Annual Report, 1988/89. 1989. Buenos Aires: Fundapaz.

Lhaka Honhat. 1995. "Memoria de cursillos, 1995." Salta: Asociación de Comunidades Aborigenes Lhaka Honhat.

Nahuel, Jorge (coordinator). 2001. "La compatibilidad entre el convenio 169 y la legislación nacional." Proceedings from Primeras Jornadas de Reflexión sobre los Derechos de los Pueblos Indígenas La Constitución Nacional y el Convenio 169 de la OIT, Panel 2: Los derechos indígenas en el Convenio 169 de la OIT sobre Pueblos Indígenas y Tribales en Países Independientes. Buenos Aires, December 6-7.

Prelature of Humahuaca. 1997. "Synthesis of Parish Meetings: Preparatory Work for the Prelature Meeting."

Ruiz, Horacio. 1993. "Institutiones: Obra claretiano para el desarrollo." *Desarrollo agroforestal y comunidad campesina: Boletín del proyecto GTZ—desarrollo agroforestal en comunidades rurales de NOA*. Salta, Argentina: GTZ. vol. 2, no. 6 (August-September): 23.

Von Bremen, Volker. 1987. *Fuentes de caza y recolección modernas: Proyectos de ayuda al desarrollo destinados a los indígenas del gran Chaco (Argentina, Paraguay, Bolivia)*. Stuttgart: Servicios de Desarrollo de las Iglesias (AG-KED). Translated from German by Carlos Fernández-Molina.

Yareta, 1997. Vol. 1, no. 1. A publication of the Prelature of Humahuaca. December 1996-January 1997.

Zapiola, Luis María. 2002. *El malón de paz*. Equipo de Pueblos Indígenas, Buenos Aires.

Index

About the Author

Laurie Occhipinti has been doing anthropological research in northwestern Argentina since 1996. She has recently begun work in the community of Otavalo in Ecuador as well. Her dissertation research examined the role of Catholic NGOs in economic development in indigenous communities. Her current interests focus on understanding the work of religious development organizations, or "faith-based organizations," in the developing world.

Dr. Occhipinti is currently an assistant professor at Clarion University of Pennsylvania. She received her Ph.D. in Anthropology in 2000, and her M.A. in 1995, from McGill University in Montreal.

www.ingramcontent.com/pod-product-compliance
Ingram Content Group UK Ltd.
Pitfield, Milton Keynes, MK11 3LW, UK
UKHW041631031026
15587UKWH00001B/200

9 780739 111109